Victory ␣

& Barrage Balloons

Victory Gardens
& *Barrage Balloons*

A collective memoir
By Frank Wetzel
and a whole bunch of other nice people

pERRy pUBLIShING

5788 Lene'a Drive NW
Bremerton, WA 98312-1114

© 1995 by Frank Wetzel
Second Edition 1997

Cover art © Beth Hendrickson-Logan.
Graphic design by John McCurdy.

ISBN 0-9622337-8-1

Library of Congress Catalog Card Number: 97-066292

Printed in the United States of America

Dedication

To those gallant men and women
who didn't survive World War II and
to those who did.

Table of Contents

Prologue

Most histories are based on official papers, institutional documents or the memoirs of public officials in positions of authority. Not this history, if so it may be called. Rather, this account is based mostly on the recollections of — well, it must be confessed: teen-agers. They aren't teen-agers now, but they were during World War II, the period covered in this book. "At every moment of history," writes Jose Ortego y Gasset, "there exists not one generation but three; the young, the mature, the old. This means that every historical actuality, every 'today,' involves three different actualities."

The "today" covered here is the today of the young. Although the grander perspectives in this book came from traditional sources, most of the material was provided by almost 150 persons who were in their teens in the '40s and who at my behest contributed their written recollections about growing up in Bremerton, Washington, during WWII.

Are their memories reliable, 50 years after the fact? They are indeed, although of course not without exception, and accuracy is abetted by the double-checking of many memories, one against another, provided by the participants in this collective memoir.

Adolescence is the most vulnerable of all ages. It's a period of exploration, of developing identities, of wild mood swings, of writing on the *tabula rasa* in indelible ink. Those experiences become deeply imbedded in our psyches and many are never forgotten; they make up our permanent adult identity. They often become prototypical. Their memories are deeply imbedded, as fixed as a photograph.

Not since the Civil War have American adolescents grown up surrounded by the grim materiel of war as we were in Bremerton during WWII. Barrage balloons and anti-aircraft units were everywhere — in school playgrounds, the empty lots next door, almost anywhere there was a small, level space. Submarine nets protected the Puget Sound Navy Yard. Smoke screens from smudge pots periodically blanketed Bremerton and the Navy Yard. There were blackouts and dim-outs and air-raid drills and late in December of 1941 there arrived the first United States battleships damaged by Japanese bombs and torpedoes at Pearl Harbor on December 7. Those ships had been preceded by a solemn reminder of the far-away war: *HMS Warspite*, a British battleship bombed in the Mediterranean by the Germans, had limped half-way round the world to Bremerton for repairs, arriving in August of 1941, four months before the United States entered the war.

Eventually, five of the battleships bombed or torpedoed at Pearl Harbor — the USS *Tennessee, Maryland, Nevada, California* and *West Virginia* — were repaired and rebuilt in Bremerton. They became part of the "Ghost Fleet" the Japanese thought they had destroyed. No other yard on the West Coast had the facilities to repair ships so big or so gravely damaged. The alternative would have been repair on the East Coast, adding crucial weeks to the turn-around time and exposing the ships to the threat of German submarines.

One other community shared most of Bremerton's experience: Vallejo, California, site of the Mare Island Navy Yard. The war hit Vallejo with a terrific impact, too. In 1939, the Navy Yard employed 6,000 and the city's population was 30,000. Five years later Mare Island employed 40,000 people and the population of greater Vallejo was nearly 100,000. But because of the topography, the population wasn't concentrated in a small area, as in Bremerton. Workers at Mare Island were scattered all over the San Francisco Bay area. Just getting to work, from Healdsburg, Calistoga, Santa Rosa, Woodland, Sacramento, Antioch, Walnut Creek, Oakland, Berkeley, San Leandro, Hayward, Richmond, Fairfax, Mill Valley, San Francisco and 30 other communities, was a major problem. But scattered above Mare Island, as at Bremerton, were scores of barrage balloons; two British warships, the *HMS Liverpool* and *HMS Orion*, were repaired at Mare Island *before* the United States entered the war, as was the *HMS Warspite* in Bremerton; and smaller ships damaged at Pearl Harbor were repaired at Mare Island. But while Mare Island concentrated on construction of destroyers, destroyer escorts, submarines and various escort vessels, it was the Puget Sound Navy Yard that repaired and renovated the big ships — the vital aircraft carriers and the battleships. (It also was the Puget Sound Navy yard that won a war bond contest with Mare Island, and led to the christening of the *USS Bremerton* by Betty McGowan.) But both yards contributed handsomely to victory in the Pacific, and nothing in this book is intended to derogate Mare Island's contributions.

Although repair of the big ships of the Pacific fleet was unique to Bremerton, much else of the war experience — the draft, rationing, dislocation — was common to all Americans. There was a unity among the American people during WWII that has not been equaled since. It was a time of camaraderie, of shared purpose, of personal involvement in the Last Good War. Bremerton represents that shared involvement, not only for the community but for the nation.

It should be noted that the United States was spared the devastation that crippled much of Europe and Asia during WWII. No attempt is made here to equate our experiences with those of people who lived — and died — in London, Dresden, Stalingrad or Tokyo. (The Imperial War Museum in London estimates that during the 20th Century wars have taken the lives of 100 million people!) That doesn't change the fact that WWII was a profound experience for Americans, particularly for WWII's teen-agers, who matured swiftly into adults because the terrible events demanded it. Boys who were only 14 or 15 when the war broke out were soldiers in combat before the war ended. Many did not survive.

Happily, most of us did. We and the United States matured together, moving from adolescence to responsible adults at a perilous time in our nation's experience that, God willing, will never be repeated.

Acknowledgments

This book was undertaken originally on the premise that Bremerton was more affected by World War II than any other community on the United States mainland. The barrage balloons, anti-aircraft guns, smoke screens, submarine nets, air-raid drills, split school shifts, war-torn ships, explosion of population — all those factors argued in favor of that premise. Now, upon completion of the book and further reflection, whether our experience in Bremerton was unique or commonplace seems unimportant. The fact is that after experiencing a devastating depression, the entire nation came together during the World War II in ways not often experienced. I am aware of the seductive allure of nostalgia and the temptation to falsely glamorize earlier times. Still, it was a time of camaraderie and sharing and caring that in these nasty times we would do well to emulate.

This is not the definitive book about Bremerton during the war years; that remains to be written. Rather, this book sees events through the eyes of teenagers and those eyes did not necessarily see the broad and inclusive perspective of Bremerton's role in World War II.

By accident, I may have stumbled into a new way of gathering information of historical interest. More than 150 people contributed to this book, and more than 50 wrote full-blown autobiographies, some of stunning felicity. The caliber of these contributions was humbling and I am grateful to all those who helped.

The "voice" that readers will note here and there in the book is mine, but I have attempted to keep that voice muted. This book was not intended to be my autobiography, but a collaborative effort among scores of others whose experiences were as vivid and perceptions as valid as mine. In stitching these life stories into a single narrative, my voice probably predominates. I hope that does not overshadow the cooperative aspect of this book.

Particular thanks must go to several contributors. Professor Jon Bridgman of the University of Washington graciously permitted extensive quotations from his Alumni Association lecture tapes about World War II. Although I have never met him, I have high esteem for his organization, scholarship, and humor.

Several friends have read the manuscript and caught some embarrassing errors. These included Myron Richards, Dr. Thomas O'Connell, and particularly Joe Stottlebower, who also offered valuable advice and counsel as the book progressed. No doubt some mistakes remain, for which I take full responsibility. But without their help there would have been many more.

Finally, my thanks to Fredi Perry, without whom this book could not have been written. In addition to being its editor and publisher, she also was chief researcher, reading microfilm of the *Bremerton Sun*, page by page, from 1941 to 1945. Her astute summaries of each day's edition were invaluable. Her knowledge of Kitsap County history filled in many gaps and her encouragement and upbeat attitude made many big problems seem small.

Frank Wetzel

Chapter 1

We Kids on Gregory Way

We kids who lived on Gregory Way in Bremerton knew war was coming long before Pearl Harbor. By 1935, when I was 9, we were fierce militarists. Oscar Nicholson, who lived in the big house down on Burwell and Anoka, had organized us into an army. His father was a Navy officer assigned to the local Puget Sound Navy Yard. From that it was assumed Oscar knew more about military matters than the rest of us. Besides, he was older. Under his command, we jostled through close-order drill, walked our posts in a parody of military manner, and sometimes were given demerits for dereliction of duty, as when we tired of Army life and went home for juice and crackers.

We carried wooden rifles rigged to fire heavy rubber bands cut from inner tubes. They stung if they hit you in the face and our mothers hated them. But no eyes were lost and they probably were safer than the fern spears that seasonally we threw at each other. The army was demobilized when Oscar's dad was transferred and the Nicholsons moved away. But by then we had moved to another battlefield, an empty lot across the street from my home on Gregory Way. Except for two fruit trees we had clear fields of fire: The terrain offered no protection from the sod clods that we flung from a labyrinth of trenches and foxholes (we didn't call them foxholes; that was U.S. Army nomenclature, adopted later).

Most of the time the enemy was imaginary, unless we could persuade Germwad to play. Germwad's real name was Gerald Lundegard but he was called that only by his family. He lived on Gregory Way, too. His mother was a French war bride from World War I; many of the men who lived on Gregory Way had been soldiers during World War I, only 16 years before. Once at dinner I expressed regret that my father hadn't been in the war. My brothers and sister hooted me down: "He might have been killed!" Well, I hadn't meant that, I replied, but a lot of the other kids' dads were in it and they came back all right. I suppose my father had been expecting the "Daddy, what did you do during the war?" question for years.

Roy, whose family briefly rented Jorgen Nelson's old house across from us on Gregory, sometimes would bring out his dad's souvenir German Army helmets, the fancy kind with a spike on top like the Kaiser's. I had supposed the spiked helmet was used to impale the enemy when the Germans lowered their heads and charged, and was disappointed when I learned that was not true. One time Roy was supposed to knight me with a bayonet by gently tapping the helmet I was wearing. Instead he whacked the helmet so hard that he dented it. I reeled home stunned but unoffended; it was time to listen to "Little Orphan Annie" anyway.

Germwad's parents apparently felt marital relations were not covered by the Armistice, for their fights were legendary — so noisy they were spectator events, like the Louis-Schmeling bouts. I once was so swept up in the exuberant energy of their door-slamming, name-calling battles that from a crowd of boys observing the fracas I tossed a rock at their house and broke a window. It was the most serious offense of my younger life. When, as partial punishment, I had to telephone my cousin Willard Parker at his hardware store to replace the glass, he guessed the damage was done playing baseball and I did not correct him. It was an important lesson: I had learned to lie without saying anything.

Anyway, when we played War we sometimes could persuade Germwad to be the enemy. Rarely, with a variety of false promises to include them in our play forevermore, we could also recruit his younger siblings, Buster and Sister. They would soon surrender, overcome by our numbers and stronger arms. Once during War Germwad thought he could blunt the fierceness of our attack by waving the American flag. When he inadvertently let the flag touch the ground, we were outraged. Poor Germwad denied the transgression, in vain. So seriously had he sinned that for a time we refused to pick on him. He would hang around on the periphery of our play, begging to be noticed. When at last someone taunted him, he brightened. He had been restored to our bad graces.

We industriously dug in the empty lot, constructing an underground command post so elaborate that the fire department, alarmed by the possibility the earthen roof would collapse, filled it in. (The firemen knew the address; some years before, at age 4 or 5, playing with matches, I had set the grass afire.)

Our militarism was stimulated by the fact that Gregory Way was only 100 yards outside the Navy Yard fence. We used the Yard's 10-foot-high cyclone fence as a backstop for our softball games. When foul balls flew behind home plate and into the

Gregory Way Gang : Jorgen Nelson, Tom Driscoll, John Gordon,
Warren Lindblad, Bernard Glavin and Frank Wetzel.
(Frank Wetzel photo.)

~

Yard, we snaked under the fence to retrieve the ball, hoping the
Marine guards wouldn't see us. Later, when I was 12 or 13 and a
caddie at the golf course in the Yard, Marine guards did catch me
climbing the fence. It happened this way: On Mondays, caddies
were permitted to play the course. Teeing off on No. 7, I hooked
my ball out of bounds onto the adjoining street. Golf balls were
precious so I scaled the fence after it. A few minutes later I was
under escort to Marine headquarters. I was let off with a mild
reprimand, saved by my truthful assertion that occasionally as
caddie I had climbed the fence to retrieve errant balls hit by the
Captain of the Yard.

At sunset the gang would sometimes quit playing softball and
walk down the hill a block to the State Street gate to watch the
Marines lower the flag. Watching the flag come down while a
bugler played Retreat was a solemn occasion. Like the guards, we
stood at attention and saluted; only civilians showed their respect
for the flag by putting their hands over their hearts and we did
not consider ourselves civilians. (We did put our hands on our
hearts at school, though, at the start of the Pledge of Allegiance.
Midway through the recitation, protocol called for us to point our

*Barrett and Frank Wetzel
at family's summer cabin
in Port Orchard, circa 1938.*
(Frank Wetzel photo.)

arms toward the flag. The result was embarrassing, although perhaps only in retrospect; with outstretched arms we looked like a gang of little fascists.)

Each summer my family moved to our cabin across the bay in Port Orchard. From there the full might of the Navy was on display. In 1936, for example, the year I was 10, the carrier *Lexington* was moored at the end of Pier 6, as were the battleships *West Virginia* and *California*. At Pier 5 were the battleships *Mississippi, Maryland,* and *Pennsylvania*. Four of the five battlewagons then present were to return later under grave circumstances. The big hammerhead crane that became Bremerton's most recognizable landmark when erected in 1933 towered over the ships. On the Fourth of July in 1933, the *USS Constitution* — "Old Ironsides" — was at the Navy Yard, part of its tour of 90 ports after it was recommissioned in Boston in 1931. On other Fourths, crews from the ships would race in their heavy longboats. Rowing those boats was the hardest work I ever saw sailors do. At night, music from ship's concerts would float across the bay, where we listened from grandmother Nana's long front porch.

On June 11, 1938, my sister Edith married a Marine officer, Naval Academy Class of '36. It was a military wedding, of course, and after exchanging their vows the couple went up the aisle under the crossed swords of the six ushers, all in full military dress. It was the first wedding I had ever attended. I was mildly surprised to learn later that sometimes people got married without the military trappings.

A year or two earlier, in 1936 or 1937, a motorist stopped in front of Camp and took photos of the Navy ships across the bay. My father unobtrusively jotted down the motorist's license number. Ordinarily, little attention would have been given to someone taking snapshots of the ships — but this man was Japanese. My father was reflecting a common attitude along the West Coast: Trouble is coming and Japan is going to cause it.

That attitude was inspired in part by racist fears of a "Yellow Peril" fostered by various newspapers. But there was reasonable basis for the attitude, too. The Japanese Army had annexed Manchuria in 1931 and sometimes when we went to the Tower Theater in Bremerton for the Saturday matinee, (after Boney had played the musical spoons during Amateur Hour but before "Flash Gordon") we would see newsreels of the war in China, including the capture of Peiping, Tientsin, Shanghai, and other Chinese cities in 1937. Some of our Central Elementary School classmates were Navy Juniors who had come to Bremerton directly from China where their fathers were stationed. As early as 1934 the U.S. ambassador was warning that Japan had designs on all of East Asia. When the *Panay*, a U.S. gunboat on the Yangtse River, was bombed on December 12, 1937, by the Japs (the common, derogatory word used for the Japanese throughout this period), we kids were outraged and swore revenge. The United States had never lost a war, we asserted wisely, parroting our parents; when the time came, we would fix those Japs in short order.

The time to start fixing those Japs was coming sooner than we thought, with a force we hadn't imagined, and it was not to be in short order.

***Don Rolstad armed with his Depression-era cowboy-and-Indian pistol at
the vacant lot on northeast corner of Seventh and Park.
Photo taken mid-1930s.***
(Photo courtesy Don Rolstad.)

Chapter 2

Peace on Earth . . . But Not for Long

The three defining events of the American mid-century were the Great Depression, the New Deal, and World War II. Of the three, the depression was the most inclusive; some escaped the war and some ignored the New Deal, but few were unaffected by the depression. For survivors the lessons of the depression linger yet; "waste not, want not" remains our watchword.

With a steady payroll at the Puget Sound Navy Yard, Bremerton escaped the worst of the depression. As late as 1940, unemployment in other Puget Sound cities was 16.8 percent. Figures for national unemployment by 1940 range from 16 percent to 20 percent. In Bremerton, however, the unemployment rate was only 6.9 percent.

Early in the depression, construction of two cruisers and a destroyer — the *USS Louisville*, launched in 1930, the *Astoria*, launched in 1933 and the *Worden*, christened in 1934 — stabilized the Navy Yard's employment. Later Congress authorized construction of five more destroyers at Bremerton and they were launched from 1935 to 1939. More important, the Navy Yard undertook repair and conversion of aircraft carriers, the ships that were to play the decisive role in the Pacific during World War II. This led in 1930 to extension of Drydock 2 to 867 feet and to completion in 1940 of Drydock 4, 998 feet long. The importance of these facilities during the war, particularly for the carriers, can hardly be overstated. Furthermore, the projects provided jobs. By 1938, about 6,000 were employed in the Navy Yard, up from 4,000 in 1929 and the low after World War I of 2,500 in 1927.

Despite the severity of the depression, for the most part it was endured stoically. At a national level, laborers and farmers and businessmen struggled with a stagnant economy over which they had no control. But shared misery is more easily borne than individual misfortune. Furthermore, national prosperity of the middle class was not assumed then, as it is now.

Members of families who escaped the depression by moving to Bremerton for war work brought with them stories of hardship faced with great courage. In Illinois, for example, Marjorie Lamb's father was a farmer who never traveled more than 100 miles from his birthplace near Bement. He died of pneumonia in January of 1929 at age 39, leaving his widow and seven children, aged 2 to 14. Marjorie's mother hired someone to manage the farm and through careful management the family survived from one crop to the next. The only thing her mother ever bought on credit was a refrigerator, which she hated until it was paid for. Then she loved it.

Labor-saving appliances were not in general use in the '30s and Marjorie's mother canned fruit and vegetables all summer in a big boiler on a corn-cob-and-coal stove in a very hot kitchen. The house was without running water. "Bathing and laundry for eight people was a major undertaking," Marjorie recalls. Plates had to be cleaned before the children got pie at supper on Saturday and Sunday. Typical of depression children, Marjorie says, "I still clean my plate."

Vi (for Violet) Magneson's father operated a creamery in Four Town, Minnesota. Forced by the depression to close it in 1931, he went to North Dakota to buy and break horses. He eventually found war work in Wisconsin before being recruited for the Navy Yard in 1943. Still, Vi believes the family of her husband, Don Olson, suffered greater hardship. His grandparents, with whom he lived, lost their farm near Mount Vernon and for some time his mother was the only one of 11 in the family with a job.

Betty Bromley grew up amid the sand storms of Colorado, where her father was a barber. Although he never missed a day of work the family ate a lot of soup, beans and corn bread. "But they were our favorite meals and still are," she says. Her grandmother made all the family's clothes. Her mother made certain each child had two pair of shoes — one pair for school and church, the other for play. "Lots of times we had cardboard in our shoes when the soles got thin," Betty says, "but we didn't know we were poor," a remark made frequently by children who had in fact been very poor.

Ruby Jewett's father ran a small logging business near Missoula, Montana. During the depression he was forced to declare bankruptcy. "He started all over with no skills but a strong back and lots of determination," she remembers. Those were important attributes but often were not enough to land a job when hundreds of others, equally strong and determined, were competing for it.

Many Bremerton families escaped the depression, thanks to employment in the Navy Yard. Here, in 1936, the Oass family (Alfred, Josephine, Virginia, Jo Ann) pose in front of their Bremerton home
(Photo courtesy Virginia Oass.)

In The Dalles, Oregon, Bert Brown's dad was a skilled auto mechanic but because of the depression took a job as chief mechanic for the Civilian Conservation Corps in Heppner, an Eastern Oregon sheep town. In 1940, Brown's father landed work as a machinist at the Navy Yard. "The move to Bremerton was a financial boon to the Brown family," says Bert. "For the first time Dad had a good wage with fringe benefits."

Jay Atherton's father was a mechanical engineer whose travel in the early '30s to Lake Charles, Louisiana, for a piping design job put the family in brief, puzzling touch with Bonnie Parker of Bonnie and Clyde notoriety.

At a motel in Memphis, Tennessee, Parker swiped the car keys from the Atherton's vehicle. Later, after she had questioned the Athertons about where they were from and where they were going, "We heard a jingle outside and there were our keys being restored."

Why she took them in the first place was never explained — nor acknowledged. Atherton says Parker wore slacks, sweater and a beret and did resemble Faye Dunaway, who played Bonnie in the movie "Bonnie and Clyde."

"I might add that the motel manager was scared to death when we checked in but we didn't know why," Atherton says. The family moved to Bremerton in 1938 when Jay's father took a job in the Navy Yard.

Geraldine Petersen, who grew up on a farm in central Utah, notes the depression was harder on some than others. "We were lucky. We owned our own land of 85 acres and managed to meet our daily needs. Of course we scraped for tax money and machinery. My parents worked hard and long hours. A dollar given to my older brother for a date was a sacrifice. We could not run our refrigerator, a gift from my grandmother, because it took $1.50 extra for electricity. With school shoes a necessity and Sunday shoes a luxury, we went mostly barefoot in summer and wore cardboard soles in winter."

Her father, a Navy electrician in World War I, eventually took a job at the Navy Yard, leaving Geraldine's older brother, who had studied farming for a year at an agriculture college, to run the farm. But in September of 1941 her brother was killed in a farm accident. The Petersens were forced to sell the farm for $7,500. They left their two-story, 12-room brick home for a project house in Eastpark, one of Bremerton's raw federal housing developments. Nevertheless, "In a way Eastpark was fun. Neighbors were close and many high school students rode the city bus home with me. On weekends we could go to Island Lake State Park for picnics and swimming. Both my parents worked, which brought prosperity to our household," she recalls.

Jim Taylor's father, a boilermaker and shipbuilder, lost his job in California with Standard Oil in 1930. A year later, the family savings depleted, the family — mother, father and three children — piled into their 1925 Buick and headed for Grandpa's in Index, Washington. "He was widowed, owned a home, was the janitor at the local school, had a woodshed chock-full, and wasn't about to let his daughter's family skip a meal," Jim says.

"My father would leave Index with a dollar in his pocket, hitchhike to Seattle, sneak on the ferry, seek employment at PSNY and return the same way with the same dollar in his pocket. He was finally hired by the yard in 1932 and the family moved to Bremerton. He pitched a tent in the City Park on Park Avenue. After a couple of paychecks we rented a house for $25 a month. By this time we had literally eaten up our old house in Compton, California, which had been sold for $900. From then on everything was sweet . . ."

Families struggled in Washington state, too. In Yakima, the depression forced Gene Gurske's father to close his candy and soda business in the mid-'30s. For the next five years he worked at any job available. These included selling Hoover vacuums and inspecting fruit for Del Monte. Young Gene salvaged metal scrap, picked wild asparagus, carried a sign-board advertising dances, sold the *Yakima Daily Republic*. The Gurske family lost their newly built home and moved to a rental across the railroad tracks. Gene slept on a screened porch, so cold during winters he would take a hot stone to bed for warmth. In late 1939, his father was hired as an electrician's helper in the Navy Yard. Gene and his mom stayed in Yakima for another year; she had a steady sewing job. Although employment in the Navy Yard eventually led to relative prosperity, the house they rented at first in Bremerton was so tiny that for a few nights Gene slept in the family auto.

Nearby Everett was also reeling, remembers Brian Corcoran, who lived there during the depression. His father, a maritime ship's officer, died of a heart attack on the *SS Grays Harbor* in Kobe, Japan, in 1933, leaving $500 in insurance and little more. Myrtle Birdell Ward Corcoran, Brian's mother, helped by her late husband's friends, became a stewardess on the *SS President Jackson*, making a number of trips to the Orient in the mid-'30s. "It was an unbelievably good job in the

Brothers Brian and Pat Corcoran were especially close after their father died and their mother worked.

(Photo courtesy Brian Corcoran.)

midst of the Great Depression," Brian remembers. But while she was away Brian and his brother Pat stayed at the Briscoe School in Kent, a boys' school operated by the Christian Brothers. "We slept in a dormitory, ate rather bad food and kept out of the way of the strictest brothers," says Brian. Later the boys stayed on a relative's 500-acre farm near Eugene, Oregon.

After about a dozen trips to the Orient, Birdell quit the sea to reunite her family and started a series of restaurants. The first, in Seattle, failed quickly. The next, a tamale stand on a parking strip in Everett, lasted a couple of years, helped by the seasonal sale of Christmas trees and fireworks. The indomitable widow's next effort was the Red Spot on Callow Avenue in Bremerton, with four booths and a six-stool counter. It supported the family but barely; members slept in a back room of the cafe. Brian and brother Pat set pins in a bowling alley and sold the *Bremerton Sun*. Eventually, Birdell realized she could make more money and work fewer hours by taking a job in the Navy Yard, where she worked in the sail loft.

Helen Jean Stubblefield's father was an optometrist in Aberdeen on Washington's coast. Timber and fishing were the main industries. Both were hard hit. "People with lovely homes could not make their monthly payments," Helen Jean says. "Professional offices closed their doors and boarded up. Banks closed their doors to those who desperately needed to get to their bank accounts. When they did open the banks for business again, they gave as little as 10 cents on every dollar deposited. For those that could wait, they gave promissory notes and even bank stock to try to appease their customers. My father was paying only about $10 a month for his office rent before we left Aberdeen and he was the only one in his building that was paying the owner anything.

"Lovely people, friends, would come in needing glasses. They would offer to work off the amount, to trade goods for services, bring eggs, vegetables, perhaps a lawnmower, but that did not pay the rent or wholesale bills, so the decision was made to make a move. Aberdeen was dying." The Stubblefields left Aberdeen for Bremerton after Helen Jean completed the first grade.

Helen Jean says, "I never felt a lack of anything. I always felt a sense of abundance and well-being and for this I am most grateful for loving parents that did not burden their child with their concerns." (One concern was passed on, however: Helen Jean was carefully instructed to hold her mother's hand tightly whenever gypsies were around, lest they steal her away.)

Although protected from the worst deprivations of the depression by the federal payroll, the Navy Yard also was vulnerable, as Congress cut appropriations or delayed approval of budgets. Myron Richards's father was transferred from the machine shop to a clerk's job with consequent loss of pay and periodic layoffs. "I remember that his salary at this time was about $125 per month," says Myron.

His family raised chickens and sold eggs from their home in Bremerton until it was found brother Lowell was allergic to chicken feathers and cow's milk. They sold the chickens and raised goats, one of unsurpassed meanness. His father sent off to the P.H. Davis company for a kit of woolen cloth samples, order forms, and directions for measuring for men's suits. "He did sell some and mother made some of the sample suit material into the most marvelous quilts for our beds. We still have two of them, and also the suitcase the samples were kept in."

As noted earlier: Waste not, want not.

"All of our heating and cooking was by wood stove," says Myron. "Sometimes we bought wood from Otto Schwab, who delivered wedges of old-growth fir in a Model T stake-bed truck. When paid off he headed straight for Pop's Inn across the alley from Doc Ellis's drug store to quench his considerable thirst.

*Even during WWII, the practice of gathering fish left in the
drained drydocks provided meals for
employees and their families.*
(Photo courtesy Larry Jacobsen.)

Legend has it that the Ford knew the way by itself to his home on
Sunnyhill Road in what is now Westpark . . ."

Dave Leathley's father was an unemployed brick mason. The
Leathleys lived in Phinney Ridge, a Seattle neighborhood. When
the children came home from school for lunch, "Dad was there in
those days, out of work, but he always had a smile for us and
asked about what we had been doing in school that morning. I
can still see him leaning up against the rail on our old Monarch
range as we ate our lunches at a small table he had made out of
apple boxes." In 1932, "Dad got a call to go to work in the Bremerton Navy Yard for six weeks. That call was to last until his
retirement 18 years later."

Ruth O'Grady grew up in Bremerton in what today would be
called a dysfunctional family. "My father had been killed in an
accident in the Navy Yard and mother got a small pension, but we
were very poor. Mother did give me a generous allowance
considering our circumstances. My mother and father were married in December, he was killed in January, and I was born in

March (of 1924). Not your conventional family. Mother had already had one mental breakdown and I guess that was just too much . . ." Somehow the family carried on although, as we shall see, not without additional calamities.

Mack Smith and his brother Roy lived at Kitsap Lake near Bremerton. Their father, also named Mack, owned the Bremerton Tire Hospital. Mack gives a succinct summary of survival skills and self-sufficiency, common traits in the '30s:

"My only recollections of the depression are (1) our father was gone to work before we got up in the morning and came home just in time to kiss us goodnight, (2) we ate a lot of rabbit, calves brains, cornmeal mush, fried apples, milk toast, and mother canned a little bit of everything in the fall of the year, (3) Roy and I made our own toys out of wood, old tires, and anything we could get our hands on, (4) we were too young to read the paper and realize how disadvantaged we were, and there was no television to inform us, and everybody we knew was in the same circumstances, so we were unable to even feel sorry for ourselves. Dad went hunting every fall, and there was always deer in the freezer, and he also grew 'the best corn in Kitsap County' in what he called the back 40 . . ."

Aileen Bellinger's father, an oil wildcatter, built a house on a $500 lot in the Bremerton neighborhood of Navy Yard City in 1933. In 1935 he added two bedrooms — and inside plumbing. "I loved to sew," remembers Aileen. "My mother and dad really sacrificed for me and got me a surprise $100 electric sewing machine (Singer) for my 13th birthday. That was a big family event. We didn't have *anything* that cost $100. No phone till I was 14 and no refrigerator till after that time."

Don Rolstad's father was a machinist. "During the depression my Dad was steadily employed in the Navy Yard but there was not much money for our family," Don says. "We ate many cornmeal patties with Karo syrup and lots of smelt, a small saltwater fish, which my Dad brought home from the Navy Yard. Whenever a ship went into drydock, there would be many schools of smelt trapped when the water was pumped out. My Dad would bring home a gunny sack of them and we would have many good meals. We had a wooden ice box to keep them for a few days."

Dolores Gutoski was born in Tacoma. "I was born into the best of times and the worst of times, just as the Great Depression descended. I saw people hungry and homeless, and I also saw generosity that has never been equaled. People cared about each other. With great pride, neighbors would share food from their gardens, firewood, clothing, toys. My father loved to fish. When he returned from Commencement Bay, everyone in the neighborhood had fish for dinner."

My own father was an early member of Bremerton's petite bourgeoisie. He had established a sheet-metal business in 1908 and he prospered during World War I. He owned his building on Second Street near the Rialto Theater and had branched into roofing, car repair and auto wrecking. His business was not thriving during the early '30s, however, and my mother was frightened. She insisted that he take a job in the Navy Yard and in 1933 he reluctantly did.

He hated it. He had worked in the Yard as a messenger when a teen-ager at the turn of the century and he felt humiliated to be back. Although the assured income was welcome, he no longer attended Kiwanis Club and the loss of social prestige was painful. To compensate, he always wore a necktie and jacket to work before changing into coveralls, perhaps the only non-supervisor or clerk to do so. Taking the Navy Yard job probably was a mistake. If he could have hung on through the leanest years in the '30s, he likely would have prospered again when preparations for war began and the economy improved.

Although we lived in a big house in a solid neighborhood, ate well, and wore neat clothes, during the depression I nevertheless felt poor. In the third grade at Central School I fell on the playground and badly cut my knee. Despite the physical pain, my biggest concern at the time was how would we pay the doctor.

But by 1940 the depression was rapidly ending, confirming John Maynard Keynes's theory that if government spending cannot end a depression, it can at least ameliorate its effects.

By then the primary purpose of the massive government spending was not to end the depression but to prepare for war. As the University of Washington's history professor Jon Bridgman relates, the world was a shambles. Totalitarian governments controlled, directly or indirectly, two-thirds of the people alive.

Most immediately threatening was Hitler's Germany, which by 1940 had conquered Europe with surprisingly small loss — only 38,000 soldiers killed (fewer than sometimes died in a single month during World War I). Hitler was opposed only by lonely, isolated Britain. In September of 1940 he tried to bomb England into submission. By the time he called off his Luftwaffe on Dec. 29, 1940, much of London was in ruins. Meanwhile, Germany and the Soviet Union, coiled like two poisonous snakes, were warily waiting for the other to strike.

Italy under Mussolini had demonstrated in its inept attack on Greece that Italians were too civilized to be effective soldiers

(Greeks suggested Italy should be nominated for the Nobel Peace Prize). But Japan had been fighting in China since 1931 and the Soviet Union had already gobbled up the Baltic states and part of Poland. Millions of people suffered under dictatorships. It seemed possible that democracy would lose everywhere.

President Franklin D. Roosevelt was an adroit politician and eager to help Britain. But he could not move faster than Congress and the electorate would permit. Still, in July of 1940 he managed to get Congress to authorize a two-ocean Navy that would be larger than the fleets of the world combined. The United States' first peacetime draft was approved by Congress in September, to last for one year. Although sometimes it seemed the country was preparing with agonizing slowness and isolationists remained vocal, nevertheless the slumbering nation was starting to stir.

The preparations injected billions and billions of dollars into the economy. In nearby Seattle, Boeing already was completing work on 90 B-17s and was about to start work on 500 more. Its backlog of orders totaled $177 million, an historic high. Seattle was starting to boom.

By Christmas of 1940, wages in the United States were the highest since 1929. People went on a pent-up buying spree; in November they purchased 400,000 cars, up 30 percent from November of 1939.

Most of the people hired at the Navy Yard were simply happy to have work. Few connected their employment with the approach of hostilities. But war was imminent. We didn't know it at the time, but that Christmas of 1940 was the last we were to celebrate at peace for almost five years.

• Chapter 3

(Headlines from the Bremerton Sun,
January-August, 1941)

Overhaul Due for Saratoga . . . Soviet, Nazis Sign New Treaty. . . Six-Day Work Week Is Likely for Entire Yard. . . Langlie Asks Three Percent Sales Tax. . . Mayor Jones Estimates Population at 25,000. . . FDR Starts Sale of Defense Bonds . . . 7 Day Week for Navy Yard . . . Aluminum Tokens To Stay. . . Nazis Push Near Leningrad . . . Bremerton/Bainbridge Ferry Operating . . . Jimmy Stewart, Ginger Rogers Win Oscars . . . Grand Coulee Dam Produces Its First Power on Saturday . . . Yard's Payroll Exceeds 13,000 . . . Britain Asks U.S. Yards Repair Warships . . . Health Officer Would Close Bawdy Houses. . . High School Double Shift Set. . . Eastpark Area Opens . . .

≈

America Awakens to Threat of War

By the start of 1941, America's defense preparations were stoking the economy and ending the depression. The 'Round Towner, a folksy unsigned column in the *Bremerton Sun,* commented:

"He may not be much else, but nobody can say Hitler isn't the world's champion employment agent. He put more people to work in six months than the brain trust did in eight years. No scheme in Washington ever hatched as many jobs as Hitler did when he started thinking about crossing the Channel."

Newspaper writers didn't know it but in 1941 Hitler had no intention of crossing the Channel. Instead, in a colossal error of judgment, he was preparing to invade the Soviet Union. It would assure Germany's defeat and take the lives of millions. Despite the misgivings of many of his generals, Hitler attacked the Soviet Union on June 22, 1941.

While most of the world looked at the growing threat in Europe, North-westerners watched "Galloping Gertie" dangle precariously over the Tacoma Narrows. She fell on November 6, 1940, and wasn't reopened until October 14, 1950.
(Photo courtesy Linc Perry.)

Since authorization of a two-ocean fleet the previous summer, the Navy had been hiring furiously in Bremerton. The *Sun* listed each new employee by name, often 60 or 70 per day, just as it named each local man drafted for a one-year hitch in the Army. By the start of 1941, Puget Sound Navy Yard employed 10,000 people, up from 6,000 in 1938.

That number wasn't enough to keep up with the work. On Jan. 17, 1941, the *Sun's* banner headline said: "Full Force To Be Employed on Saturdays." For the first time since the Yard was established in 1891, the *Sun* said, all employees would work six days per week. The *Sun* said repair work had been choking new construction, although two night shifts already had been added. Workers were to be paid time and a half for the extra shift.

The money was welcome and stretched far. Safeway advertised pot roasts for 21 cents per pound, beefsteak for 29 cents, ground beef two pounds for 35 cents. A fresh pint of Pacific oysters was 21 cents and a 12-ounce bottle of ketchup 10 cents. Sears was selling double-duty overalls for 79 cents, dress shirts for 44 cents, work oxfords for $3.49. Kaufman-Lebo advertised manual lawnmowers for $9.95, only 25 cents down. A Nash sedan cost $971. A fancy six-passenger Packard wasn't much more: $990, delivery in Detroit. Income taxes, due on March 15, averaged $109 per taxpayer and for the nation totaled only $14.3 billion.

When the Navy Yard expanded its work week, Bremerton's merchants generously decided to help the war effort by selling more goods. In a full-page ad, they said:

"Six-day week in the Navy Yard makes it difficult for Navy Yard workers to do what shopping they have to do. It also makes it difficult for them to shop with their wives for the things they purchase together. It is with this thought in mind — and an earnest desire to serve you better — that Bremerton merchants have decided upon a later closing hour. Recognizing your needs, beginning tomorrow stores will remain open until 6 p.m. every evening until further notice." Such thoughtfulness!

Printing this information was the *Bremerton Sun*, audaciously established in 1935 to challenge the old *Bremerton News-Searchlight* owned by the Jessup family. (The challenge was successful. The *Sun* bought out the *Searchlight* in 1945).

Serving a town almost entirely dependent upon the Navy, the *Sun* naturally supported war preparations. The editorial page often printed crude syndicated cartoons depicting Hitler and Mussolini as bully boys astride an enslaved Europe. A typical editorial page in early January of 1941 also included a continuing fiction story by Edward Churchill, "She Wanted Wings," and Jimmy Fidler's Hollywood gossip column. Page 3 included dress patterns and needle-work service. On the same page was a story about election of Rainbow officers: Virginia Laing, worthy adviser, to succeed Margaret Jolley. There's also a story about the Camp Fire Girls and a comic strip, Abby and Slats.

Page 4 included the Port Orchard briefs: "Patty Miller was hostess with a 'watch' party on New Year's Eve. Her guests enjoyed an evening of cootie and a midnight supper." At the bottom of the page was a comic strip, Freckles and His Friends. The *Sun's* news service was United Press; the *News-Searchlight* was a member of The Associated Press, the older, bigger news service (in those days members could blackball competitors from joining the AP).

On Page 5 was a picture of 13 young men who were members of Port Orchard Boy Scout Troop 521 receiving the rank of Eagle Scout. Also Tracyton briefs and the comic strip Flyin' Jenny, which seemed somehow to be connected with combat in Spain or Latin America. (A friend claims he learned to become an aviator by reading the footnotes to a similar strip, Smilin' Jack.)

Racial identifications such as "Negro" or "colored" were routinely printed, usually in connection with crime. A sports story about boxer Bob Montgomery refers to him as a former "pickaninny school boy" and "mahogany-colored Philadelphian." Civil rights were violated without outcry; in February, the respected Judge H.G. Sutton of Kitsap County Superior Court held six youngsters, ages 15 to 17, indefinitely and without formal charges in the county jail "until they get a little less sassy." The judge wanted them to "think over ways and means of improving their automobile driving manners."

That spring the Navy fired nine Yard workers, apparently as security risks but without public explanation. A month later Yard workers were required to sign affidavits swearing they would not participate in subversive organizations. The *Sun* said "Thousands of employees at PSNY have flocked to sign statements of American loyalty and freedom from all subversive policies." In August the Seattle Industrial Labor Union Council said 39 men had been fired from the Navy Yard while "dozens of members of an assertedly pro-Fascist organization (Christian Front or Silver Shirts) continue working at the yard." The labor council said all but two of the dismissed men had been active in trade unions.

In June a young local woman, a British subject, was denied citizenship because she said it was a sin to kill and on those grounds would refuse to bear arms for the United States.

Such civil-rights violations got short shrift in the *Sun* but generally no social item was too trivial; on February 19, for example, the paper listed the ten guests at a surprise 15th birthday party for Helen Jean Stubblefield. The same edition said Mrs. C. Ron Hubbard, wife of the well-known local author, had addressed the Bremerton Pen Club. There was nothing sophisticated about the *Bremerton Sun*. But then, there was nothing much sophisticated about Bremerton, either.

As employment increased in the Navy Yard in early 1941, Bremerton boomed. In March, Mayor Homer Jones estimated the city population at 25,000, up from the 1940 census figure of 15,134. Building permits jumped in April by 585 percent over the previous April and the total value of the permits — $737,073 — outstripped every city of the state save Seattle.

The *Sun* reported happily on the new construction. Chief Kitsap Jr., editor Julius Gius's weekly editorial column, congratulated Maurice and Isaac Soriano: "Everyone is marveling at the face-lifting job you have nearly completed on the old St. James hotel building at Burwell Street and Pacific Avenue. You have turned an eyesore into a handsome structure."

Bremerton's Population Boomed as War in Europe Exploded.
(Puget Sound Naval History Collection, Kitsap Regional Library.)

~

In March, Bill Gates, grandfather of the Microsoft tycoon, obtained a permit to build and lease out a new Ice Creamery on Sixth Street. Cost: $4,000. Another popular spot for teen-agers, Milt's Donuts, which the *Sun* said would make 500 dozen doughnuts a day, opened in June farther down Sixth Street, operated by brothers Milton and Arthur Shelly. Even more important for youngsters was the new Roxy Theater on Fourth Street, advertised to cost $150,000 for construction and equipment. The Roxy hired the best-looking girls in town as usherettes; they were permissive in letting their friends sometimes sneak (local vernacular was "leach") into the theater without charge and also, some said, in other ways as well.

The Roxy opened on May 31 with Hollywood-type searchlights probing the sky and a swing band led by Jackie Souders. The opening attraction was "The Devil and Miss Jones." Film of the opening ceremony catches 15-year-olds Lincoln Perry and Brian Corcoran sneaking into the theater, the first of many such excursions by Perry and his cohort.

In June, the Bremer family, whose members owned much of downtown Bremerton, built a one-story building next to Milt's Donuts for the Firestone Home and Auto Supply Store. More important, the Bremers also started construction of a new J.C.

Penney building in the heart of downtown at Pacific and Burwell. Later in the year construction started on Bremerton's first A&P grocery store, on Callow in Charleston. In one year the number of telephones in Kitsap County increased from 4,850 to 5,517. The boom was well under way.

Elsewhere, the democratic world was crumbling. In April of 1941 a coup d'état in Yugoslavia prompted Hitler to attack. With only 5,000 casualties, the Germans swept through Yugoslavia and Albania and into Greece, capturing 500,000 prisoners and quickly occupying Athens. On May 20, the Germans invaded Crete. After stiff fighting the English were forced to evacuate. It was another stunning success for Nazi Germany. At the end of April, *Life Magazine* proclaimed, "Democracy is in its darkest hour."

While rolling through the Balkans the Germans simultaneously resurrected the air blitz on England. On May 17 they hit London with the largest air raid of the war, killing 1,000 people. The German bombs destroyed the British House of Commons and inflicted the only damage of the war on St. Paul's Cathedral when a bomb fell through the high altar and into the crypt. For Britain's wartime prime minister, Winston Churchill, it was his darkest but finest hour.

On March 11, President Roosevelt managed to get a lend-lease bill through Congress. The *Sun* celebrated: "Students of American history for decades to come will regard it as one of the significant turning points in the life of the republic. It terminates drastically and completely the 21-year period during which the isolationists ruled this country."

In April the United States occupied Greenland, accepting an unauthorized gift from the Danish ambassador to Washington. On May 21, in a speech heard by 85 million people including a hook-up in England, Roosevelt declared an unlimited national emergency. It was unclear at first what that meant. In fact, it was FDR's way of tugging the United States toward active involvement in the war; he was chary of getting too far ahead of public opinion, which was still sharply divided between the interventionists and the isolationists.

Finally, at first light on June 22, Hitler sent his army into the Soviet Union. By August the Germans had cut through the Baltic states and were within 100 miles of Leningrad and 400 miles of Moscow. Casualties were horrible: The Germans killed or wounded a half-million in the first seven or eight weeks of the campaign, themselves taking 213,000 casualties, 50,000 of them dead.

Churchill and Roosevelt were ecstatic at the opening of an Eastern front. The invasion gave Britain and the United States a respite to build up their strength. The Japanese were even more pleased, because it removed the Soviet Union as a threat to their rear. The Japanese soon sent forces into southern French Indochina, outflanking the Philippines and putting them within bomber range of Singapore. It also gave them access to oil, which had been cut off by a U.S. embargo. Japan's aggressive steps were turning the Pacific into a possible theater of war. U.S. preparations for war intensified.

Seattle held its first test blackout. The *Sun* reported, "There were some things impossible to black out. There was, for instance, a half-moon. Lights gleamed brightly at the big Boeing plant and the Todd-Seattle shipyards on Lake Washington, both so busy on national defense orders that they could not stop for 15 minutes for a practice blackout. The most popular place in town was a ballroom which had advertised a 'blackout dance' — 15 minutes of waltzing without lights."

Chief Kitsap Jr., the *Sun's* editorial alter ego, was unimpressed. He told Seattle: "Don't get all swelled up about that blackout of yours last night. Bremerton held a blackout months ago, and it was a spanking success, too."

Gas mask training started in April for Yard workers and in August the Navy proposed that civilians be trained, too. Such training for civilians must have been unusual; Universal Newsreel came to Bremerton to film it. In war games, an invading force captured Bellingham and Mount Vernon before mechanized troops from Fort Lewis and Fort Lawton halted them. In another training exercise, an enemy tank battalion captured Shelton.

That summer of 1941, the Navy Yard payroll topped 12,000. The first 600 permanent housing units built under the U.S. Housing Authority were filling rapidly at Westpark. More than a half-century later, many are still in use. At another project in Manette, imaginatively named Eastpark, 560 units opened in August. Monthly rent ranged from $17 to $50 per month, depending upon the annual salary of occupants. Gas, water, electricity, and garbage cost $4.50 per month. Some central facilities such as lawn mowers and a laundry room were provided. In Westpark, each family was assigned two hours a week to do laundry. At first there were no outside clothes lines and a drying room adjacent to the laundry room was inadequate.

Washing and Drying and Working in Shifts at Westpark.
(Puget Sound Naval History Collection, Kitsap Regional Library.)

~

Still, occupants of the federal projects were lucky; the local housing shortage was wretched. As The *Sun's* 'Round Towner noted, "Everything with shingles on it seems to have someone living under it. The garages are all full; the chicken houses have waiting lists; woodsheds are nice homes; boat houses are grand, and if this keeps on, 'Chick Sales' homes will be next." ("Chick Sales" were outhouses, named for a humorist who wrote of such amenities). Long-time residents were not notably hospitable. A woman who lived in a trailer camp complained, "The people in Bremerton treat us like dirt under their feet just because we live in trailers. Why do they feel that way? We're decent people, not bums!"

Residents of the housing projects also complained of a cool reception. But they quickly developed their own social stratification; those who moved into Westpark felt superior to later arrivals in Eastpark.

Enrollment at Bremerton High reflected rapid growth of the city. The school was built to accommodate 900 students. In the years 1939-40, students numbered 1,133; 1941-42, 1,570; 1942-43 (the year double shifts began), 1,705; 1943-44, 1,807, and 1944-45, 2,053.

Opportunity brought new residents to Bremerton from all over the United States. Sometimes just getting to Bremerton was an adventure. Patricia Henning wrote of her family's move:

"In 1936, we were living in San Diego, California, where my Dad was stationed on the *USS Holland*, a submarine tender. By this time he had been promoted to chief warrant officer and as such had the rate he needed to command a vessel. In June or July, my dad was transferred to the Bremerton Navy Yard and assumed the command of a Navy tug, the *USS Challenge.*

***Edith and Pat Henning
at Illahee Dock, 1941.***
(Photo courtesy Pat Henning)

~

"In September, 1936, my mother packed up and with my 16-year-old brother driving, seven other kids and our puppy we started out for Bremerton. We had a big old black Packard car, which was a limo to us before we had to spend six days and nights in it. While in California with lots of sunshine, we slept on beaches in blankets, roasted weinies over the fire, etc. As we headed into Northern California my brother was having a lot of problems with his eyes so one day we picked up a sailor who was hitchhiking to Portland. The condition for a ride was he had to know how to drive so he could spell my brother. It worked out really well as he was young and adventurous. Mostly we slept in the car. Every now and then Mom would buy us a hot hamburger or a hot dog but we mostly ate bologna sandwiches, lots of fruit, and milk. No bathing, but we did stop at gas stations to take a sponge bath.

"In Salem, Oregon, our car broke an axle and it took almost all day to get the part and make repairs. In order to keep us organized my Mom sent us to movies right across the street from the garage. When we came out of the first show she shoved us in again. We saw two feature movies three times. I will never forget the name of the movie, "Moon over Miami." It took us another two full days to arrive in Bremerton.

"When we drove into the Navy Yard and to my Dad's boat, we were dirty, tired, crabby, and very hungry. I'll never forget the look on Dad's face when he saw what his family looked like. Needless to say, he got us out of there before anyone saw us."

Jo Peterson came to Bremerton at the age of 17, preceded by her father. Of the trip from North Dakota she wrote:

"By February of '43 my Dad had enough money saved up and housing arranged (you had to wait your turn) to send for my Mother and us six kids. We left Hatton by train. We were so excited but sad also to leave. The high school was allowed to come down to see us off. Then when we got to Northwood, the next little town, there were some girls at the depot to see me off. So I thought, but realized later it was my brother Howard they were really interested in. My Mother had packed a very large lunch for us as we would not be able to afford to go to the dining car. That night in Montana the water pipes for the heating system froze and broke on the train. We woke up to water on the floor. It was very cold. We were able to share our extra warm clothes with some young mothers who were on the way to meet their servicemen husbands. I had a coat with a zip-in lining and was able to wear the lining while I shared the coat. Also our big lunch came in handy as it was quite messy with the water on the floor to try to get to the dining room.

"That was when I first became aware that my Mother could be attractive to someone else other than my Dad. A nice looking man came and invited my Mother to go to the dining room for dinner. All of us kids were very pleased because by this time our lunch was getting very low!

"On February 15, 1943, we arrived at the King Street Station in Seattle. My Dad was there to meet us and we all carried our suitcases and walked down to the Bremerton ferry on Marion Street. We were so excited and, as cold as we had been, we were warm by the time we got to the ferry. We rode on the top deck of the ferry so we could see everything. It must have been fairly cold but we sure didn't notice it. We went by bus to our little two-bedroom house on Anderson Cove. Dad had three mattresses on the floor and a few small tables he had made from crating . . .

"The first days after we arrived Dad would read the want ads in the *Bremerton Sun* to find used furniture but he was always too late because we had to wait for Uncle Darl to drive him to the addresses. One day they finally reached a place out in the Sunnyslope area and the furniture wasn't sold yet. The lady told them to go out to the shed and pick out what they wanted. The problem was it was covered with chicken manure so no one else wanted it. But Mom and Dad weren't too proud to clean it up and underneath the manure was a nice bedroom set and round oak dining room table and six chairs, which we used many years. A dresser from this set is still in use. . ."

During the turbulence of early 1941 — the world in flames, the nation moving to war footing, the city bursting with new residents, and the Navy Yard working three shifts per day, seven days per week — what most excited Bremerton's adolescents?

Easy question. On Saturday night, March 22, Bremerton High School won the state basketball championship. We were euphoric.

The Wildcats had finished the regular season tied with Lincoln of Tacoma for second place in the tough Cross-State League. In the most exciting game of the early season, Bremerton matched its man-to-man defense against Everett's zone defense and won, 19-17. Nearly 1,500 fans cheered; the Seagulls' coach, Jimmy Ennis, almost got into a fight with a Bremerton spectator. Maurice Campbell, inevitably nicknamed Soupy, scored 7 points for Bremerton. Steady Bill Long scored 2, Allen Maul 4, Mack Adams 4, and Les Eathorne 2.

But on January 24, Bremerton lost at Bellingham, 34-32, and after the game Maul, Campbell, and substitute Ray Hall didn't get back to the team's hotel until 1:30. Coach Ken Wills promptly suspended all three, saying he had "plenty of boys on his squad who want to play basketball enough to keep training rules." The next night, with none of the three playing, the Wildcats lost at Everett.

The trio was restored to the team the next week and as the season neared an end, big Roger Wiley, his height variously listed between 6 feet 5 inches and 6 feet 8, won increased playing time. In the district championship Wiley was top scorer with 15 points as Bremerton whipped North Bend 57-31, and in the first game of the state tournament in Seattle he scored 11 as Bremerton defeated West Valley of Spokane 49-28. In the second round Bremerton barely beat Lincoln of Tacoma, 30-29, on Campbell's free throw with 10 seconds remaining. Then the Wildcats played their best game of the tournament, beating the Cross-State League champions, Yakima, to which they had lost twice during the regular season, 39-24. That put Bremerton in the finals against tiny St. John from Eastern Washington. A special ferry took excited Bremerton fans through the Lake Union boat locks to the game, played at the University of Washington's Pavilion.

St. John was led by two genuine stars, the Leifer brothers, Bob and Irwin. It's worth a play-by-play account of the final minutes to recapture the tension, the highlight of a tumultuous year for Bremerton's teen-agers.

With five minutes remaining, Hal Worland hit a long shot to put Bremerton ahead, 26-20. Then Bremerton's best player, lefty Allen Maul, fouled out, Wiley replacing him. Bob Leifer made both free throws awarded on Maul's foul, 26-22. But then he fouled Bob Engstrom, who made the second free throw, 27-22. Mack Adams fouled Bob Leifer on a jump ball and Leifer made the free throw, 27-23. Bob Lindley made a long shot for St. John, 27-25. Again Hal Worland hit a crucial basket for Bremerton, dribbling to the basket to make it 29-25. Wiley was fouled and he made it 30-25 for Bremerton. Irwin Leifer dribbled to the right side and swished it, 30-27. Then Bob Lindley sank another for St. John with a minute left, 30-29. With time almost gone, Irwin Leifer fouled Les Eathorne. It was Leifer's fourth and final foul. Bremerton elected to take the ball out of bounds instead of shooting and stalled the final few seconds.

State champions!

It was Bremerton's first state championship. Maul scored 6, Campbell 4, Worland 8, Engstrom 2 and Wiley 10. Maul was named center on the all-state team, Worland was named to the second team and Wiley won honorable mention. After the game the Bremerton captain, Bob Engstrom, brought laughs when he said Coach Wills "was a great athlete in his day." Engstrom amended his statement by saying, "Ken can still run circles around any of us."

Wills said, "These kids have been playing together ever since they were freshmen. They have worked hard and they deserved to win. They're great boys and it has been a pleasure to coach them."

Are wars won on the fields of Eton, or in the gyms of American high schools? Certainly not. Wars are won by economic might. But those who are physically fit and accustomed to tough training and teamwork are a great national asset, too.

Imperial Japan was already planning to test both U.S. economic might and physical fiber — and before the year was out.

- **Chapter 4**

*(Headlines from Bremerton Sun,
August-December 1, 1941)*

High School Double Shift Set. . . Eastpark Area Opens Monday. . . New Bridge Over Narrows Gets Priority. . . Sen. Truman Visits PSNY. . . Civilians Advised on Control of Incendiary Bombs . . . Axis Girds for Sea Combat Against U.S. . . Annual Pay All Teachers Boosted $60. . . Fair Rent Committee To Visit Homes . . . Sub Invasion Causes Alarm in City, Yard. . . Moscow Digging in for Decisive Battle. . . Lime-Burned Wildcats Play at Shelton . . . Chrome Banned from New Cars . . . American Warship Sunk . . . Navy Families Ordered to Leave Island of Guam. . . All Soldiers on Alert in Hawaii . . . Auto Rates on Ferries Cut by Black Ball . . . Crisis in Pacific Remains Unresolved . . . Japan Feels Peace Formula Still Possible . . . Bremerton Opens Prep Casaba Season with 45-23 Triumph

≈

County Opens Heart to Warspite's Crew

America's pre-war heroes came from baseball. Not the flamboyant heroes of the '20s and '30s, such as Babe Ruth or Ty Cobb. The heroes of the '40s came from the Depression. Bobby Feller, probably the fastest pitcher of all time but the dullest man in the world, lived with his parents on an Iowa farm, where he built them a two-story Tudor. But he was a true star; he had started the 1940 season with a no-hitter and his hopping fastball won 27 games that year.

In baseball's long history, few years were more classic than 1941. There was sadness, too; Lou Gehrig, who had played in 2,130 consecutive games for the Yankees and whose lifetime batting average was .341, died on June 2. Even Westbrook Pegler, the choleric columnist, praised Gehrig. He was good, simple, and decent, Pegler wrote, a person of character. (But it's no credit to the human race that that was noteworthy, Pegler added with characteristic venom.)

Two weeks before Gehrig died, on May 15, Joe DiMaggio, the Yankee Clipper, scratched out a single off Cotton Ed Smith of the Chicago White Sox. Then DiMag kept hitting, and hitting, and hitting, for 56 consecutive games, a record that still stands. (But earlier, in the Pacific Coast League for the San Francisco Seals, he had hit safely in 61 consecutive games). Not until August 16, when third baseman Ken Keltner and shortstop Lou Boudreau of Cleveland made outstanding plays against him, was he held hitless.

Ted Williams, the Splendid Splinter of the Boston Red Sox, was hitting .3995 going into the final game of the 1941 season, a mark that would go into the record books as .400. His manager asked Williams if he wanted to sit out the game to guarantee a .400 season. Instead, Williams chose to play — and went 6-for-8 in the final day's doubleheader, boosting his average to .406. No one has hit over .400 since. Despite Williams' marvelous average, DiMaggio was named the American League's most valuable player, probably because he played for a better team; the Yankees won the American League pennant and the World Series, beating the Dodgers, four games to one. (Before the 1942 season started, DiMaggio was asked to take a $2,500 salary cut; the Yankee management feared the war would cut into attendance and receipts. Quite naturally he refused. He eventually ended up with a raise of $5,000, and went into the service at the end of the season).

Bremerton's closest connection to that glorious baseball season was Joe Sullivan of Tracyton. Sullivan, 5 feet 11 inches and 175 pounds, was a left-handed spot starter and relief pitcher. He compiled a 25-11 season's record for the Hollywood Stars of the Coast League in 1934. The next year he went to the major leagues with the Detroit Tigers and put together a 6-6 won-lost record and a respectable earned run average of 3.51. The Tigers won the World Series that season, 4-2 from the Cubs, but Sullivan didn't play in the series. His record slipped in 1936 to 2-5 and Sullivan went back to the minor leagues. He didn't return until 1939 with the Boston Braves of the National League. He was 6-9

He was 2-2 with the Braves in 1941 before he was sold to the Pittsburgh Pirates, where, despite a suspension for breaking training rules, he was 4-1. It was his last year in the majors. His overall record was 30-37 with an ERA of 4.01. Bobby Feller he was not — just a solid, journeyman pitcher who today would be earning a couple of million per season.

The Summer of '41 was a time for fun at the beach. (Upper left) Ray "Soupy" Schutt, Jim Blume and Frank Morella at the Illahee dock. (Pat Henning.) (Upper right) Floreine Laes near the old road to Gorst with a President Line's ship held here in storage before the war. (Harry Harkness.) Dorothy Jessup and Barrett Wetzel enjoying the good life on Hood Canal. (Frank Wetzel.)

While Americans followed baseball that summer of 1941, the Nazis were conquering the Balkans and invading the Soviet Union. The conflict seemed distant. But on August 11, the war came quietly to Bremerton. Under dark, gray skies, a badly damaged British warship slipped through Sinclair Inlet, past Manette toward a berth in the Navy Yard. For us kids and probably the adults, too, the war up to that time had been real but far away — headlines in the paper, bulletins on the radio. Here was tangible evidence that people were fighting and dying. Arrival of the ship made the possibility of our own involvement in the war imaginable.

The British warship was *HMS Warspite*. Much earlier, during World War I, the *Warspite* had proved that British battleships could take a hammering. One account of the Battle of Jutland says the *Warspite* "received from 13 to 22 direct hits (reports conflicted) from heavy shells without suffering serious damage." By 1941 the *Warspite* was old; she had been launched in 1913, one of five of the Queen Elizabeth class. She was 639 feet long, displaced 30,600 tons and carried eight 15-inch guns.

In April of 1941 the *Warspite* and other British ships had bombarded the harbor of Tripoli to interrupt the supply lines of Marshal Rommel's Afrika Korps. The war was going badly; Western Europe was lost and recently the Germans had invaded Central Europe. They swiftly swept south through Greece toward Crete in the Mediterranean. On May 23, shore-based German planes (a former *Warspite* crewman said Messerschmitt 109s but more likely they were Stukas) attacked the British fleet defending Crete. A 500-pound German bomb hit the starboard side of the *HMS Warspite's* forecastle. Four-inch guns were blown completely overboard. Four of the six-inch guns and a boiler room were knocked out of action. One officer was killed, 37 ratings (enlisted men) were killed or died of wounds, and 31 were wounded.

The *Warspite* made her way under her own power to nearby Alexandria in Egypt and was patched up there. Then she started her odyssey halfway round the world, eventually bringing graphic awareness of the war to Bremerton.

The *Warspite* stopped in Honolulu on August 2 and on August 10 dropped off 284 men at Esquimalt, British Columbia, near Victoria. She arrived in Bremerton on August 11. My family was at our summer cabin in Port Orchard and had a good view of her arrival. Mom's diary notes the ship was welcomed by hard rain. "The big thrill this morning was the arrival of the long awaited English ship," she wrote. (How she knew the *Warspite* was coming I don't know; probably it was Navy Yard scuttlebutt brought home by my father). "It looks different from our battleships and of course was flying the British flag." Then, she notes, she dutifully went ahead with the washing despite the rain. Of course: It was Monday.

The *Warspite* was Bremerton's intimate introduction to World War II. She was not a pretty sight. Clyde C. Caldart, a shipfitter apprentice (his pay before deductions was $2.88 per day), in a reminiscence written in 1986, says:

"Having no refrigeration aboard, livestock had been slaughtered as needed. Evidences remained, both sight and smell. Having to give first attention to enemy action for so long, it had been difficult to maintain good housekeeping in various compartments aboard. Enlisted men's heads, reached by vertical ladders into sunken compartments, were mostly flooded. Our first assignment was to tag and ship to shop the urinals, reinstalling after refurbishing."

Caldart remembers the traditional lineup of the *Warspite* crew each day for grog. "We apprentice boys could only observe, not imbibe," he notes wistfully.

"Surprisingly, the youngest members of ship's company were 15- and 16-year-olds, earning their keep as midshipmen. Ship's company included a Royal Marine Band contingent. They were most impressive with their crisp precision, even when marching to waltz time up and down the dock alongside. They performed in several locations around the general area, including British Columbia. The entire ship's company was well received during their stay. Discipline for minor offenses included running up and down the dock/pier at attention, rifle held high above them."

Bremerton opened its heart to the *Warspite* crew. They were lionized, treated like heroes. Remembers Jack Bender, "All our families would have the surviving sailors over for supper to find out 'what it was really like'." Bender also speaks of rumors that dead sailors were still in the *Warspite's* hold when the ship arrived, rumors I have not been able to confirm.

Communication with the *Warspite's* crew was not always easy, particularly with the Cockneys. "They spoke our language but strangely," says Brian Corcoran. He thought they looked emaciated, with bad teeth. "The British didn't resemble the traditional version of a WASP; the sailors were really different in their speech and bedraggled looks." Furthermore, says Corcoran, downtown Bremerton was invaded by large rats about the time the *Warspite* arrived; it was assumed the rodents came down the lines from the ship. Poison eventually took care of the problem, says Corcoran.

***Audrey Thompson and English
sailors from The Warspite.***
(Photo Courtesy Audrey Thompson)

~

Still, the crew was usually welcomed warmly. Harold Engebretson remembers that his sister's cabin on Hood Canal was
often turned over to crewmen on leave.   During a party on
Christmas Eve in 1941 his sisters, Thelma and Lucille, started to
sing a Christmas carol in German before their embarrassed
mother attempted to hush them. "The Brits apparently were not
bothered and joined in singing in German," Harold remembers.

Says Bert Brown, "We had a couple of British sailors out to
dinner. I recall we had a hard time understanding them —they
were 'Cockneys.' And they had a hard time with our 'corn-on-the-
cob.' We felt closely allied to the British because Mom had a sister
who was in the middle of the London Blitz."   The Leathleys,
parents of Dave and Ellen, were originally from Yorkshire and
they frequently entertained the *Warspite's* crew, too, particularly
a 19-year-old Royal Marine, Doug Jones.

Harry McIntyre, then a Western Union messenger, recalls
delivering a message to the *Warspite's* captain. "The captain, an
elderly man of perhaps 50 (I think Harry is joking here; he was 16
in 1941 but 69 when he wrote this), took the extended message,
looked at it briefly and handed it off to an orderly for decoding. I
turned to go when the captain asked me to sit down. I was
surprised but sat in the offered chair. He leaned back in his chair
with his hands behind his head, smiled and said, 'Do you know
anything about the Olympic Mountains'?"

"I told him that I'd been a Boy Scout and had been through
them three times. This impressed him (and me) and he shot a
stream of questions about them at me for about 15 minutes.

"As I left, my escort said, 'My God, I never saw the old man
talk to anyone like that'."

Asked to elaborate on the visit, McIntyre wrote, "His interest in the mountains was reminiscent of one who had never been around anything so spectacular. He asked how to get there and I flippantly said, 'Oh, just take a car.'

"His reply was something like, 'I certainly don't have access to an automobile.' Somehow I had the impression that he had never had access to an automobile. It was like I was giving him a glimpse into a world that he had never experienced; neither the world of autos or mountains. He was like a little boy filled with wonder.

"I picture him aboard his battleship being towed stern-first" (my recollection is that the *Warspite* arrived under her own power) "down the Strait of Juan de Fuca with the Olympic Mountains at his right elbow, towering and majestic. It would be a sight for someone who came from England and that part of the world."

Caldart, the apprentice shipfitter, remembers that the skipper, wary after combat, insisted on isolation of the pier where the *Warspite* was moored in the Navy Yard. "A barrier was erected at the inshore end, and no one was permitted entry," Coldart wrote. "That stand-off was shortly resolved, and much needed on-board renovations proceeded. To limit access, however, a special badge was issued — No. 126."

The *Warspite* brought the war closer to Bremerton but mostly the conflict remained distant. (A young student at BHS also helped personalize the war. He was Peter Elder, who had been evacuated during the Blitz a year earlier from London. He was graduated from BHS in 1942 and eventually returned to Britain.)

Looking through my mother's diary for the summer of 1941 I find notations about family life as usual far outnumbered the occasional expressions of concern about war. Sometimes the two overlapped: Her diary notes that on May 5 her daughter (my sister Edith) sailed for Honolulu aboard the *Lurline* with her infant daughter, Jann, to join her husband. Edie happily telephoned on June 25 that he had been promoted to captain in the Marine Corps. Thereafter mother tried to time her letters to catch the Pan American Clippers as they flew to the islands.

Other entries give a picture of one family's life that summer:

May 17: "Frank went in to caddy (in the Navy Yard) for the first time since his operation." (I had an appendectomy on April 17). "We had our dinner a bit early so Scott and I could go to the show and see *The Road To Zanzibar*. We got a big kick out of it."

June 5: "We are all enjoying Frank's "Booster" (school annual) and the pictures and comments. We listened to our usual Thursday night programs and part of the ball game." Broadcast, of course, by the nasal Leo Lassen.

June 10: "I couldn't sleep because Frank was out on the highway and was alarmed when I heard sirens, and more so when the phone rang. It was Frank saying he was at the fire — which turned out to be Willard's hardware store where Frank was to work this summer." (Willard Parker was my cousin; the fire destroyed Parker Lumber and the hardware store. I had been at Twanoh State Park with Shirley Eskridge, who was still in her bathing suit at the fire and drew many admiring looks.)

June 19: "Doris (Adley, a teacher at South Kitsap High) came and I asked her to stay for dinner. She was in slacks and hesitated since we were having the Truaxes but finally stayed. . ." (In those straitlaced times, heaven forfend that a school teacher would wear slacks.)

June 25: "After dinner the boys started working on their Dad and got him to go and look at new cars. They came in a beautiful Oldsmobile and took me for a ride. We talked prices and terms to the dealer and decided to take the car. Boys are completely sold on it and Scott thinks it is a good deal. We didn't sleep much from all the excitement."

June 27: "Frank and Joe Stottlebower went to Seattle to play tennis in a tournament and won their first day's play. Go tomorrow for the finals." (We lost.)

June 30: "The new tenants (as usual, we rented our house on Gregory Way and moved to our summer camp in Port Orchard) are reserve officers taking a 16-week training course at Keyport. All have four years of college — 3 months at Annapolis — 3 months at sea and now 4 months torpedo work." (When we moved back in October the young officers left the house in a mess. Mom was angry.)

July 14, en route home from Salt Lake City and San Francisco via Highway 101: "We got behind a motor caravan of men and equipment going from California to Camp Lewis and the going was slow and tough."

September 3: "Frank had to go to school today but he is going just in the afternoon as the school is on a split shift. . . ."

(Three days later at a meeting in the old Imperial Palace in Tokyo, the Japanese Cabinet and the Supreme Command told Emperor Hirohito that if their diplomats could not, by the first week of November, persuade President Roosevelt to lift his embargo on oil and other raw materials, they would attack the Pacific territories of the United States, Britain and the Netherlands.)

Mother was not prescient, of course, but that fall her diary entries are increasingly somber:

October 9: "After dinner we all read and discussed the war situation."

October 18: "Japan is getting restless again and since it may affect our kids out there we are very interested."

November 2: "Two couples from the *Saratoga* came to look at our rooms and took the two front ones."

November 16: "The big thrill of the day was Edith's call from Honolulu that she might come home for a month or more."

December 4: "Found a letter from Edith here when I got home yesterday saying she wouldn't be home for a while as there were no reservations available for two months. I shall have to try and get her packages off soon as so many boats are going off the run to Honolulu."

And finally, December 7:

"About noon we got word to listen to Kaltenborn and heard the terrible news of Honolulu's bombing. Tried to put a call through to Edithann for we are crazy with worry. . ."

The call could not be completed. We were at war.

December 7, 1941, the Japanese attack at Pearl Harbor:
Battleships Tennessee and West Virginia.
(Photo courtesy Larry Jacobsen.)

Chapter 5

(Headlines from Bremerton Sun, December 8-10, 1941)

**Japan's Attack Comes As Shock to City,
But No Sign of War Hysteria . . .
Air Raid Volunteers Wanted . . . Bremerton Watershed
Guarded . . . Civilians Mobilized in City-County . . .
Two Ferries Disabled — But No Sabotage . . .
Sheriff Will Pick Up Some Japanese Here . . .
Invoke Censorship of Navy Yard News . . . Navy Wives
Stoic . . . Blackout Tonight from 12:30 To Dawn . . .
Seven-Day Week Ordered for Navy Yard . . . FD Warns of
Sneak Punch on Coastlines . . .
Guns Will Practice Here Each Morning . . . Schools Will
Make Test Evacuation . . . Nurses Asked To Register . . .
Taverns Must Close During Blackouts . . .
Flaming Arrows, Guide for Raiders, Found on Peninsula**

≈

Japs Bomb Pearl Harbor; Is Bremerton Next?

The sun rose over Oahu at 6:26 that Sunday morning, December 7, 1941. Seven vessels were lined up on Battleship Row in the center of Pearl Harbor. The *California* was at the southwestern end of the row. Then, moored in pairs, were the *Maryland* and the *Oklahoma*, the *Tennessee* and the *West Virginia*, the *Arizona* and the repair ship *Vestal*. Finally, at the northeastern end of the row, the *Nevada*. The eighth battleship, the flagship *Pennsylvania*, was in dry dock with the destroyers *Cassin* and *Downes* across the channel from Battleship Row. Nine cruisers, 29 more destroyers and various smaller ships were in the harbor, 94 in all, with only one channel to the open sea.

Mitsuo Fuchida, 39-year-old commander of the Japanese planes approaching Pearl Harbor, peered in surprise through his binoculars. Never, even in the deepest peace, he recalled later, had he seen a target so completely unprotected.

Despite numerous warnings, the U.S. armed forces were utterly surprised. The Chief of Naval Operations, Admiral H.R. Stark, had told Pacific admirals on November 27, "This dispatch is to be considered a war warning. . . An aggressive move by Japan is expected within the next few days." But Stark had also said the evidence pointed toward amphibious operations "against the Philippines, Thai or Kra Peninsula or possibly Borneo." There was no mention of Hawaii.

This is not the place to examine responsibility for the worst defeat in U.S. naval history; volumes have already been written about that. Suffice it to say the surprise was so complete and the destruction so devastating that an attack on the U.S. mainland by the Japanese force seemed possible, even likely. Even more inexplicable than Pearl Harbor was the devastation leveled by Japanese aircraft on Clark Field in the Philippines near Manila, 12 hours *after* the attack on Pearl Harbor. Recalls Saburo Sakai, a Zero pilot: "Instead of encountering a swarm of American fighters diving at us in attack, we looked down and saw some 60 enemy bombers and fighters neatly parked along the airfield runways. They squatted there like sitting ducks."

Jon Bridgman, professor of history at the University of Washington and expert on WWII, says 18 of the 35 B-17s and 56 of the fighters were lost, still on the ground. "Almost criminal negligence," he says.

The next morning, President Roosevelt gave his famous "date that will live in infamy" speech to a joint session of Congress. His speech was only 500 words and lasted three or four minutes. As he requested, Congress swiftly declared war against Japan; it was a unanimous vote in the Senate and only Jeanette Rankin, a Republican pacifist from Montana, opposed the declaration in the House (she had also opposed the declaration of war against Germany in 1917).

Disaster followed disaster. On December 10 Guam fell, virtually undefended. The Japanese hit Wake Island the next day but 300 Marines drove them off and immediately became American heroes. The Japanese stormed back on December 23 and took the island. Only a week after arriving in the Pacific, the British Navy's *Prince of Wales* and *Repulse* were lost to Japanese torpedoes and bombs. In northern Malaya the Australian and Indian divisions started to crumble. The Japanese mounted their first landings in the Philippines. Hong Kong fell on December 25.

The next day Manila was declared an open city and American forces withdrew to Bataan Peninsula.

By the end of the month virtually no Allied planes were left in the Pacific — and not many ships, either. Admiral Husband E. Kimmel was relieved of duty as commander in chief in the Pacific; he was replaced by Chester V. Nimitz, who had often visited Bremerton while assigned sea duty. Lt. Gen. Walter C. Short, the Army commander in Hawaii, likewise was sacked. For the most part, however, Americans were unflummoxed and thought the tide would turn.

In Bremerton that morning of December 7, we kids were being good citizens. We were at mass at Our Lady Star of the Sea or in Sunday school at First Presbyterian. We were caddying, babysitting, setting pins at a bowling alley, stocking grocery shelves.

Frank Harlow was helping his father cut firewood. Gordon Moen and his dad were digging a sewer trench. Al Stewart and his father were putting shingles on a roof. Gene Gurske, Brian Corcoran, and Harry McIntyre were setting pins at the bowling alley on Callow Avenue. Frances Clement, baby-sitting for a Marine colonel in the Navy Yard, had just answered the telephone; Washington was on the line.

Others were doing what teen-agers do best: goofing around. Marilyne White and Ray Walton were driving home from Fleming's grocery at 11th and North Callow, singing with the car radio, "I Don't Want To Set the World on Fire." Les Eathorne was walking along Warren Avenue to the high school gym, where Ken Wills, the basketball coach, already had unlocked the doors. Duane Norgren had just made a fast right turn onto Tenth Street in his newly acquired Model A Ford.

Memories of that day, more than 50 years later, remain shiny bright: sharper than V-E Day, V-J Day, sharper even than memories of the assassination of JFK 22 years later. It was a day that turned our lives upside down. No one was unaffected.

Small things loomed large, such as unexpected profanity. Eleanor Boyle heard the radio station announce the bombing and called to her father, who was cutting wood at the beach on Oyster Bay, to ask what it meant.

"My father never used profanity around his family but he swore at me — said I'd heard wrong," she recalls. "Nevertheless, he ran for the house and before he could change his clothes the phone rang and my father, a master moulder in the Navy Yard, left and didn't return for three days."

December 7 — Possibly the USS Shaw at Pearl Harbor.
(Photo courtesy Larry Jacobsen.)

~

Al Stewart and his father were putting shingles on the roof of their new home at 13th and Rainier. "Mom ran out of our house next door and yelled up to us that the Japs had attacked Pearl Harbor. Dad, who never cursed, said, 'Those yellow SOBs!' and threw his shingling hatchet off the roof and narrowly missed me in the effort."

Virginia Oass was coming home from church with her mother and the Schairers when her Dad came to their porch on Gregory Way and shouted, "The Japs have bombed Pearl Harbor!" Her father was an engineer in the Yard and her mother was captain of the Red Cross Motor Corps.

"I remember packing our survival kits, assembling gear and outfits to jump into on a moment's notice, and improvising blackout curtains so that not a sliver of light escaped," Virginia recalls. "Hearing over and over again that an air raid was coming at any moment gave all of us the motivation to comply precisely with instructions. Perhaps my most poignant memory was kissing Mother good night, knowing that in the event of an air raid she would immediately don her uniform and head off for the Red

Cross control center — and not knowing if I would ever see her again."

America in general and the Navy Yard in particular mobilized quickly.

Harry Harkness: "Within an hour our telephone rang and it was my dad's supervisor. 'Get into your work clothes, pack a change or two for an overnight stay' he said. 'You're driving our largest flatbed to Astoria to pick up ammunition and return as fast as you can.'"

Joan Baer: "The Marine next door pounded on our door and asked, 'Mr. Baer — have you heard? The Japs have bombed Pearl Harbor!' At first, Dad thought he was joking, but the Marine's obvious nervousness and paleness of face soon convinced my Dad. He quickly got into uniform and drove to the base. We didn't see him (or the car) until Dec. 12."

Fear in Bremerton was almost palpable. After their stunning success at Pearl Harbor, would the Japanese attempt a knockout blow on the vital repair facilities at the Navy Yard in Bremerton?

Doreen Burton: "I remember being very frightened because of the Navy Yard. I really thought we were in danger of being bombed."

Roger Wiley, babysitting his nephews in Charleston on a hill overlooking the Navy Yard: "I immediately thought to myself what would I do if I saw Japanese planes coming over the horizon and bombing the yard."

Ed Bejeault: "We kept our ears glued to the radio and our eyes glued to the skies over the Yard. We expected to see Jap fighters and bombers at any minute."

Robert Romberg: "I remember. . . the rumors of a giant burning arrow in the Port Angeles area pointing to Bremerton." (The rumor apparently was prompted by routine slash burning eight miles east of Port Angeles. A newspaper account said, "The 'arrows' consisted of a series of cedar brush fires on each side of a road pointing toward Seattle and Bremerton. They were set by men clearing land whose names were given to the Army and FBI.")

Not everyone was upset by the Japanese attack; sailors aboard the *HMS Warspite* under repair in Bremerton were jubilant. Rudy Onstad's parents had invited two British sailors to dinner. "I remember the two of them whooping and cheering, saying 'You're in it with us now'," said Onstad. Less affable was an English soldier seen staggering down a street by Patricia Goodwin, who remembers him saying, "It's about time you blokes got in it. Should have been in it long ago."

In it we were. The day after the attack on Pearl Harbor, men thronged to recruiting stations. Jim Taylor remembers high school administrators trying to dissuade students from leaving high school to enlist. Students listened to FDR's speech that morning at an assembly in the high school auditorium.

Almost all the able-bodied boys from BHS's classes from 1941 through 1945 went into the service; too many didn't return. Lt. Wes Wager, president of the high school student body in 1941, was shot down over Croatia but was rescued. Pete Burmaster, president in 1942, became a second lieutenant of infantry and died on Okinawa. Xie Olanie, president in 1943, fought in Italy with the 10th Mountain Division and, happily, survived. Jack Carlson, right guard on the football team, was lost at sea. Recalls Brian Corcoran: "My brother Pat, only 17 years old, was serving in the Army in the Philippines. We lost him a few months later on Bataan — but his death was not confirmed until 1945."

Still, it would be wrong to conclude that those were only grim, desperate times. In truth, for teen-agers it was a time of newly found independence and exuberance. We had jobs and money and freedom from parents who were preoccupied with the war — a war that united America as seldom before, and never since.

December 7 was, as FDR said, a date that would live in infamy. But more, for teen-agers, it was a day of fear and uncertainty and growing up, a day that is secretly remembered, a half-century later, with an odd mixture of embarrassment and regret: for nothing since has provided quite the same excitement.

Chapter 6

(Headlines from Bremerton Sun, December 12-31, 1941)

**Navy's Recruits Get Hurry-Up Orders ...
Four Japanese Picked Up In This County ...
Draft Hearings To Open ... America's Entry into War
Spurts Activity of Red Cross ...
Hen Houses Blacked Out by Poultrymen ... Yard Adopts
7-Day Working Schedule ... Sand Bags Placed against
Phone Office ... Rose Bowl Game To Be Played in East ...
Teachers, Pupils Told What To Do in Air Raid. .. U.S.
Planes Attack Enemy Sub Off Coast ... Civilian Defenders
Refute Rumor of Mass Evacuation ...**

≈

Picking Up the Shattered Pieces

Young Gene Gurske's experience as a pin-setter at a Callow Avenue bowling alley the morning of December 7 provides the perfect metaphor for America's reaction to the attack on Pearl Harbor. "The public address system came on for an important announcement," he recalls. "Then came the shocking news that the Japanese had bombed Pearl Harbor, and that all service personnel were to report immediately to their bases. Everyone stood dumbfounded. It seemed weird to be there in a bowling alley in which everyone stood motionless and not a sound was heard. It was as though time stood still. Then one brave soul picked up a ball and sent it down the lane, breaking the silence. Gradually, everyone continued their games."

And so it was elsewhere: Stunned at first, we silently digested the dreadful news. Then, with a figurative shrug of the shoulders, we slowly resumed our lives, continuing our games almost reflexively. They were not games that we resumed, however, but our daily routines, now fraught with anxiety. For the first time we teen-agers saw fright and uncertainty in our parents and other adults. Of course our lives will be disrupted, we told ourselves, but let's hang onto the ordinary for as long as possible.

At my home on Gregory Way, preparations for a meeting of Chapter AH, PEO, had been under way for weeks. The acronym PEO is supposed to be secret but it was common knowledge among the Wetzel children that it stood for Philanthropic Education Organization. PEO played a very big part in Mother's life. She was president of her chapter in 1940. Holding the meeting at her home was an important occasion. We kids dreaded it because in the best of times it put Mother on edge and she involved the entire family in the house-cleaning. This time Mother was truly upset, for there was no word from Honolulu on whether Edie, her Marine husband and her infant daughter had survived. Still, Mother seems to have given little thought to canceling the meeting. Her diary for December 8 reads:

"Turned on the radio for news the first thing and the reports of yesterday's bombing are worse than at first. I cried myself into a headache and found it hard to get ready for PEO. The house looked nice with lots of red candles and holly and the food prepared by Winona (Schutt) and Floy (Gordon) was delicious. Fannie (McDowell) helped serve and she and I ate in the kitchen after serving 26 at the tables. The program was very good and the gifts afforded a lot of fun. I kept up pretty well, only having one really bad crying spell. Got the house back in order."

Members of her generation put a high premium on uncomplaining courage, a trait they nurtured in their offspring. When Mother wept she must have done it privately, for I cannot remember ever seeing her cry.

Her diary entry for the next day, Dec. 9, carried good tidings: "The phone woke me at 2:30 this morning and it was Western Union with a wire from Edithann which said, 'Everything all right.' It was certainly good news, for we think of her constantly and worry over her welfare. We had the radio on all night as this is the first night of the blackout. Had to get breakfast in the dark, which wasn't too easy."

Evidently we hadn't put up adequate blackout curtains.

The U.S. did not at first admit the dimensions of the disaster in Hawaii. Ironically, the Japanese reports were far more specific and accurate. The banner headline in the *Sun* on Dec. 8 said: "U.S. Loses One Battleship/War Declaration Voted, Signed by FDR." The story said the White House had confirmed the loss in Pearl Harbor of "one old battleship" and a destroyer, which was blown up. But another front-page story in the same edition under a Tokyo dateline said, "The Japanese naval command claims sinking of U.S. battleships *Oklahoma* and *West Virginia*; damage to four other battleships, damage to four heavy cruisers, heavy destruction of U.S. planes, probable sinking of a U.S. aircraft carrier (rumored to be the *Langley*); capture of 'many enemy ships; sinking of minesweeper *Penguin* at Guam'." Fortunately, the Japanese were wrong about sinking of a carrier although loss of the *Langley*, a converted collier, would not have been a serious blow.

The *Sun* recounted Bremerton's experiences on Pearl Harbor day:

A highlight of the historic day's events was the order for many yard workmen engaged in repairing U.S. warships and *HMS Warspite* to report immediately to the yard for work. A prominent sign in the Bremerton Navy YMCA specifically ordered all Yard electricians to report at once.

Meanwhile, local ears were glued to downtown and residential radios and to the frequent extra editions of newspapers as each bulletin and news flash of the day's fast-breaking events was confirmed. Listeners and readers clustered in groups downtown and strolled dazedly about the Bremerton business section. The UP Teletype printer in the *Sun's* window on Fourth Street, usually idle on Sundays, started receiving special leased wire service shortly after noon. Large, grim-faced throngs gathered in front of the office to read the bulletins posted on windows as they came over the Teletype.

One development of yesterday's startling events was the emergency meeting of Bremerton and Kitsap officials and civilian defense heads, held last night at City Hall. The meeting had originally been scheduled for tonight. A large part of the throng which milled around downtown thronged the City Hall corridors and rooms eager to take part in the defense activities which were coordinated here last night. . .

Bremerton's streets were almost devoid of American enlisted men last night, while seamen of the HMS Warspite set about town at various business establishments, taking no part in the multitude of conversations regarding the war actions.

Blowing of the Navy Yard fire whistle last night caused many residents to wonder whether the signal, for a five-minute fire at the naval base, was a "general alarm." A U.S. Marine sprinted down Pacific Avenue when the signal sounded to take any necessary station at the yard, but the main gates had been closed by the time he arrived and the "secure" signal for end of fires was sounded soon after his alert action.

The *Sun's* edition the next day said:

Bremerton's first "for keeps" blackout plunged the city and PSNY into total darkness from 11 o'clock last night until early today. Two blackouts were held, the first extending from 7 p.m. when the Navy Yard was plunged into darkness following the trial general alarm whistle, until 9:30 p.m. Some 350 volunteer air raid precautions workers bearing "Air Raid Warden" sleeve bands were on duty throughout the night under the direction of ARP (for air raid personnel) Chief Ted Hubbard.

The secure signal following the general alarm is two blasts of the yard whistle. When these two blasts are sounded, residents may turn on their lights and return to normal activity. During blackouts, all motor traffic should pull to the side of the road and park until the sounding of the secure signal or return of street lights. However, according to Police Chief Rod Murphy, autos may run in a blackout at their own risk with all lights, including dimmers, out. Emergency vehicles including police cars, fire trucks, ambulances and civilian defense autos will run in blackouts. Buses also will be allowed to continue operation in blackouts. All lights which are not absolutely necessary for the prosecution of Yard work will be extinguished from sundown to sunrise. In the event of an air raid alarm, the Yard will sound the general alarm signal — "33" — three blasts blown twice, and this repeated four times on the Navy Yard whistle.

The next day, December 10, the *Sun* reported the deaths of two Marines who had been on duty enforcing the blackout. Their bus, loaded with defense workers and enlisted men from the torpedo station at Keyport, had collided with a truck.

The *Sun* also told readers not to be surprised by gunnery practice each morning. "The sound of anti-aircraft firing was heard in Bremerton for the first time today, but gun crews in the Puget Sound Navy Yard were only practicing their marksmanship. The anti-aircraft drill will be held each morning beginning at 9 until further notice. Hearing the 'pom-pom' reports of the guns is no cause for alarm by residents." The gunnery practice was short-lived.

The *Sun* reported that a practice evacuation of students in Bremerton public schools would be held the next day. "Policy of the school officials is to send students to their homes to be cared for there by their parents. There are not enough school buses to take care of both grade and high school students, thus students of the High School will be required to look out for themselves so that the younger children in grade and junior high may be evacuated to their homes by buses available." This policy was changed later, when high school students from outlying areas were assigned shelter in homes near the school.

On December 11 the *Sun* reported:

Surprisingly good cooperation from the business houses and residence occupants in regard to obeying the strange new blackout restrictions was reported by ARP workers.

Shortly after 11 p.m., the entire city was blackened. The first blackout caught many diners unawares in downtown cafes. Waitresses served meals in the dark and patrons accepted the inconvenience in a light-hearted mood. Taverns were emptied and closed soon after the blackout became effective and theaters presented one complete show and then were closed for the night.

The blackout followed yesterday's enrollment of nearly 1,000 Bremerton civilians volunteering for all phases of civil defense work. (Sixty-eight were students from BHS, Lincoln and Washington Junior highs, who volunteered for service as messengers). ARP workers were on patrol duty throughout the night, many of them reporting for work today in Puget Sound Navy Yard and in Bremerton and Kitsap business establishments after their London-like all-night stint.

Major casualty of the blackout was a large plate glass window of the National Dollar Store, which was smashed by unidentified persons during the early hours of total darkness.

The store was owned by Chinese, not Japanese as the assailants may have thought.

The same edition of the *Sun* quoted the Western Air Command as warning that an air attack on the Pacific Northwest coast was still imminent. Blackouts would continue each night. For fear of showing light, the third shift in the Navy Yard was briefly canceled. A *Sun* editorial said many in the city failed to understand "how close war had come to our shores until the radio stations were silenced and the eerie blackouts became effective. The war is as near as the waters of the Pacific. Things we have thought about as war 'sacrifices' will appear as nothing compared with what we soon will be expected to sacrifice."

The war and fear of invasion dominated everything. "This is war," declared Lt. Gen. John L. DeWitt, chief of West Coast defenses. "Death and destruction may come from the skies at any moment."

A book[1] written in 1944 after censorship had been relaxed, breathlessly reported:

> During the dark days when the great ships of the American fleet lay at the bottom of Pearl Harbor, no single facility was more important than the Bremerton Navy Yard. It was the only yard in the entire Pacific capable of handling the large battleships and aircraft carriers, repairing them and returning them to service. The Japanese knew this. They were expected to strike at the yard. A successful air raid would have meant that all the damaged ships would have had to be taken through the Panama Canal, or around the Horn, to the Atlantic for repairs.
>
> For that reason extraordinary precautions were taken. The Army rushed troops and artillery to this area. Fighters and bombers were concentrated upon Puget Sound fields. The first barrage balloons went into the air around the Navy Yard. Air patrols spotted and sank submarines too close for comfort, but the defense was successful.
>
> One by one the great first line ships were lifted from the mud of Pearl Harbor, floated to Bremerton, and repaired. Aircraft carriers, wounded in the first engagements, accompanied them. The manpower and shops of the Bremerton Yard refitted them, and in each case, returned them to the fleet, stronger and more effective weapons than they had been before.

In the meantime, the Red Cross equipped six first-aid stations in Bremerton. Bandage cutters reported to a new office in the basement of the Enetai Inn on Washington Avenue. The Post Office lobby, formerly open all night for the Christmas season, closed at 11 p.m. until the blackout ended each morning. An ad

---

[1] Ritchie, Arthur J. *The Pacific Northwest Goes to War (state of Washington).* Seattle: Art Ritchie and William J. Davis, publishers. Circa 1944.

by the Night Owl on the Sun's entertainment page began, "It is the duty of every citizen to serve his community in any capacity for which he is fitted in order that our preparation for war may be total." Then, comically finding the silver lining in the war clouds, the wise owl added: "Dancing is good exercise. It will keep us fit and equal to meet any emergency that may arise."

The exterior color of the officers' quarters in the Navy Yard was changed from white to dark green. Oil tanks near the golf course were covered with camouflage netting. Barrels of sand were placed on roofs in case incendiary bombs fell. Gun emplacements were spotted about the Navy Yard.

Reports that relatives had survived the attack on Pearl Harbor were mingled with the first sad newspaper notices that others had been killed. "Pretty young Mrs. Arthur B. Curtis Jr. (nee Eleanore Austin), Bremerton High School graduate, received Navy Department notification of the death of her husband Sunday during the initial Japanese attack on Hawaii. . . She was working at Woolworth's when she received the tragic tidings." So also perished Ensign Robert N. Brooks, 21, president of his class at North Kitsap High, among the first of too many who were killed during the next four and a half years.

On December 18 a *Sun* headline acknowledged what everyone in Bremerton already knew: "Anti-Aircraft Gun Crews Keep on Alert."

Numbers and locations are secret but scores of Bremerton and Kitsap County residents have seen the weapons being set up and unlimbered for possible action in defense of the county's strategic Puget Sound Navy Yard, Keyport torpedo station and Ostrich Bay ammunition depot. Gun crews accompanying the weapons have been on 24-hour alert. The large majority of the men are sleeping in pup tents, many of which have been pitched on the rain-sodden earth. The public is warned to stay indoors during air raids and out of the way of falling fragments from anti-aircraft shells.

Writing about the Northwest, the *National Geographic Magazine* of October, 1942, said:

No housewife is astonished if, rising some morning to get breakfast, she finds Army tents in her backyard and soldiers setting up anti-aircraft guns or inflating a barrage balloon.

Notice machine guns in left foreground. Tents, replaced in 1942, were headquarters for the barrage balloon unit sent to Kitsap County early in the War. (Looking east from Chester.)
(Photo courtesy James S. Webb.)

That was the experience of Berenice Lee, then 15, who lived with her family on an 18-acre chicken ranch four miles outside Chico. She remembers feeling concerned and unprotected those first days after Pearl Harbor. "I guess someone in Washington, D.C., was also aware of our vulnerability for several days later I awoke to find the Chico school yard next door filled with trucks and soldiers; as we drove to school, we saw that the local golf course was full of tents. We found out later that at least the Chico group was part of a National Guard unit from Chicago; they had been on maneuvers in Louisiana on December 7 and shortly thereafter put on trains and sent to Bremerton.

"In the next day or two, the Army spread out into our field and that of our next-door neighbors, the Olsons. I suppose there must have been some dry days, but I always remember the soldiers slogging through the rain in six inches of mud. Those trucks really tore up the ground.

"After about a week a group of soldiers came to our back door and asked if they could sleep in our barn. My parents said yes, so they moved in right away. It was just a small barn, and the soldiers lived where we had used to put the hay, a room about 15 by 15. Then my Mother started worrying about the barn not being heated, so she sent me down with a big dish of chicken and dumplings to warm them up. I think they were surprised to see me, but they thanked me nicely, and the next day brought back the pan all washed and scoured. Thus started a friendship that lasted for some until the unit moved, others much longer."

One of those with whom the friendship lasted much longer was Sgt. Harold Ziegler, who with his wife Ruth remained in Bremerton after the war and were friends of the senior Lees for as long as the Lees lived. Another was Cpl. Louis G. Mueller, who later applied to the Army Air Corps, became a co-pilot of a B-17 and, writes Berenice, "married my sister shortly before he shipped out for England."

Yet another who married a soldier from the 202nd was Jean Naish. A friend's mother invited soldiers who were camped in her backyard into her home on their birthdays. Jean met one of them, Clyde Grindle, on April 20, 1942, and they were married later that year on New Year's Eve. She followed her husband from camp to camp for the next four years. Housing near Army camps was sometimes so hard to find, Jean remembers, that she found shelter one night in jail, although not behind bars, and unknowingly spent part of another night in a Newport News whorehouse, escaping unscathed but frightened and less naive.

Art McCarty remembers how fatigued the soldiers were when they arrived. "Tents were all over Forest Ridge Park and soon the searchlights were at work. It was only a couple of days when an Army sergeant showed up at the door asking if we had room to house any of the GIs in the garage or elsewhere. We had about eight guys sleeping in our garage. Later tarpaper barracks were built and they moved out. Things were pretty tight up around the park and the observation tower there."

Jim Braman found reassurance in realizing the best anti-aircraft weapons around were aboard *HMS Warspite* "and had sailors who knew how to use them!"

Congress unanimously declared war on Germany and Italy on December 11, wrote my Mother, "after Hitler in a fiery speech to the Reichstag had reviled the U.S. and its people and policy and declared a state of war existed between the U.S. and Germany. Mussolini followed suit in Italy." She said the war felt very close, not only from concern about Edith and her husband and baby "but in our blacked out nights and silent radio. Getting breakfast in the dark is quite an adventure. . . ." However, on December 12, she notes, "Didn't have to get breakfast in the dark this morning as our blackouts are lifted temporarily." On December 14 she invited the Guy Wetzels from Port Orchard for dinner. "They were held up for half an hour by the Army moving in." Then, forgetting that loose lips sink ships, she listed several places where anti-aircraft units were being installed.

Bremerton's population grew and grew. In three years it more than tripled. Almost all the established families opened their doors to the newcomers. At my house, almost always a Navy couple or two occupied the upstairs bedrooms. Mother was a soft touch. By some mysterious process, perhaps chalk marks left on the sidewalk as the hobos used to do, Navy officers knew that rooms were sometimes available at our home. Telegrams or letters would arrive unexpectedly, asking for the room when so-and-so's ship departed. Typical was a note in Mother's diary in 1944, "A nice Navy wife was here looking for a room. I decided to give her my room until the Clines (other Navy renters) leave." Many of the renters became part of our larger family. Mother's diary notes that an officer "brought in wood for the fire place. They made a drink for us in the evening and sat in the living room for quite awhile." On the second wedding anniversary of a Navy couple, Mother wrote, "I got her a plant which pleased her as her husband is quite ill. She joined us at dinner and had some ice cream with us." One couple, Tom and Eileen O'Gara, were particular favorites. They stayed at our house for several months early in the war and when they returned, Mother was delighted. Early in 1945, she wrote, "We had hardly finished breakfast when the phone rang and a nice masculine voice said, 'Rosalie?' I said 'Tom!' and in a short time the O'Gara's were here bag and baggage." Two days later she wrote, "We are enjoying our guests so very much. Our meals are pleasant and our games of bridge fun. We cut in and out so everyone has a chance to play." Still later, she said, "It seems so good to have the O'Garas here for they are one of the favorite couples we have ever known."

Given the circumstances, my family's Christmas was remarkably ordinary. Brother Barrett, preceded by his laundry, was home from Washington State College. A new Christmas tree replaced the bedraggled one left from the PEO party on December 8. (In those days, Bremerton families cut their own trees, almost as an entitlement, from whatever forest in which the trees happened to be growing.) Two Army wives, new renters in our home, came down from their upstairs rooms on Christmas Eve "and we talked and enjoyed the fire until two o'clock," writes Mother. "Finally got the stockings filled and to bed." Mary Robbins, whose father had been commanding officer of the hospital in the Yard, spent Christmas day with us from the university. "Kate (Bender) brought her whole family here and we played a little bridge and had pie." That may well have been the start of the bridge game that, save for an occasional hiatus, lasted the duration of the war. Well, so it seemed.

The next day was Edith's birthday. There had been no word since her brief wire on December 9 and Mother was depressed for lack of information. That afternoon a letter arrived from Edie. Mother wrote, "It was the best present I had received this whole unhappy season for not only is she being cared for but John (Edie's husband) too is OK." Meanwhile, life went on: That night Barrett took Doris Scully to the Crystal Ball while I worked, setting pins at the Officers' Club bowling alley. One day I must remind him of that.

Submarine nets were installed in Rich Passage,
opening only when a ferry went through.
(Puget Sound Naval Collection, Kitsap Regional Library.)

Chapter 7

(Headlines from the Bremerton Sun in 1942)

**Tire Rationing Board Set up in Bremerton ...
Searchlight Drills Here This Evening ... American Troops
Going to Great Britain ... 1,000 New Houses To Be
Fabricated ... OPM Order Stops Sale of New Autos ...
Order Brothels Closed ... Yes, Those Things in Sky Are
Balloons ... Whistle Drills Made Today in Navy Yard ...
Jobs Available for Single Girls in Gas Stations ... Sugar
Ration Books Soon To Be Distributed ...
Submarine Net 'Traps' Ferryboat**

≈

Pearl Harbor Ghosts Return from Graveyard

Two days before the end of 1941, a surprise visitor appeared at the Navy Yard — the *USS Tennessee*, her after-section bombed, blasted and burned at Pearl Harbor. The Japanese thought they had sunk her on December 7, but the *Tennessee* was the first of the Pearl Harbor Ghosts to return from the graveyard. She was followed to Bremerton the next day by the *USS Maryland*. Both ships traveled under their own power. They were the least damaged battleships hit at Pearl Harbor.

Yard employees were already working three shifts a day, seven days per week, on routine repair and new construction. But the Navy desperately needed the two battlewagons. Construction was put aside while workers concentrated on their repairs. And more than just repairs: On the *Tennessee's* turrets they installed 14-inch rifles, replaced her old anti-aircraft guns with 20- and 40-millimeter batteries, and constructed 130 watertight compartments. On the *Maryland* they completely rebuilt the after section, added blisters and 745 tons of armor plate as

***USS Tennessee** overhauled after Pearl Harbor*
devastation prepares to leave PSNY Feb. 26, 1942. (Note balloons.)
(Photo courtesy Larry Jacobsen.)

well as eighteen quad 40 mm anti-aircraft guns. *Nipsic to Nimitz,*[1] the centennial history book of the Navy Yard, says the two battleships, rebuilt and modernized, departed only 53 days after arrival.

None too soon. After Pearl Harbor, the Japanese Imperial Navy ruled the ocean. On December 7, the U.S. Navy had nine battleships in the Pacific; eight were at Pearl Harbor. The ninth, the *USS Colorado,* was in Bremerton for overhaul. Five of the battleships at Pearl Harbor were sunk in shallow water, heavily damaged. Three battleships in the Atlantic fleet — the *New Mexico,* *Idaho* and *Mississippi* — were transferred to the Pacific and in March were joined by the *Tennessee* and *Maryland,* by then hastily repaired in Bremerton. Still, they were no match, at least numerically, for the 10 battleships of the Japanese. Fortunately, no carriers were at Pearl Harbor at the time of the attack, but the *Saratoga* was torpedoed on January 11. (When the wounded *Saratoga* arrived in Bremerton for repair, it was decided to refurbish and modernize her as well.) As it turned out, carriers were more important than battleships in the Pacific, and the earlier construction of the big drydocks that could accommodate carriers in Bremerton demonstrates that despite being caught asleep at Pearl Harbor, some U.S. preparedness had been prudent and timely.

Jim Braman: "On the rainy night of Sunday, December 14, in our home at Sixth and Highland, we heard trucks begin to rumble

---

[1] Reh, Louise and Helen L. Ross. *Nipsic to Nimitz.* Bremerton: Federal Managers' Association. 1991.

past. A look outside showed a long line of Army trucks. The next day anti-aircraft guns had sprouted up in parks, playgrounds and school yards. They had arrived from Texas and we finally had a sense of protection."

Not until months later, writes Braman, did we learn why an anti-aircraft unit stationed at nearby Fort Lewis hadn't come to Bremerton. "It went instead immediately to the Coast, where it was stationed as the only available force to repel a possible enemy invasion. The state of panic was such that even anti-aircraft batteries, which certainly wouldn't substitute for coastal artillery, were considered better than nothing."

The Army unit was the 202nd Coast Artillery. One of its officers was 1st Lt. James Bounds, an engineer who had been commissioned through the Reserve Officers Training Corps at the University of Kansas. He later married Betty Bender, a member of one of Bremerton's oldest and most prominent families. "He wore a sidearm at all times, even at the club," she recalled in a telephone interview in 1995. "That frightened me for what it boded."

The nucleus of the 202nd came from Chicago, but replacements came from all over the U.S. When they first arrived, the soldiers lived in tents. But, Betty remembers, "A colonel glommed onto a cabin near Kitsap Lake. He told Jim to see that a fireplace was added. Jim did — and it was so over-engineered that it almost blew you out of the place."

Paul Linder, who later became superintendent of Central Kitsap schools, also arrived with the 202nd. He married a local woman, Roberta Bussett. A playfield adjacent to Jenne-Wright school is named Linder Field for him, as is the street alongside, Linder Way.

The 303rd Barrage Balloon Battalion arrived three weeks later. It was ordered to Bremerton on December 26 from Camp Davis, North Carolina. An advance party included Lt. James S. Webb. He and two other officers flew ahead to Bremerton and settled on the Girl Scout Lodge at 11th and Warren for the 303rd's headquarters. On New Year's Eve the three officers slept on cots on the stage of the auditorium at the Veterans' Home in Retsil, the best accommodations they could find.

The four batteries and headquarters unit of the 303rd arrived by rail at Fort Lewis, then quickly deployed their balloons around the Navy Yard. "It was January and pouring rain," said Webb in an interview in 1994. "The Warren Avenue playground was a sea of mud. We pitched tents. Some officers rented rooms so they would have a warm place to sleep. They also stayed at the Navy BOQ in the Yard.

**Barrage Balloons
hovered over all
parts of Kitsap
County. From
Bremerton scrap-
books, unathor-
ized photos. All
photos were taken
in 1942:** *(From Up-
per right photos cour-
tesy of Virginia Oass,
Adena Brown, Adena
Brown, Audrey
Thompson.)*

"The Navy was happy to see the Army; they had wild ideas about the Japs dropping bombs on us. They really feared a Japanese attack.

"The balloons were English design but were built in this country. On Britain, they held up the island, the English said. The top half was hydrogen, the lower part air. Helium wasn't available. The balloons were highly explosive. Maximum altitude was 6,000 feet. They were secured with quarter-inch cable. Theory was, we were concerned about torpedo attacks by Japanese planes; we learned a little bit from Pearl Harbor. If they hit the cable they would shear off a wing or something. Also a small grenade was attached to the cable. It would slide straight down the cable and hit the plane. Balloons were anchored by concrete blocks, tied down by a whole circle of them. It looked like Stonehenge. Powerful winches were mounted in concrete, too. The balloons were about 60 feet long, diameter 12 or 15 feet.

"The 308th Barrage Balloon Battalion was at Silverdale and the 202nd Coast Artillery AA Battalion manned the guns. There were barrage balloons around Boeing Field, too.

"When it was windy we were very careful to bring the balloons down. We would tether them down. But one day in June of 1942 a wind came up quickly and we had the balloons at 5,000 or 6,000 feet. We lost more than 100.

"The broken cables would wrap around chimneys and just yank them out. They took out power lines, you could see one section after another go dark. In Seattle people were caught in elevators. The Canadians sent up the RCAF to shoot them down. We sent out parties to locate and bring them back. It took them months to retrieve. The Colonel was looking at the control board, walking up and down and growling."

A recovery party of two officers and 20 men that ventured onto Hood Canal's Dabob Bay in search of blown-away balloons was missing briefly, causing concern at their headquarters. A search party that included Coast Guard planes eventually found the group bivouacked at Camp Parsons near Brinnon. They had recovered two empty balloons.

Jim Braman also remembers balloons breaking away during storms. "One evening at dusk . . . a squall swept the city," he says. "From an upstairs window on our hilltop home we could see lights go out in section after section of the city as balloons broke loose, trailing steel cables that shorted out power lines. One balloon for some reason deflated, and slowly settled down over a house up the street from us on Highland Avenue. Though I didn't see it personally, neighbors said that the occupants of the house came crawling out from under the edge of the balloon, wondering why everything had gone black all of a sudden."

Presence of the balloons was mentioned offhandedly in the *Bremerton Sun* on January 16, saying "All barrage balloons which broke away and disrupted power service Monday have been recovered. The last recovered was drifting toward the Cascade Mountains to the eastward."

Four days later, the *Sun* acknowledged more formally that yes, those things in the sky are balloons. "An undisclosed number of barrage balloons are being utilized to protect military objectives in the Pacific Northwest," said the *Sun*. "Swaying thousands of feet above the earth, the balloons are moored by thin steel cables that would be almost invisible to enemy pilots but which would cause any plane which struck them to crash." The article said the balloons were about 100 feet long, much bigger than Lt. Webb's description. Webb says, "The balloons were supposed to be up all the time — they weren't any good on the ground. But weather and maintenance required us to keep some down. Yes, they were very flammable. Clouds would build up quite a charge and generate sparks. They would explode in midair — poof! Just like that and drop straight down."

At least once during the war a balloon exploded on the ground in Bremerton. In February of 1943 a balloon at Sixth Street and Lafayette Avenue exploded, critically injuring a New York City sergeant and seriously burning six other soldiers. A newspaper account says the balloon exploded when additional fuel was being added. "It was while in the process of further inflation that the terrific concussion and ensuing fire occurred," said the news account. The explosion shook houses throughout the west side of Bremerton.

Webb recalls, "There was a squad of men at each site. They lived in tents for months, heated with cone-shaped stoves. When barracks were built, we had regular toilet facilities and showers, just like small, temporary barracks. Each battery had a kitchen and they delivered meals to the sites by truck, just like today's Meals on Wheels. Every site had a .50-caliber machine-gun. The AA units scattered outside Bremerton had 75-millimeter guns."

Webb said the soldiers were welcomed wholeheartedly. "The hospitality was a marvelous thing. I'm from Maryland and North Carolina but I've never seen Southern hospitality to equal. They invited our boys into their homes for showers, fed them, women would drive up in station wagons in front of headquarters, unloading maybe 50 cakes at a time."

"The units became part of the community, people were so hospitable. A lot married local girls and are still here." Among them is Webb, who married Fern Rogers. They live near Silverdale. "I met Fern on the first of February and we were married on 27 March, 1942. Mrs. H. H. (Bernice) Lang, the Girl Scout commissioner with whom we negotiated the lease for the headquarters, said she would like to entertain some officers at dinner. I was first in line when we arrived so I could inspect the girls. I spotted Fern — she said something cute and I sat down beside her. End of story." (High school students of that time will remember Mrs. Lang as the mother of Bill and Jim Daulph).

Phyllis Ford of Bremerton also married an officer from the 303rd, Engel Brooks. Agnes Sadler, whose family owned City Hand Laundry in Bremerton, married Jacob Weiss, also of the 303rd.

Virginia Oass remembers the barrage ballooners' song:

We don't have to march like the infantry
Shoot like the artillery
Ride like the cavalry
We don't have to fly over Germany.
We're in the balloon barrage.

Many of the Army installations went up on school property, including the sports field called the Bowl adjacent to the high school. Carolyn L. Ferguson, in her thesis *"Bremerton Schools: Bremerton in the 1940s"* notes the school board did deny one Army request: "To use the high school gymnasium for machine-gun firing. The gun, a pneumatic type which fired celluloid pellets, was not a problem. What caused officials to refuse permission was the prospect of men in GI shoes tramping across the gym floor." Ken Wills, the basketball coach, who guarded the floor fiercely, must have been pleased. The Navy intruded into school life, too. Gene Gurske says sailors were being trained in the school's machine-shop course. "As a result, we high school students were unable to use the metal lathes because the sailors had priority. So we never had much hands-on experience."

Presence of the Army resulted in closure at last of Bremerton's notorious brothels. The *Sun* said County Prosecutor Fred Cohen and Sheriff Fred Vetters would cooperate with Bremerton officials to prevent prostitutes from moving to outlying areas. "As a general practice throughout the nation, brothels are being closed in the vicinity of Army cantonments," said the *Sun*. "Today's closing order was the first issued to Bremerton brothels since August, 1935, when Admiral T.T. Craven, then commandant of PSNY, called on the city to take similar action. The houses were opened four weeks later, however."

Later in the war, the *Sun* published an unusually perceptive look at downtown Bremerton:

Wartime Bremerton streets, like those of other vital war centers, are usually littered and the litter often tells a story. Any alert observer may take an early morning stroll and deduct from the signs what happened the night before. A broken whisky bottle and a minute trail of blood at one intersection, probably indicated a street fight. At another point several persons probably held a conference with popcorn as refreshments, for the area was littered and the fragments trampled. Three cigarette stubs lay together and one was lipstick smeared, indicating two men and a girl. At other intervals one is rather unpleasantly reminded someone has had far too much to drink. A couple of toothpicks are mute reminders of a dinner. But above all the litter often rising to the proportions of filth on the once-clean streets fairly shriek war.

Joe Stottlebower offered another snapshot of Bremerton in those times:

"It was eerie. At 4:44 p.m. down on the main street amid all the shops in the Navy Yard in the early '40s no one was in sight. Where was everybody? The silence was overwhelming. Then the 4:45 whistle blew. Tumult. Machinists, sheetmetal workers, shipfitters, riggers, boilermakers, pipefitters, electricians, painters, foundrymen, shipwrights, toolmakers, woodworkers, draftsmen, engineers, boatwrights, patternmakers poured out of the shops toward the gates.

"Once they emerged from behind the cyclone fence, the workers' pace slowed dramatically. Their shoulders slumped, the black metal lunch bucket seemed permanently attached to one hand, and they seemed to trudge sadly home always by themselves, never in groups. That is, at all the gates but one.

"If anything, once the workers cleared the main gate, the pell-mell rush became serious. The sidewalk was not wide enough. The speed in which newspapers were purchased set records. It could have been a prison break or the Oklahoma land rush. The buses waited eagerly to swallow up the workers not headed for the Port Orchard and Seattle ferries. The workers with the most frenetic facial expressions were the ones designated to capture a card table for their group on the *Chippewa* or *Kalakala* or another Seattle ferry. The flow of a faceless society moved with purpose to fulfill individual and dedicated lives."

Joe pinpointed the importance of the Navy Yard whistle, which regulated schedules both inside and outside the Yard.

"Come home when the whistle blows," was a common admonition of Bremerton mothers when their children were playing outside. The whistle was a double-bell steam whistle in the Central Power plant. It was blown at 8 a.m., noon, 12:45, 4:45, 8:30 and 9 p.m. In March of 1944, those times were changed and the whistle blew at 7:45, 11:45 a.m., 12:30, 4:30, 8 and 8:30 p.m. The whistle was blown on special occasions, too. A month after the war started, a long blast, a test, at 7:15 a.m. caused confusion among residents who thought they had overslept until the 8 a.m. whistle. The whistle was also to be blown as the general alarm signal. In 1945 when FDR died, the five-minute interval of silence observed throughout the Yard was signaled by the whistle.

By mid-January of 1942, Bremerton was an armed camp. AA guns were atop buildings in the Yard and sprinkled throughout the area. Balloons were tethered to barges in the bay and from any flat place that could be found. Dimouts had replaced black-outs but the air-raid drills continued. Jim Braman recalls, "Occasionally the smudge pots around the perimeter of the Yard were fired up as a test, their purpose being to obscure any specific targets of possible aerial attack. These tests came at pre-announced times, and some nearby residents who forgot to take in their laundry learned to pay more attention to the schedule."

For the most part we adolescents took the warlike atmosphere with equanimity. We hadn't experienced a war before and hadn't known exactly what to expect. (Neither had our parents, but we didn't realize that). A lot depended on how old we were; there's an immense difference between being 13 and 18. Those who were 17 or 18 realized they would be personally involved in the war soon. Those of us who were only 13 or 14 did not project that far

Smudge pots and barrage balloons were meant to protect Bremerton from surprise air attack.
(Puget Sound Naval History Collection, Kitsap Regional Library.)

into the future; we were still getting accustomed to the big deal of being in high school.

Not all youngsters reacted that way, however. Martha Jane Schuh said that at best being a teen-ager is a hard job, and "being a fragile gentle teen filled with innocent optimism in World War II was overwhelming and horrendous. I have always hated war and I still ache when I think of all those lovely young people that were killed, world wide. I was not prepared for the uprooting of my family. I felt betrayed and violated . . . The necessity for restriction on material commodities in World War II was a shock and sacrifice, I was frightened: The black drapes at the window, the night-time hum of Army trucks coming up the hill and past our door, the air-raid drills, the bomb extinguisher on our back porch, the screeching sirens, the blackout curfew, the oppressive, huge balloons guarding our city and obscuring a view of the sky, my Mom's air raid warden meetings in our living room, all the strange, unusual, single women from out of town who came to work in the Navy Yard and lived in our little house next door, the sadness of being able to go to school only four hours a day, the crowded classrooms, my parents' nervous tension and fears, and rules which kept me isolated from the thousands of new people coming into town was oppressive! I sat dazed among the ruins of a world I thought I knew. The certainty of permanence was gone."

Perhaps more typical of the younger age was Patti Serry. Fifty-three years after the fact she wrote:

"We lived on the top of a hill, and we had a large window (actually French doors) that looked across all of West Bremerton (still called Charleston in those days) and across Sinclair Inlet to Port Orchard. The Navy Yard was laid out in front of us, the golf course, the Naval Hospital, the Officers' Club and some of the officer's quarters, the Marine barracks, and their parade field and a big baseball field. We could see Bremerton up past the Naval Avenue gate, and east and north to a few lights in Manette. And all of a sudden it was all blacked out! And when you turned out all the lights and opened the heavy blue velvet curtains (they once were the stage curtains from the Rialto Theater — and they were *our* drapes, *our* bed spreads, *our* couch covers. Mother still has a faded blue 'plush' pillow.) it was black. No house lights, no street lights, no lights on the ships in the Navy Yard, no car lights, and no sparkling Christmas lights! It was a week before Christmas, and my parents had gone to play cards with the neighbors. My brother was probably doing his duty as an air-raid warden. Perhaps up on the tower at the Boy Scout Park (now called Forest Ridge) looking for the planes that we truly expected to be coming every night.

"I had turned out all the lights, opened the curtains, closed the doors on the console radio so the dial light wouldn't show, and looked out across the darkness. Occasionally (very occasionally) a dim light would make a faint glow for a moment in the Shipyard. Everyone was still getting used to operating in a blackout, and it must have been very difficult for swing- and grave-yard shifts to work in the dark. It was overcast, but I could see the water, beyond the docks and across to Port Orchard, reflected in the glow from the sky. Bing Crosby was singing on the radio — and I, for the first time realized that *this* was *not* fun. That patriotism — and pride in our 'brave boys' — was not exciting, and things would never be the same.

"So I did what any 13-year-old (I would be 14 in January) would do. *I didn't think about it that deeply again.* But you had better believe that from that moment on, I *hated* those sneaky, yellow, slant-eyed dirty little JAPS that had destroyed my peace of mind; and being well propagandized, I hated Germans and Hitler, and Italians and Mussolini, and knew that they were my *real* and *very present* enemies."

At some level, most of us did as Patti did and managed to push the war out of our lives. One way was through school sports, which, after being suspended briefly at the outset of the war, were quickly resumed.

As we have seen, Bremerton High won its first state basketball championship in 1941, and it had an outstanding team in 1942, too. It won 22 straight games and the tough Cross-State League championship and lost only one game (to Everett) prior to the district tournament in Bothell. Les Eathorne, Ray Volz, and Roger Wiley were back from the 1941 team and they had strong support from Frank Wright, Duane Thompson, Bob Romberg, Ed Devaney, Art McCarty, Al Kean, Frank Pease, and Joe Stottlebower.

The Wildcats easily won their first game at the district tournament, whipping Bothell 53-32. Eathorne scored 20 points. They had a tougher time the next night against Fife, which led 36-33 with 90 seconds to go. Eathorne hit a long shot to make it 36-35. Wiley missed a foul shot but the rebound was batted to Eathorne in the corner. He knocked in an impossible shot to put the Wildcats ahead, 37-36. Fife was unable to score on the next possession and Eathorne passed to Devaney, who slipped the ball into Wiley under the basket. The big center dropped in the clincher and Bremerton won, 39-36.

On February 28, Bremerton played and lost a strange game to Clover Park. The clock malfunctioned and the final 30 seconds were replayed. Volz sat out the game with a sore throat and

Eathorne fouled out in the fourth quarter. Late in the game, Romberg forgot to report to an official when he entered the game but a minute later made amends with a 15-footer that put Bremerton ahead, 31-30. Those were the last points Bremerton was able to collect. Clover Park won, 33-31.

In the consolation game Monday night, Bremerton backed into the state tournament, beating Bothell again, 37-26. Wiley led the Cats with 16 points.

The state tournament in Seattle started on March 11. Bremerton swamped Wenatchee in the first game, 53-32, and it appeared the Wildcats were back on track. They took the lead at 24-9 and were never headed. The second team played the fourth quarter, except for Eathorne, who re-entered near the end to enhance the possibility of winning all-state honors. He scored 10; Volz had 13 and Devaney 11. In the second game, Bremerton met Lewis and Clark of Spokane, which played without a single substitution. The score was tied at 25 at the end of the third period but Bremerton led by five points near the end after Wright knocked in a shot. After Lewis and Clark scored a basket, Bremerton stalled the final minute and won, 33-30.

In the semi-finals, Bremerton scored the second highest total in the history of the tournament, swamping Vancouver, 56-29. The Wildcats were ahead 35-10 at halftime. Eathorne scored 15, Wiley 10, Volz 8, Wright 7, Devaney and McCarty 6. The second team played much of the final quarter.

The victory put Bremerton into the state finals against Hoquiam. If they won, the Cats would be only the second team in history to repeat as state champions. But Hoquiam, vowing to win for its coach, Elmer Huhta, who was leaving to become freshman football coach at the University of Washington, was inspired. The game was a nail-biter: Hoquiam led 9-7 at the first quarter, 22-20 at halftime and 28-26 at the third quarter. Walt Haney, captain of the Hoquiam team, made a rebound with a minute to go for the final advantage, 36-34. Bremerton had two ball possessions after Haney's basket, but was unable to score.

Eathorne was named to the all-state team. Wiley was chosen for the second team and Volz won honorable mention. In accepting the second-place trophy, Eathorne was a gracious loser. "They not only outplayed us, they scored more points than we did," he said. The *Sun* reported: "The assembled thousands broke loose with a cheer for him and his courageous mates."

Some of the players contend the 1942 Bremerton High team was better than the 1941 team that won the state championship. They may be right — many from the '42 team had illustrious basketball careers in college — but they didn't win that final game. Close, but no cigar.

Bremerton's team in 1943 was strong, too. Four of the starting five players were over 6 feet — big for the time. Furthermore, remembers Duane Thompson, the '43 team was "light years quicker than the Ponderous Percherons of '42 who almost made it." All five starters — Pease, Thompson, Romberg, Wright and Kean — had played in '42 and during the regular season won 17 of 20 games and the Cross-State League championship. The team seemed poised to win the state championship except for one thing: The government decided the expenditure of energy to get players and fans to the tournament would detract from the war effort. The tournament wasn't played that year.

In 1944, the usual starting lineup was Russ Parthemer, Jack Hansen, George Bayer, Jack Dunn, and Joe Stottlebower, the team captain. Bayer played most of the season expecting to be drafted at any moment, but he managed to stay for the entire season. (He later became one of Bremerton's most successful professional athletes, playing football for the Washington Redskins and winning the Canadian Open and other big tournaments on the golf circuit.) Bremerton won all its pre-season games but in late January were only 2-2 in the Cross-State standings. The next month the Wildcats lost at home to Everett, 21-19, notable because it was Bremerton's first home-floor loss in three years. But they won the district tournament and once again qualified for the state tournament, which had been resumed.

Bremerton won its first two games at the state tournament, beating Peshastin 35-27 and edging Everett, 31-30, the latter a particularly sweet victory because Bremerton had lost twice to Everett earlier in the season. In the semi-finals, Bremerton met Lincoln of Tacoma, a team it had twice defeated earlier in the season, and seemed to have a good chance of waltzing into the finals. Not this time, however; Lincoln knocked Bremerton out of the championship round, 34-24. The final night, Bremerton lost to Colfax, 44-28, placing sixth in the state. Lewis and Clark of Spokane edged Lincoln, 41-38, for the title. Stottlebower was named to the all-state second team. A few days later, George Thompson wrote in the *Sun*, "Bremerton did not have ONE natural basketball player on the team. It succeeded through will power and determination of the coach."

No doubt the will power and determination of Coach Ken Wills was shared by his players. That's almost as good as a championship.

Well, OK, that's stretching it a bit. Still, not bad for a gang without natural talent.

Many local students found employment at
Bremerton's theaters. The Rialto and Rex
were located on Second Street.
(Photo courtesy Fredi Perry.)

Chapter 8

G-Men Raid Japs' Homes on Bainbridge for Contraband . . . Third Ferry Snared by Anti-Sub Net . . . Harlem Globe Trotters Here . . . Don't Forget To Set Your Clock . . . High School Girl, Refusing To Salute Flag, Is Expelled . . . New Navy Yard Badges . . . Navy Requests 'Loan' of Binoculars . . . High School Doing Part in Civil Defense . . . Coast Refinery Shelled; Japs' Aim Is Poor . . . Clover Park Stops Bremerton

≈

Once Scarce Jobs Now Chasing Kids

The U.S. reacted resolutely to Pearl Harbor and, considering the magnitude of the Japanese successes, reacted with relative aplomb to the serious setbacks in the Philippines and Singapore in January of 1942 as well. Winston Churchill, the prime minister of Britain, helped morale when he arrived at the White House for three weeks on December 23 and made a wildly popular speech to Congress.

Although we had faced the immediate outbreak of war with equanimity, the nation was unprepared for the disasters that followed. The University of Washington's professor of history, Jon Bridgman, remarks, "Everything seemed to go wrong." He lists the losses of February, 1942:

Field Marshal Rommel gained back all the ground lost by his Afrika Korps in North Africa. Japanese forces swept through Malaya. On February 9, the great liner Normandy caught fire in New York and turned turtle. The German battle cruisers, Scharnhorst and Gneisenau, succeeded in a surprise daylight dash up the English Channel from Brest to the relative safety of German ports on the North Sea; the RAF lost 42 planes trying to knock out the ships, leaving the English aghast. On February 15,

Singapore surrendered. Three weeks later, the Dutch East Indies fell. At the battle of Java Sea late in the month five cruisers and seven destroyers were sunk, including the USS Houston with loss of 500 men. Northern Australia had been bombed, and the Japanese had complete control of the South Pacific. German subs sank tanker after tanker on the East Coast.

Senator Walsh of Massachusetts said the West Coast of the United States was defenseless and suggested American forces be pulled back to the Rocky Mountains and defended from there. Life Magazine published a story that outlined six ways the U.S. might be invaded. One arrow on a map printed with the story showed the invaders coming through Washington state.

The situation was not all bleak, however. It was not clear at the time, but the Japanese had reached the limits of their expansion on March 8. Furthermore, the Nazis had failed in Hitler's hope of knocking the Soviet Union out of the war. In addition, the U.S. had started a massive ship-building program in 1940. It took 18 months for Essex-class carriers to become operational, and they would not join the fleet until late in 1942, but when they came they came in astonishing numbers. Independence-class carriers were also coming; 16 carriers joined the fleet in 1943.

Meantime the Navy Yard was hiring workers as fast as they could be found, the armed forces were sucking up the able-bodied young men, and consumer demand was high for whatever merchandise could be found, creating jobs for anyone who wanted one — including high school students.

A survey of BHS students reported by the *Sun* in 1944 showed 634 with outside jobs. The majority were clerks. But girls also were office workers, waitresses, usherettes, cashiers, nurse's aides, telephone operators, messengers, or caretakers of children. Two were dancing teachers, two were beauticians, and two were floral designers. Boys worked in the Navy Yard, carried papers, pumped gas, drove trucks, pushed brooms. They worked on farms, or as messengers, watchmen, laundry workers. Girls worked an average of 21.3 hours per week. Boys worked an average of 24.1 hours per week.

"The Woolworth and Kress Dime stores were almost completely staffed with kids from high school," remembers Helen Jean Stubblefield. "Bremers Department Store had a few but they all looked like they were afraid to talk to anyone. Downtown Bremerton was like an extension of the student body." She says that one day during a stroll through downtown Bremerton she received five unsolicited job offers.

One who worked at Woolworth's was Gerry Petersen, who had moved to Bremerton from Utah. "I believe Woolworth paid 35 cents an hour." she says. "I remember seeing for the first time a young lady smoking at the Woolworth counter, a shock to my virgin eyes." Later she worked at the National Bank of Commerce for $100 per month. "I saw a $15,000 mortgage at 5 1/2 percent and thought surely it would never be paid for in this lifetime."

Catherine Anderson worked at Woolworth's, too, earning $15 per week ($14.85 after Social Security was deducted). "I can't say that my experience at Woolworth's is one of my fondest memories. For years, I could not stand to go near a dime store. It had something to do with the way the place smelled — a combination of stale popcorn, candy, and God knows what." The Monday after she graduated from high school in 1943, she became a police court clerk in Bremerton's City Hall at a salary of $100 per month.

Like many other students, Berenice Eicher worked in a clothing store. "I got a job working at a dress shop on Callow Avenue for 20 cents an hour. I lasted exactly one week. I think what did me in was my inability to tell a customer that she looked lovely in a dress that I privately thought she looked awful in. The best I could manage was a 'mmmm'."

Another who worked while still in high school was Rosalind Gillie, who remembers: "There were numerous opportunities for employment in Bremerton. In the early years there were babysitting jobs. Then when I was 15 I got my Social Security card (I had to lie and say I was 16) and I got a job as a pinboy/girl in the bowling alley, before the days of automatic pinsetters. We had to pick up the fallen pins, put them in the rack and at the end of the frame push the rack down to reset the pins for the next frame. We were paid 10 cents per line, and I think I made over $20 on my first pay day. I can still feel the euphoria with which I rode home on my bicycle upon collecting my first real pay dirt.

"Then there was the job in the hardware department of a local 10-cent store. A friend and I applied, probably in November, and I asked the boss if he was going to fire us after Christmas. He assured me that he wouldn't do that. So after Christmas when he let us go I reminded him and he replied that he wasn't firing us, merely laying us off. From age 16 until V-J Day I worked in the Navy Yard, 48 hours a week during summer vacations, four hours a day during school time, with another four being at school, and evening hours devoted mostly to roller skating at the rink or dancing as a junior hostess at the USO and YMCA. It was a full and satisfying life. My Navy Yard job was that of a shipfitter-helper-learner, and I enjoyed it. I would be a 'gopher' to get tools from the tool shop, grind pieces of metal smooth on the giant grinding wheels, do some tack welding, and worked on a test gang on four destroyer escorts that were under construction. We would test the air-tight compartments for leaks by painting around the hatches with a thick liquid soap, and if there were any leaks the soap would blow bubbles. The pay was $4.64 per eight-hour day. Surprisingly, it added up, with time-and-half on Saturdays."

In the middle of Marian Booth's junior year of high school, she also became a third-class shipfitter in the Navy Yard. She was issued a hard hat and a photographer took her picture for her identity badge, which all Yard employees wore. "We were told to get hard-toed safety shoes, bib overalls and to tie our hair up in a bandanna. We were assigned to a shipfitter named Homer Washburn, who told us to follow him, keep our eyes and ears open and our mouths shut. We went aboard a battleship that was in drydock. We were given grinders and goggles. Our job was to grind off the tops of rivets that were sticking up on the iron decking. We learned that our ship was the *USS West Virginia* that had been nearly destroyed by the Japanese attack at Pearl Harbor. We also worked on the *USS California* while these two ships were to be refurbished and sent back into service. They were rusty, smelly hulks that bore no resemblance to the freshly painted, sharp-looking warships that slipped out of the shipyard before daylight a year or so later."

Virginia Eddy, fresh out of high school and 18 years old, also became a shipfitter. She remembers: "To familiarize the new employees with shipboard language, we attended a class to learn about port and starboard, forward and aft, the bow and the stern, bulkheads, decks, frames, below decks, hatches, main decks, and on the carriers, the flight deck, the gangplank, etc. We took a gas mask test. We were instructed to wear our hard hats, our hair would be wrapped to avoid being caught in any machinery, and hot dog, we would wear steel-toed shoes! The painful blisters are still etched in my memory! I was hired as a shipfitter's helper. The first week I was placed in the shipfitter's shop with a hefty lady who was to show me the ropes of some machinery. She explained, right off, 'Don't sit on the steel, honey, it will give you piles.'

"The second week, I was put on swing shift, (we were given a choice) and was led out to the piers among these battered warships. A different world this was, and the reality of the war that we had watched in the movie newsreels and on the radio was becoming obviously stark. My leading man, Mr. Rand, led me out to the battleship, *USS West Virginia*, being repaired from the damage of Pearl Harbor. As we headed for the gang plank, a line of somber, hard-hatted young ladies was being escorted off the ship by a 'matron,' a woman who was a type of security person of the women employees. I asked Mr. Rand what was going on, to be told 'These girls are recruits that came up here for the wrong reasons!' My gosh!

"Work aboard ship was a mesmerizing experience I shall never, ever forget. It was like an ant's nest of activity around the clock. A world of shipfitters, welders, burners, chippers and caulkers, drillers, riggers, machinists, painters, etc., were coming and going. Sailors and Marines, officers, etc., made the whole scene just plain exciting. At first I retrieved tools for the shipfitter that I was assigned to, then I helped snap lines, then to center punch those lines, (the burners would cut out the steel so designated). Then I used the grinder to smooth out the welder's slag. I enjoyed it all, felt pretty smug learning all this 'important' stuff. On one of the carriers, I was given a phone, and crawled into the crevices of the armor plating, and as the shipfitter gave me the directions, I would relate it to the rigger on the pier, lining up the replacing plates of steel."

Later Virginia remembered that tension could run high during the frantic ship repair, and behavior to deal with the stress included lots of kidding and joking. "This one summer evening, the riggers were near where I was working with the shipfitters. They were signaling the crane to fill the loading bucket to move material off or on the pier. I was doing my share of making crazy remarks. The crane brought an empty bucket up for loading when I found myself hoisted by 'Mac,' (an ex-wrestler-rigger now) into the bucket. Amazed, I was given a free ride to the end of the pier, and unloaded. Oh, boy. Those fellas thought that was pretty funny as I made my way back to the ship. They were like a bunch of big brothers. Thinking of it now, I imagine they would have gotten a warning slip, or worse. But nothing ever was said."

Harry McIntyre supported himself through high school, occasionally living with a relative but just as often paying for his lodging elsewhere. He held many jobs. He tells of one: "Remember the Army-Navy YMCA on the corner of First and Washington? Well, I used to be a desk clerk there in 1942. I worked swing shift mostly, from 4 p.m. until 11 p.m. This allowed me time to go to school from 8 a.m. and have the afternoon off for courting my girl friend, Gloria Stivers, and sundry other things. The YMCA was a micro world all of its own. Many men and a few women called it home while they sought more suitable housing for themselves and often their families back home. I would walk into the lobby and every chair would be occupied. Not just temporarily but permanently. At least until the occupant had to go to work —whether swing shift, nights or days.

"Occasionally we had a room for rent and they went quickly. Each night I, along with several helpers, set up 100 cots on the canvas-covered gym floor and these rented immediately at 50 cents apiece. When I pulled the covers on the seven pool tables at 10 each evening two men would make their bed for the night there.

"The bathrooms and showers were busy 24 hours a day and so was the lunch counter. Only now it served three meals a day, around the clock. The sailors would come in and check their peacoats with me because it wasn't *cool* to wear a peacoat to Seattle and cover up your tailored blues. They streamed back six hours later to pick them up and go back to the ship. I remember chipping in money with a waitress so there would be enough money for a hungry man to have a meal at the lunch counter. They often arrived with little or no money and had to survive for up to two weeks to get a pay check. More than once an argument would be generated over property rights for a chair to sleep in for the night or day.

"The YMCA's program, run by the secretary, Mark Harader (later to own Flowers by Mark) was survival. No dances, no games, no contests of skill — just survival. Get the guys bedded down, fed, washed, toileted, etc., seven days a week, 24 hours a day. That was the YMCA at the corner of First and Washington; now it's torn down and serves as ferry boat parking. Then it was a *live thing* providing the necessities of life for men and a few women in transition from farms and towns all over the U.S. There to fight the civilian side of the war. For some, there to have the first paying job they'd had in a long time."

McIntyre remembers another job: "Speaking of brothels — we were, weren't we? — well, I was a Western Union messenger for a while in '41 and had the downtown route. About 75 percent of my time was spent running messages between the 'girls' in the 12 brothels in town and the sailors on the ships in the Navy Yard. I would be told by my boss to go to the Fleet Rooms, for example, and ask for Katie. She wanted to send a message into the Yard. I would jump on my bike and head out through the traffic to carry out my mission. At the door I would walk in — through an electric eye usually — a buzzer would go off — a face would appear either down the hall or at the top of the stairs — followed by a greeting like 'There's a man in the house.' This always pleased me because I was 15 or 16 at the time.

"I would ask for Katie and sometimes she would come, usually scantily dressed, to me and hand me a hand-written note in an envelope or the madam would give me the note. If I remember correctly, the charge was 50 cents and I could always count on a tip, usually a quarter (I accepted only monetary tips). The sailor on the other end usually took a bit of ribbing from his buddies but they always were happy to get the messages. Occasionally there would be a message back but sailors usually spent their money in other ways. And I guess the notes were more 'directives' than questions to be answered."

Donald Rolstad also made deliveries to a house of ill repute. "At Fugitt's Grocery downtown I would deliver a large sack of groceries three times a week to a house of prostitution on Burwell and Pacific. It was an old hotel located above a store. I would climb the old rickety steps to the door and buzz the bell. Usually I had to go in and give the groceries to the madam. The 'girls' who answered the door would make an announcement that Don had arrived. Some of the other 'girls' would come out to the entry hall and tease me. The madam would pay me and I would hightail it out of there."

Duane Thompson was a clerk at Walt's Mixer Shop. "Bremerton was by then a U.S. Navy boom-town, and it was educational," Duane remembers. "Walt sheltered me from these customers, but once I delivered cases of mixer to the Rae Rooms on Washington — as a hooker cheerily bade good-bye, her sated U.S. Marine client slunk on down the stairs. The next time the madam called in an order, she asked Walt to 'send over that cute blond kid.' He didn't.

"On another occasion Walt and I delivered all the mix and beer his Ford would hold to the Fleet Rooms, after hours. We carried in the cases and it was quite an experience to see the painted ladies drinking with the sailors and Marines."

Rachel Morrill worked at Forget-Me-Not Florists. She remembers lots of flowers being sent to the brothels. The women also would come into the shop to order flowers. Rachel would peek at the personal notes they sent. "They were steamy but not lewd," she says.

Bremerton wasn't the only Puget Sound city with brothels. Brian Corcoran sold ice cream bars to lumber mill workers bordering Everett's red-light district on the east side of town near the Snohomish River. "Mill workers would stand along lower Hewitt Avenue during their lunch break. Ladies were upstairs in the red-brick buildings, many looking out the windows onto the street where their prospective customers stood. 'Here's a dime,' one fellow said to me one day. 'See that lady in the window upstairs?' It was easy to spot the grinning face. 'Take her an ice cream bar and point me out,' he ordered.

"I pocketed the coin and climbed the stairs in the back of the building. Inside, I found a large open room with a row of curtained beds. There were a number of ladies, including the one to receive the ice cream bar. She was delighted, and she waved at her smiling benefactor on the street below. I sold a couple of other bars before I left the building. It was my most memorable sale. Ironically, the man I would eventually work for many years in Washington, D.C., was a young county prosecutor in Everett and had his eye on the houses of prostitution in the Riverside district. I told Senator Jackson many years later that I could understand why he did it, but when he wiped out the Riverside red-light district he had made a dent in my ice cream business."

Adrienne Johnson worked at the Officers' Club in the Yard: "When the school turned us first-shifters loose around 11:30 I would dash over to the State Street gate, show my pass to the Marine on duty, hurry past the machine-gun emplacement there pointed toward the gate, on past Officers' Row and up to the Club, into the waitresses' room to change into my uniform, then a mad dash to the dining room to be on deck in time to serve lunch. It was fun, and the best part came when the chef dished up plates of lunch for the dining-room help. It was always welcome and often my first and last meal of the day.

"Between the end of lunch and dinner time we would busy ourselves with the silver, linen, coffee pots and all that. I worked from noon to 8 p.m. week days, eight hours on Saturday, including the dinner dance, and sometimes was even scheduled for Sunday breakfast and lunch. We made fifty cents an hour and no tips ever. I heard one officer tell a newcomer, 'We don't tip here'. Oh well, there were other perks like the celebrities who passed through. I waited on Ginger Rogers when she came to the Yard for a bond rally. She was seated at a table for 12, with an admiral on each side of her who were just about falling into her plate trying to be nice to her. The famous Metropolitan Opera tenor, Richard Crooks, also ate at one of my tables, and he was also there for a bond rally. He was a jovial person and when I served dessert, apple pie, he pretended to slip it under his coat so he could eat it later after he sang. Ever after when I would hear his great voice on records or radio I remembered the apple pie.

Adrienne Johnson in crepe dress, purchased from wages at Officers' Club. She was caught in a rain storm and the dress shrunk "until it would fit a 5-year-old."
(Photo courtesy Adrienne Johnson.)

"By far the most important person I saw there, but I didn't know just how important, nor did any one else at the time, was a slender, well-tanned young man of medium height. Officers were flocking around him and one of the other waitresses said he was very wealthy and that his father was the ambassador to Great Britain. It was John Kennedy and he was on his way to the South Pacific."

As noted, McIntyre held many jobs, although some didn't last long. For instance: "I said I was going to write about being a doorman at the Rex Theatre but there's really not much to that. I'm not sure what motivated me to apply for the job but I did. The manager, a short fat man whose office was on the second floor of the Rialto Theatre across the street from the Rex, puffed on his cigar as he looked me over like a buyer sizing up a side of beef. I seemed to fit the bill and he had me start as soon as I could be fitted for a uniform. When I reported for work, to my surprise and pleasure I found Mitzi Verbon worked there. She was the girl friend of my boy friend, Don Young. The job required about 15 minutes of instruction and then I was a full-fledged doorman. I think the pay was 50 cents an hour plus free admission to the other theatres in town. This was a reciprocal agreement.

"The people that frequented the Rex were the working stiffs from the day and graveyard shifts from the Navy Yard mostly — and the friends that I let in free. This cost me my job after just a few short weeks at the Rex. I had just finished football season prior to taking this job in '42 and I had let in a few of my ex-teammates one afternoon. Wouldn't you know that the word got around and I think half the team showed up the next day. Well, what with peer pressure and a laissez-faire attitude anyhow, I flagged in the group. Unfortunately, my boss was looking out of his office window at that precise moment. The phone rang and I was summoned to the holy of holies.

"I remember listening to this fellow rant and rave for a while, feeling like ten cents worth of cat shit and turning in my beautiful uniform. It's the only time I can remember getting fired and I do remember that it does nothing for your self-esteem. So much for show biz."

Helen Jean Stubblefield had better luck across the street: "I well remember one night going with my friends to the Rialto Theater. After we had been escorted down the aisle and had taken our seats, Cleo Frances, the head usherette, came down and asked us to step into the lobby. We wondered what could be the problem. Mary Lou Flieder, Susan Swanson, Pat Bryant and I were asked to accompany her to the manager's office where we were offered jobs as usherettes. This was the summer of our sophomore year of high school and I was so excited that one would think that I had been elected Queen of the May. A first real job, with paycheck of my own!"

Parents of the girls were not so enthralled, however. They met with the manager and set up rules. "It was agreed that parents took on the chore of picking us up each evening. We never left the theater on our own. .Three of us were allowed to accept jobs at the Rialto that summer. I loved the uniforms! They were furnished by the theater. Gorgeous fabric. They really fit and we thought most flattering. We had to make a special trip to Seattle for the fitting. It was like going to an exciting event every night and getting paid for it. We saw our friends, knew who was seeing whom, saw all the current movies and had our own spending money."

Patricia Henning's experience shows why conscientious parents kept close tab on kids' employment: "My first job in high school was as an usherette at the Admiral Theater on Sixth and Pacific. One time I told my Mom that a young Marine had patted my rear end. She told Dad and that was the end of my working career."

Some kids quit school to work. One was Brian Corcoran, who dropped out in 1942. He rode a Harley Davidson motorcycle around the Navy Yard, delivering messages. One day he entered the Yard's administrative building. Going up in the elevator, he noticed a Navy man looking at him. "Kid," said the man, "you're pretty damned young. How old are you?"

"I'm, uh, 16," lied Brian.

"What are you doing here?"

"I'm a messenger."

"Big deal," said the unknown man. "Why aren't you back in school? Get rid of that damn badge and get back to school."

Brian was startled at the unsolicited comments. But the following fall, he heeded the man's advice and returned to school, years later becoming Sen. Jackson's long-time press secretary and a key figure in two runs by Jackson for the Democratic presidential nomination. Still later he became chairman of the Snohomish County Commission.

Another of Corcoran's jobs was doorman at the Roxy. He also became a sports reporter for the *News-Searchlight*. He has the distinction of once covering an American Legion baseball game in which he played second base.

Gene Gurske worked at one of Bremerton's focal points: The Black Ball ferry terminal. Many Yard workers lived in Seattle and made the 55-minute trip daily. Almost as many Bremerton residents made frequent, casual trips to Seattle to shop, to see movies or shows, take music lessons, eat dinner, or prowl the arcades. Black Ball increased the number of trips during the war until by 1945 ferries left at intervals of 15 to 25 minutes during the daytime, more than 30 per day. Ferries on the run included at various times the *Chippewa, Enetai, Malahat, Willapa, Quinault, Sacra-*

mento and the most famous of them all, the *Kalakala,* notorious for its shake, rattle and roll, but also adorned with a piano and luxurious ladies' lounge. (One of Virginia Oass's favorite stories about her loquacious mother was when she chattered so intently with a group of her friends on the Seattle ferry that they forgot to get off in Bremerton.

The Kalakala
(Photo courtesy Fredi Perry.)

"It was a long round-trip back home," Virginia said.)

At the terminal, Gene Gurske took tickets, parked vehicles and raised and lowered the car and passenger ramps. "Gangs of sailors would run for the ferries, or they would jump into the back of a truck. That made it nearly impossible to take tickets. Sometimes, it paid to look the other way."

Aileen Bellinger held a variety of lunch-counter jobs — at an ice-cream parlor on Callow, at Horluck's, Olberg's Drug, and the Arctic Circle. "By the next year as a junior my grades started to slip," Aileen recalls. "Working in restaurants you always had to clean up on your own time and everything had to sparkle and the grill scrubbed off with the soapstone, which made it late getting home lots of times. Close up at 11 and clean up till 12, etc. I got a D in a class and went to sleep in Miss Wagner's class. I hated that. I loved her so much and to think that I did that to her has haunted me always."

Harry McIntyre put himself through high school with a variety of jobs, and paid a toll in fatigue. "I seldom went to school on Mondays for lack of sleep," he says. "Therefore, when Miss Holman, my ex-fifth grade teacher, rang the doorbell that Monday morning she found me home. Not only home but sprawled in an overstuffed chair and smoking a cigarette. I opened the door, for we had seen each other through the door glass and I'm sure that surprise was written all over my face.

"She said, 'Hi, Harry. I'm the new truant officer. I looked down my list of kids to check on and I recognized your name so you are my very first person to see'."

"I said, 'Well, isn't that nice. It's always a pleasure to see you, Miss Holman.' I really don't remember the conversation after that." (If I were casting Harry in a movie, Jack Nicholson would be my choice.)

Ronald H. Bailey[1] writes that the experiences of Aileen and Harry were not unusual:

"Many states had to relax their child-labor laws to allow minors to work. By '43, almost 3 million American boys and girls were working, half a million in defense plants. Between '40 and '44, the number of teenage workers in America increased by 1.9 million; the number attending school declined by 1.25 million. Many who tried to combine school and work fell asleep in class.

"The teen-ager acquired a new independence through the breakdown of normal family life and the availability of jobs that paid well. Aided by ready access to plenty of easy money and the relaxation of social constraints, the wartime crop of teen-agers developed into a highly specialized subculture, with its own clothing styles, interests and problems."

Lack of parental supervision also may have led to juvenile delinquency. "These youngsters were perhaps the hidden scandal of the war-worker army," writes Richard R. Lingeman[2] in his book, *Don't You Know There's a War On?* "People alternately viewed them with alarm or ignored them; hard-pressed personnel officers continued to lure them, even in violation of the law; and parents of many of them continued to look the other way, if indeed they were around to look at all, and sometimes even encouraged the youthful breadwinners to contribute to the family pot."

Another book,[3] says WWII was profoundly important in American social history. The old idea that women's place was in the home was shaken by the huge number of married women in the workplace. The materialism of the years after 1945 was fostered in part by the financial security produced by a second family income. The good life was expensive and women had to contribute their share.

When the war ended, returning GIs reclaimed their old jobs and many women returned to a domestic life. Although the workplace again became mostly masculine, the seeds of feminism had been planted. Traditional family values were turned upside down. The wartime experience began the process of accommodation between family and work and pointed the way to a greater degree of choice for American women.

A half-century later, the ripples from the huge splash made on employment by WWII are still being felt.

---

[1] Bailey, Ronald H. *The Homefront: U.S.A.* Alexandria, Virginia: Time-Life Books. 1978.

[2] Lingeman. Ibid.

[3] Anderson, Karen. *Wartime Women: Sex Roles, Family Relations and the Status of Women During World War II.* Westport, Connecticut: Greenwood Press. 1981.

- **Chapter 9**

(Headlines from the Bremerton Sun in 1942)

**All Japs in County Face Removal. . .
OPA Orders Rent Slashes Here. . .
Bremerton Overcomes Fife, Enters State Tournament . . . Your Tires Good? US May Seize Them
Soon . . . No Spring Vacation at BHS . . . East Side
Site Chosen for New Housing . . . Card Rationing
of Gasoline Due Soon . . . Shirley Samson Named
Queen of HS Ball . . . Jap Population of
Bainbridge Moved Out in Four Hours . . .
Harold Shidler Quits Post as HS Coach**

≈

Easy Aces, Casablanca Brought Laughter, Tears

The Japanese spent April and May of 1942 tidying up. They had fulfilled their pre-war hopes. And more: Victory had come with unexpected ease. But never again could they feel so smug. On May 6 and 7, at the battle of Coral Sea, they won tactically because they sank many of our ships, including the *Lexington*, and seriously damaged the *Yorktown*. But they lost strategically; they had lost forever the naval power to threaten Australia.

The *USS Lexington* was a favorite in Bremerton but even more beloved in Tacoma. In 1929, drought and an unusual cold spell had reduced the flow of water over dams at Lake Cushman and the Nisqually River, sources of Tacoma's hydropower. On December 15, the *Lex* tied up on Tacoma's waterfront and for the next several weeks generated 20,000 kilowatts of power for 12 hours a day, providing power to the city and permitting water to build up behind the dams.

By the spring of 1942 the novelty of being at war was wearing off for Bremerton High School students. The halls were thronged with almost 2,000 students in buildings built for 900. It was joked that driver's education and sex education were taught in the same car. Even with two shifts, morning and afternoon, it was crowded. Almost all the juniors and seniors attending the morning shift held jobs in the afternoon. But that did not preclude pursuit of what teen-agers do so well: Having fun. One of the ways we did that — listening to the radio — may strike the generations that followed as mundane. But the radio was at least as vital then as television is now.

During World War II, Bremerton had no radio station but Seattle's stations came in loud and clear. For the first time, thanks to radio, current news and professional entertainment were available everywhere in the nation — without direct cost. (The indirect cost was having to listen to commercials). The effect was profound. When television came along later, Americans were already accustomed to swift broadcast of news (CBS, NBC's Red and Blue Networks, Mutual), tear-jerking soap operas (Stella Dallas, Ma Perkins), comedy (Bob Hope, Jack Benny) and classical music (Standard Symphony, Ford Hour).

Radio in the '90s bears little resemblance. Studio orchestras have long since disappeared. So have most news staffs. Instead, stations stick to formats — talk, country western, classical, jazz — aimed at a narrow segment of the audience. There are many more stations now than in the '30s and '40s — there were no commercial FM stations then — and so variety has been preserved, not by individual stations but by their aggregate.

The *Sun* published comprehensive radio schedules. The schedule for a Sunday in early 1941 included Major Bowes on KIRO, followed by the Salt Lake City Tabernacle Choir. The New York Symphony (presumably today's Philharmonic) played on KVI at noon. At 2:30 on KOL was The Shadow. At 5 on KOMO was Charlie McCarthy; at 5:30, Sherlock Holmes. At 6 on KIRO was the Ford Evening Hour. At 8:30 on KOMO was Jack Benny, at 9 Walter Winchell. At 10 on KOMO came the Richfield Reporter, with this introduction, remembered 50 years later:

"News flashes, by Richfield! And a good, good evening, ladies and gentlemen . . ."

Also stuck in my memory are the lyrics to the song that introduced Little Orphan Annie:

"Who's that little chatterbox?
"The one with pretty auburn locks
"Who can it be
"But Little Orphan Annie." .

Granted, the jingle was not a great foot-tapper. But at the start of 1941 it was better than most music played on the radio. That's because on January 1, 1941, ASCAP — the American Society of Composers, Authors and Publishers — demanded more money of the radio networks for the performance of the songs it licensed. So the networks quit playing ASCAP songs. That included almost everything then popular. The ASCAP ban lasted until late 1941, when the networks and ASCAP compromised and a new contract was signed. During this period, Stephen Foster's warhorse, "I Dream of Jeannie With the Light Brown Hair" was played to the point of distraction. It was in the public domain and could be played without payment of royalties.

The music industry stumbled again on August 1, 1942, when James C. Petrillo, president of the American Federation of Musicians, took his union on strike against the record companies. This ban lasted for 13 months, when a pact was agreed upon. The record industry also suffered from a wartime shortage of shellac. The industry set up collection points for old records, which were melted and reused. It was a bum trade. Thousands of excellent records were lost, replaced by mediocre platters produced during the war years.

My family listened to the radio faithfully. Mother's favorite program was Information Please, a quiz show moderated by Clifton Fadiman during which listeners tried to stump columnist Franklin P. Adams, journalist John Kieran and other experts whose names I don't remember. Our family also enjoyed the popular comedians, too: Jack Benny, Fred Allen, Fibber McGee and Molly, Edgar Bergen and Charlie McCarthy (particularly when Charlie traded insults with the misanthropic W.C. Fields). Mother thought it worth entering in her diary on November 26, 1941, that Fred Allen had traded insults with Edna Mae Oliver, the droll, equine-faced actress. We listened to Bob Hope, too, but Mother didn't like him; she thought he was salacious.

Other Bremerton families listened with equal faithfulness. LaVerne Jacobson says her family enjoyed Fibber McGee and Molly, Jack Benny, Fred Allen, Myrt and Marge, One Man's Family, The Shadow, Inner Sanctum, and Lux Radio Theater. The kids listened to Jack Armstrong ("the Alllll-American Boy!"), Little Orphan Annie, The Lone Ranger and the Cisco Kid. "We sent for everything, all decoding devices, rings, etc. that didn't cost any money," LaVerne remembers.

We didn't pay attention to it at the time, but males were invariably featured in the adventure programs aimed at kids. As William M. Tuttle[1] points out in his book *Daddy's Gone To War,* "On children's radio adventure and crime shows, as well as their comic books and animated cartoons and their movies and serials, men were invariably the heroes, the action figures, the ones who took the risks." About the only exception was Wonder Woman, a comic book.

Other popular programs included the Bill Sterns Sports Show, Bing Crosby, Kate Smith, Aldrich Family, Meet Corliss Archer, and newscasters Gabriel Heater ("There's good news tonight!") and H.V. Kaltenborn. The comedy team of Amos 'n' Andy was not mentioned by any of my Bremerton correspondents nor in several reference books, although the show enjoyed phenomenal popularity in the early '30s. Perhaps that was too early to be remembered by those who contributed to this book. More likely it's because in retrospect we realize it gave a skewed picture of blacks and is seen as racist. ("I'se regusted," said Kingfish was typical dialogue). Others who weren't mentioned, although for other reasons, included Eddie Cantor, one of the first comedians to stage a mock campaign for president (he sang that he would kill all the red ink in Washington); Ed Wynn, the Texaco fire chief with the loony laugh, and Joe Penner, whose query, "Wanna buy a duck" always brought a good laugh. And wasn't there a Baron Munchausen, who told fantastic, funny stories about his heroic exploits?

Alice Jane Levin says her grandmother loved the soaps and when Alice Jane stayed with her they would listen to John's Other Wife, Ma Perkins, Back Stage Wife and Vic and Sade. Alice Jane's mother listened to Myrt and Marge, and Easy Aces. "Jane Ace had a drawling, nasal voice and a way of turning a phrase," says Alice Jane. "I remember her saying when someone asked her if she played the piano that she played 'for my own amazement.' Her answer to everything was 'Just fine.' Once her husband fell asleep and dreamed that the United States had just elected its first woman president. The strains to 'Hail To the Chief' were heard and the announcer said the president would now give her State of the Union address. Jane's voice said, 'Just fine.' Ace's reaction to most of these events was, 'Isn't that awful?'

---

[1] Tuttle, William M., Jr. *Daddy's Gone to War.* New York: Oxford University Press. 1993.

and my Dad adopted that as one of his pet expressions but we all thought that Mom was more like Gracie Allen."

I associate all the daytime soaps with being sick. A whiff of Vick's Vapo-Rub can instantly stimulate memories of Helen Trent ("Can a woman of 35," etc.) or John's Other Wife. The only time I heard Pretty Kitty Kelly or Ma Perkins was when I had the measles (I had at least four varieties) or 'flu and was home from school. I should make it clear that listening to the soaps didn't make me sick; that was an existing condition.

By consensus, the favorite radio program was One Man's Family, an evening serial that began on the West Coast in 1932 and became a popular network feature the following year. It was written by Carleton E. Morse and set in San Francisco, in those days everybody's favorite city. Nothing much ever seemed to happen, which may be why it seemed so realistic, like our own families. I can still draw a laugh from other aficionados by sighing in resignation, "Yes, yes, Fannie," in the manner of Father Barbour. "Everyone listened to it," says David Leathley. He also remembers a program no one else mentioned: Rocky Gordon, Engineer, the saga of a railroad engineer. Gordon Lecair mentions Joe Louis's fights but adds, "The one I remember best was One Man's Family. I guess it was because it had a character for each member of my family (or so it seemed)."

Dorothy Fick says listening to the radio stimulated the imagination, a mental faculty crippled later by television. With radio, she says, "We could picture everything that went on." She's right. I remember my disappointment when my grandmother Nana sent off for a photograph of the Barbours of One Man's Family. The actors didn't look at all like the characters I had imagined. It took awhile for my own imagination to take over again.

Listening was often a group experience. Jim Braman, whose home on Sixth Street became an unofficial hospitality house for servicemen, speaks of a parade of sailors, marines, and soldiers joining the Bramans "in listening to radio favorites such as the Jack Benny show (funny), Inner Sanctum (spooky), Manhattan Merry-Go-Round (melodic), and Lux Theatre (dramatic)."

The radio sets themselves often were elegant. Dorothy Fick remembers her family's cabinet Zenith. Patti Serry's big console had doors that she closed to contain the dial light during blackouts. Myron Richards said his parents bought a second-hand Majestic for $15 from the Rev. Mr. Pyle of Charleston Baptist Church. "The set was in the most magnificent piece of cabinetry you can imagine with much inlaid wood of different colors." Later he traded a Model A car, for which he and his brother Lowell had paid $15, for a radio.

Sponsor identification was powerful. Myron remembers these lyrics for a West Coast gasoline:

> *Red Lion Oil, Gilmore Gas,*
> *Put them in your motor*
> *They'll add a lot of class.*
> *There's no one on the highway*
> *That you can't pass,*
> *Unless they're using Gilmore Tooooo.*

Naughty little boys, attempting to be bawdy, would change the last line:

> *That you can't pass,*
> *But you'll be skidding*
> *on your . . . behind.*

One of the strongest sponsor identifications was established by Ovaltine with a children's program, Little Orphan Annie. Anyone who coveted standing with his or her classmates in the third grade sent away for products offered by Ovaltine, a drink mix that tasted like cocoa. When you are 9, the wait for arrival of the product by mail seems interminable. Sometimes the expectation exceeded actuality.

Virginia Eddy: "In grade school, sister Hedy listened to Orphan Annie and Tarzan, and at one point sent for an Ovaltine 'unbreakable' shaker. It cost a quarter and an Ovaltine label. Anxiously Hedy waited, and when the package arrived, she took out the shaker and said, 'Watch, it's unbreakable!' She then slammed it on the floor to demonstrate this magic, only to find it split the side. So much for unbreakables."

Alice Jane Levin: "I waited impatiently for the end of each Orphan Annie episode so I could copy down the letters and decode the secret messages that more often than not were reminders to 'drink your Ovaltine'."

Berenice Lee: "Yes, I did have a decoder, gotten after I promised to drink Ovaltine that we had to buy to get the aluminum seal to mail away for the decoder. Years later, the Ovaltine was still standing on the pantry shelf."

Patricia Henning, proving that the sins of siblings are never forgotten, remembers from a half-century ago: "My brother stole my decoder and broke it."

Harry Harkness turned his remarks about Little Orphan Annie into a wonderful True-Confession type digression: "Sure I had a decoder pin when I lived next door to Rodney Abacherli on

Olympic Street. . . my very best friend from tricycles to cars. We even stole a car from a used-car lot at Naval and Burwell . . . Rodney died at age 33 of cancer. We used to pee in the corner of Mrs. Stewart's garage at age 4 and 5. This was our tricycle turn-around spot. Once when we were both home on leave from the service (Rod was in the Navy, me in the Army Air Corps) we raced up Fourth Street in both our parent's cars and survived an accident on the lawn of the Christian Science Church. What a mess we made of the shrubs and lawn."

Patti Serry more sedately recalls: "I would crouch in front of the radio with the doors semi-closed on each side of me. Jack Armstrong and Little Orphan Annie had gone to war along with Lucky Strike Green. The Andrews Sisters warned us, 'Don't Sit Under the Apple Tree' and we knew . . . just what rude noise to make "Right in der Fuehrer's Face" while we laughed with Fred Allen or Fibber McGee and Mollie.

"We listened constantly. How else would we know if the West Coast would be invaded. The radio was our link to the world around us; our lifeline, so to speak. It advised what to do in case of bombing, how to survive an invasion, and it gave us the latest news. It exhorted us to buy War Bonds, asked us to conserve food and clothing and shoes, and told us to give our aluminum pans and scrap metal to the War Effort.

"And there was always the music . . . swing and jazz and boogie-woogie, and the bittersweet songs that told us 'We'll Meet Again.' And who can forget President Roosevelt's Fireside Chats?"

Or the Hit Parade, which told us what were the week's most popular songs.

Radio created a national community of shared experiences. We laughed together when we heard Jack Benny's echoing footsteps and the creaky opening of his bank vault or when Fibber McGee opened the door to his cluttered closet. Jack, Doc and Reggie of "I Love a Mystery" were at least as well known as Larry, Curley and Mo, the Three Stooges. Gildersleeve's pitiful sigh, "Heee, heee" always brought laughter and applause from the studio audiences.

After the war started, radio played an even bigger role. A survey in November of 1942 estimated that three-quarters of Americans used radio as their major source of information about hostilities.

Catherine Anderson's father had emigrated from Norway before World War I. "I can still see my father twiddling the dial on the radio to hear the latest news from Europe, and when Germany invaded Norway he was beside himself," recalls Catherine. "We listened to all the news. We heard William L. Shirer reporting from Berlin, and we heard the buzz bombs over London and Churchill's marvelous speeches."

Richard R. Lingeman[2] notes, "To millions of Americans the radio became a primary source of information abut the war. In a commercial medium, news was a commercial success. By 1944 NBC alone was devoting 20 percent of its airtime to news, compared with 3 percent in 1939; 30 percent of Columbia Broadcasting System's programming was devoted to war news . . . "

For pure entertainment, however, nothing equaled the movies (that may still be true). In the '30s and '40s, movies were part of almost everyone's life. In a population of 130 million, 80 million to 90 million went to the movies *every week*. There were about 20,000 theaters across the country. In Bremerton, the Rialto and the Tower were the early first-run theaters, joined in 1941 by the Roxy and the next year by the Admiral. The Rex showed second-run films and so did the Grand in Charleston. The Saturday matinees at the Tower cost us kids 10 cents. Popcorn was a nickel or dime. So were candy bars.

A Seattle motion-picture chain had reported in 1938 that weekly attendance averaged 62,000; by 1943 it had increased to 116,000 — an 85 percent jump, notes James R. Warren.[3]

Attendance figures probably don't include special showings for the military during the war. Don Fry remembers, "Through the Operators' Club at school I got work with the YMCA going out to the barrage balloon sites and showing full-length movies to the Army personnel at the sites."

I wrote home in 1944 from Buckley Field near Denver, where I was taking Army Air Corps basic training, that I had seen "Going My Way," "Double Indemnity," and "Arsenic and Old Lace." For a few days after seeing "Arsenic" my buddies and I shouted "Charge!" whenever we dashed up a flight of stairs, as Teddy Roosevelt had done in the film. I remember all three movies with affection.

During the Great Depression, theaters offered weekly Bank Nights — drawings at which the door prize might be several hundred dollars, a whopping figure in those times. Bank Night was so popular in Bremerton the police would rope off the streets and the whole town would turn out. LaVerne Jacobson remembers that you had to be present to win. "We never missed the two-mile round-trip walk downtown when the weather allowed."

---

[2] Lingeman. Ibid.

[3] Warren, James R. *King County and Its Queen City, Seattle.* Woodland Hills, California: Winsor Publications. 1981.

Gordon Lecair speaks of Bank Night at the Rialto and Rex theaters: "When Dad was not working the swing shift in the Yard, we would go to the movie on Thursday night when they drew a name for the prize of about $300. When Dad was working, Mom and I would go down and stand in the street between the theaters to wait for the announcement. The street was always full of people waiting for the chance that they might be the winner. We never were. On one of those nights we were at the Rex watching Charlie Chaplin in 'Modern Times.' My father started to laugh and just couldn't stop. I remember that he had to go outside to calm down but on return he would start again. It was a good time for all."

Movies provided up to three hours of entertainment: The main feature, a second feature, newsreel, previews, sometimes a travelogue, and at least one cartoon. Once started, they ran continuously; the lights never came on. Only the fussy timed their entry for the start of a film; usually, we entered when convenient and remained until we had seen everything that was being shown. And sometimes longer.

Hollywood at first ignored Pearl Harbor; author Lingeman quoted Hollywood producers as saying, "We felt it wise to leave Pearl Harbor out of it, for all this can do is remind us of defeat." It was not until March, 1942, in "A Yank on the Burma Road" that an actor first denounced Japanese perfidy at Pearl Harbor. Most war movies of the time were awful; it wasn't until after the war was over that the good ones were made. Lingeman also said the attitude of audiences changed. Gone was the silent reverence and gratitude for escape of the Depression. Furthermore, theaters became social centers for parking kids, for necking, and for footloose teen-agers. Wrote Lingeman:[4]

"There was the ecstatic release in watching John Wayne driving a steam shovel at an enemy tank, picking it up and dropping it over a cliff. Or Andy Devine shooting down an enemy plane with a shotgun. Or the insouciant fastidiousness with which Errol Flynn spat out a hand-grenade pin, like spitting out grape seeds."

Lingeman also said you could count on a variety of patriotic movie clichés to pop up, such as: "Well, looks like this is it." . . . "Now go, darling, and don't even look back." . . . "I don't want any dead heroes in this outfit." . . ."Synchronize your watches, gentlemen." . . . "Don't try to win the war by yourself, kid."

The UW's Jon Bridgman says the movies maintained a remarkably high level of writing and also achieved a high technical

---

4 Lingeman. Op. cit.

gloss. A few were high art. The studios had fairly well known styles; MGM was known as the Cadillac that did everything well. "Paramount was sophisticated, Warner Brothers did tough, hard, sort of proletarian films; when making the final cut they looked for ways to tighten and shorten." Every theater showed something like 104 films per year. To make money the movies had to avoid controversy. They accurately portrayed background, such as hardware, stoves, clothes, hair styles and language. But the Andy Hardy movies had little more connection with reality than did the "Leave It To Beaver" television series later. The Hollywood moguls censored their own movies to conform with the Legion of Decency of the Catholic Church. Professor Bridgman says that when Rhett Butler said, "Frankly, my dear, I don't give a damn," near the end of "Gone with the Wind," it was the only profane word in any American film in the '30s and '40s.

In 1941 the *Sun* listed the movies being shown on April 15:

Rialto: Barbara Stanwyck and Henry Fonda in "The Lady Eve" and Orrin Turner and Bonnie Baker in "You're the One"

Rex: Frank Morgan and Virginia Grey in "Hullabaloo" and John Howard and Ellen Drew in "Texas Rangers Ride Again".

Tower: Anna Neagle in "No, No, Nanette" and Guy Kibbee in "Scattergood Baines".

Grand: Claudette Colbert and Ray Milland in "Arise, My Love" and selected short subjects.

By 1942, Bremerton's movies had become more warlike:

Roxy: Victor McLaglen, Edmond Lowe in "Call Out the Marines" and "Sing Your Worries Away."

Tower: Abbott and Costello in "Keep 'Em Flying" and Jane Frazee and the Merrymacs in "Moonlight in Hawaii."

Admiral: Dorothy Lamour in "The Fleet's In."

Rialto: Wallace Beery, Lewis Stone in "The Bugle Sounds" and Lew Ayres, Lionel Barrymore in "Dr. Kildare's Victory."

Rex: Nelson Eddy, Rise Stevens in "The Chocolate Soldier" and Lynn Bari, Charles Ruggles in "The Perfect Snob."

Grand: Ronald Colman in "Lost Horizon" and "Westward Ho Hum."

By then, the national anthem was being played at the start of the main feature in Bremerton. The audience would stand and with Old Glory fluttering on the screen, we would sing, or try to sing, "The Star Spangled Banner." This brought up sad memories for Brian Corcoran, who felt guilty that he was watching a movie while his 17-year-old brother Pat was fighting the Japanese on Bataan. "I couldn't survive those emotional moments without a flow of tears," he remembers. "It wasn't fair that I was comfortable in a Bremerton theater, but Pat was in a jungle, prison camp or worse. I walked out of theaters time and again with wet eyes no matter what the subject of the films."

Virginia Oass remembers that when she and sister Jo Ann were young, movies were important in their choice of who would be their baby sitters. "Before deciding what sitters got to come, we would dicker with them to see what movies each had seen recently, and how many each would tell us after were tucked in for the night. They were frequently disgusted with me when I would ask the next day what had happened after a certain point in the movie and they discovered I had fallen asleep soon after the start of the movie. One night Pat (Driscoll) talked close to two hours to herself!"

In the summer of 1942, the dreams of Virginia and her close friend, Jeanie Schairer, came true: They went with their mothers to California; first a stop in San Franciso and then on to Hollywood itself. More than 50 years later the thrill is still apparent:

"For two movie-struck 15 year olds, the trip proved to be a dazzling experience never to be forgotten. We were treated to the Top of the Mark in San Francisco, lunch at the Brown Derby, footprints at Grauman's Chinese Theater, a bus tour of the homes of Hollywood stars, swims at Santa Monica, and, best of all, tickets to the world premier of 'Mrs. Minniver' starring Greer Garson and Walter Pidgeon. That night, one after another of the black limousines pulled up, spilling out Hollywood's most glamorous stars decked out in full regalia. From start to finish, Jeanie and I (and even our mothers) collected over a hundred autographs from Gregory Peck, Lana Turner, Joan Crawford, Dick Powell, June Haver, Katherine Hepburn, Bob Hope, Shirley Temple, Deanna Durbin, Irene Dunne, Dorothy Lamour, Joel McCrea, Clark Gable . . . Our star-studded dream — while sitting at the fountain of the Rex Drug in Bremerton savoring sundaes as we read the latest movie magazines — had become a reality."

Among other movie memories, Virginia mentions her sympathy for Jeanie Schairer "after her mother sighted her leaving 'Gone with the Wind,' her seventh viewing, during school hours."

Patricia Henning remembers social aspects of movie-going. "My girlfriend and I used to go to the Rialto or the Rex on Second Street. We really preferred the Rialto because it had a balcony. We used to meet lots of cute sailors there and go for cokes after."

Presiding over the Mickey Mouse matinee at the Tower Theater on Saturdays was Uncle Ralph — Ralph Trathen, sometime composer and manager of the Tower. He helped youngsters prepare their performances for the amateur segment of the program and acted as master of ceremonies. The only performer I remember was Boney, who wasn't — how to say this gently — completely bright and played the musical spoons. (Myron Richards says Boney got his name from playing on hardwood sticks that were called "bones." Says Myron: "He could play drums also, and post-war I played a gig with him at the Sunnyslope Community Hall. He played drums, and bones, and I played string bass.") I think most of us wanted to see the movies, not the performers, and didn't react politely to their presentations. But the kids hooted and ran up and down the aisles during the newsreel and previews, too, so the real-life performers weren't persecuted inordinately.

Alice Jane Levin says hers was a movie-going family that never missed a Jeanette MacDonald-Nelson Eddy musical and always attended when the Marx Brothers, Wheeler and Woolsey or the Ritz Brothers were showing. Movies she remembers included "It Happened One Night," "Rebecca," all the Betty Grable, June Haver musicals, "Lost Horizon," the Fred Astaire-Ginger Rogers musicals "and all the horror movies the Tower Theater used to show on Saturday afternoon at the supposed children's Mickey Mouse Matinee. Many years later they were aired on late-night TV and my kids thought they were great, Bela Lugosi, Lon Chaney Jr., Boris Karloff."

Don Rolstad said no Saturday was complete unless he attended the matinee at the Tower. "The matinee consisted of a newsreel, cartoon, a Western serial and a movie. I lived from week to week to see that serial and if I missed, it was a major disaster. My favorite Western stars were Tom Mix and Ken Maynard."

We walked or rode our bikes to the Saturday matinees. Getting there and back was not necessarily prosaic; imaginative kids can make an adventure out of anything.

Art McCarty remembers: "One day Bob Romberg and I walked home using only the parking strip and making a complete circle around everything on the strip, telephone and power poles, cars, anything. Took us a couple of hours."

How come they don't make movies like that any more — that send us home reeling, eager for adventure, dizzy with the joy of being alive? Or is it only that, like Art McCarty and Bob Romberg, we were young then, and that was very long ago?

Chapter 10

(Headlines from the Bremerton Sun, 1942)

Boeing Unions Lift Ban on Negroes ...
Dwight Scheyer Bremerton Football Coach ...
City Census: 26,966 ...
Gas To Be Rationed Beginning June 1 ...
324 Students, Largest Senior Class in City's History, Will
Graduate ... Survey of Air Raid Shelters Completed ...
Bob Crosby's Band Due Here Tuesday ...

≈

Schoolboy Patrol, Ink Wells and Standing Tall

I went straight through the Bremerton school system, except for a few brief interludes at elementary school in Port Orchard when we hadn't moved back yet from summers at Camp. My first six grades were at Central School. If pressed, I could go trace my schooling even earlier, to a kindergarten at the Baptist Church across the street from Central, which was between Fourth and Fifth streets on Warren Avenue. I don't remember much about kindergarten except playing drum on a cylindrical Quaker Oats cereal container in a rhythm band. Images of Central's teachers remain vivid, however, and not only for me. Sixty years after sitting in Central's classrooms, an astute classmate, Joe Stottlebower, offered these taut characterizations of our teachers: First grade, Mrs. Marsh: kind. Second grade, Miss Wood: sensible. Third grade, Miss Giovannini; smiling, flexible. Fourth grade, Miss Spencer: Austere. Fifth grade, Miss Hendrickson: Organized. Sixth grade, Miss Thompson: Crusader.

My memories are similar but not identical. For instance, I remember Miss Spencer, not austere so much as tall and dignified, sitting beside me at my desk to make certain I understood a problem of fractions. I remember Miss Hendrickson, the principal, red-haired and volatile, upset because the interludes at Port Orchard elementary put me out of synch with her teaching schedule at Central. I remember that Miss Thompson lived at the Helena Apartments on Burwell — no significance to that, except it's one of those fragments that stick inexplicably in my mind — with whom we listened to the Standard Symphony on the radio, I think on Thursday mornings. She could barely suppress her laughter when in class one day I told her I customarily held my breath crossing the street to avoid inhaling carbon monoxide from car exhausts. An environmentalist ahead of his time.

Bremerton elementary schools offered a sound fundamental education. I remember Central as a no-frills, straight-forward school that today would seem old-fashioned for such things as its dirt play field, the ink wells in each desk, and exercises in Palmer penmanship. More important than the spare physical facilities, however, was this: In the '30s, teachers still had time to take a personal interest in their pupils. Even more important than that, however, were the lasting friendships established during six years at Central. In many cases, the children I met in first grade were still classmates when a dozen years later we were seniors in high school. In a few cases they remain close friends today, 60 years later, remarkable in this mobile age: Joe Stottlebower, Jorgen Nelson, David Poll, Bill Gates, Don Haskell, Dick Kint (who left Central after the first grade but with whom I was happily reunited in Alva Hugenin's World History class as freshmen at BHS). I don't see them often but I still feel close to Mary Lou Flieder, Susan Swanson, Helen Jean Stubblefield, Phyllis Johnson, my cousin Mary Lou Parker. Of some I've lost track: The Chinn sisters, Mary and Lena; Mary Smith, Bruce Zimmerman, Morry Brooks, Eric Felton. Some were a half-grade ahead or behind and might be in 2A when I was in 2B. Or vice versa.

Memories of Central School in the '30s are still bright but come now in fragments: Refereeing a fight prompted when James Penn called Dave Poll a damned Jew, and wondering what was a Jew? . . . . Kicking a rock all the way home from school, hearing Warren Lindblad's mother scold him for doing so, and wisely deciding not to tell my own mother . . . . Leaving class periodically with my flute under arm for a special music class offered at Smith School . . . . Bungling the Christmas wreath I was cutting out in third grade, finding Mary Smith's fancy one on the floor, erasing her name from it and listening sympathetically when Mary told the teacher she had lost hers . . . . Proudly leaving class for duty with the Schoolboy Patrol, hoping it would rain so I could wear the Patrol's yellow slickers, telling the little kids when it was safe to cross the street, attending Police Lt. Art Morken's safety meetings at City Hall, followed by a movie . . . . The fleece-lined aviator's helmets worn by many young boys, the flaps warming our ears in winter, my goggles soon lost . . . . Wearing knickers until the fifth grade, wondering why my mother inflicted such pain when, gee whiz, Mom, all the other guys get to wear long pants . . . . And my knee-high boots, called "loggers," that laced up to the knees . . . . On the way to school, Warren Lindblad carefully lifting angle worms from sidewalks to lawns because on rainy days he thought they were drowning . . . . Jorgen Nelson's compulsion to walk in step with his companions and the fun of trying to frustrate him by skipping to change the pace . . . . Miss Condy, a visiting teacher and nasty old biddy, raising welts on my palm from her ruler — and my gratitude when some girls in the class told our regular teacher I had been nailed on a bum rap.

The posture contests at Central were dominated by Shirley Braendlein, whose father was postmaster. Even as a young girl, she stood tall and stately, as straight as a strong sapling. Although in high school she grew her hair so long that she could sit on it, even then you knew she had good posture. Her shoulders were back and her chin was up. She walked like royalty. So did her sisters, Dolly and Bunny, despite their proletarian names. Posture was important then, back in the '30s, almost as important as penmanship. Several times a week we practiced the round O's and the up-and-down l's of the Palmer method of writing. One special day Mr. Palmer himself visited our class and praised our penmanship. At least I think it was Mr. Palmer; you know how it is in grade school, all men in suits look alike. Maybe it was only Tillman Peterson, the school superintendent.

Under the Palmer system of penmanship, everything was supposed to be arm movement. I think motion was supposed to come from the shoulder, or maybe it was the elbow. It was kind of like writing with a long stick; it felt like the paper was 10 feet away. Anyway, the wrist and fingers were supposed to be kept stiff. If the teacher saw you move your fingers, you could expect a swift admonition. A whole classroom of pupils doing their round O's and up-and-down l's could get up quite a head of steam. On rainy days when we couldn't go outside during recess and the kids really got into it, the windows would drip with condensation.

Our desks had holes at the top, on the right side, for ink bottles. The school provided the ink. Not, of course, for the little kids in the first or second grades, who could be trusted to spill it or do something dumb with it. But when you got older, in the third grade, say, then the teacher came around once or twice a year with a bottle of ink and a spout and poured ink into your bottle. We wrote with straight pens. They had disposable points. If you were careful, they would last a whole school year. We were careful, believe me; this, I will remind you, was during the Great Depression.

A straight pen with a sharp, disposable point makes a mighty weapon. I made that discovery when I dropped mine under my desk and in retrieving it inadvertently goosed the girl sitting in front of me. Neither the girl nor the teacher believed it was accidental. I was not the first innocent person to be punished for an offense committed with neither intent nor premeditation. My pen never again achieved a reaction so swift or dramatic.

In the lower grades we had periodic inspections for clean fingernails. I was caught after a particularly rowdy recess one time and attempted to clean my nails with a pencil. The lead made the nails look even dirtier, of course, a point that Miss Woods triumphantly pointed out to the entire second-grade class.

I have no idea why the emphasis on posture, whether it was a symbolic reaction to the slumping economy — a little joke, there — or a bee in the bonnet of Pearl Wanamaker, the state school superintendent. It was emphasized out of school, too. "Stand up, boy," my father would bark. As near as I could figure, that meant pulling your shoulders back into an unnatural position and holding them there until you were out of a patriarchal sight. I still do that when passing a woman. I was once reminded that state law directs teachers to impress on pupils the principles of morality, truth, justice, temperance, humanity and patriotism. Well, in the spirit of Ronald Reagan, I suppose the posture contests helped America stand tall.

Central was of course superior to the other elementary schools in Bremerton for a simple reason: It was where I went to school. Of the other elementary schools, kids with learning disabilities went to Smith (not all of the pupils at Smith were special students but it was fun to pretend they were; Dorothy Fick recalls calling it "the dummy school," although she couldn't remember why). Hillcrest was way out in the sticks — Charleston or some distant place like that, for heaven's sake. Naval Avenue school was OK, I guess, but didn't draw from the distinguished Gregory Way group of which I was a member. But Dick Grace remembers his Naval Avenue grade school friends with fondness: Among them Don McCoard, Wayne Lichter, Al Stewart, Bob Caughie and Kenny Fick. So I am forced to concede that the other grade schools had some of the same virtues. But not as many as Central, you understand.

Harry McIntyre also attended Naval Avenue school. His recollections of the Schoolboy Patrol are like mine. "When I was in Miss Hendricks' fifth-grade class at Naval Avenue School she called me to her desk one day and asked me if I would like to be a schoolboy patrolman. Well, would I ever. I don't remember all of the particulars but the next thing I remember is that I'm walking out of class 10 minutes early to get down to the intersection of Sixth and Naval to stop traffic and allow students to safely walk to the other side of the street. It's hard to imagine now that a 10-year-old kid with an eight-foot-long piece of bamboo with a triangular stop sign on the end would stand a chance in traffic there. But this was another era when Bremerton was 10,000 people and Sixth and Naval wasn't the main thoroughfare that it is today.

"I remember the Red & White Grocery store on the northwest corner of the street that I stood in front of while I waited for the kids to start pouring down the sidewalk hurrying to get home after class.

"Wow, here comes that cute girl in my class who lives in the Navy Yard. She is about as worldly as they come because she even takes French lessons, I'm told. She gives her braids a little toss as she floats by me and crosses safely because I have brought traffic to a halt with my magic wand and my white Sam Brown belt with the silver badge. Life just doesn't get any better than this.

"My long-time friend Duane Thompson is also a school boy patrolman and sometimes we work as a pair. Eleventh and Naval is another hot spot that we patrol but not our favorite because it's gravel and it can get dusty in dry weather.

"This brings me to the yellow slicker raincoat which has to be the ultimate in fashion. Of course because I was short my main problem was getting one that cleared the ground. These of course were worn only when it rained.

"If you can believe it — the city schoolboy patrol met once a month at the police station and guess who presided. None other than Art Morken, all decked out in his flawless uniform and knee-high black leather boots. Other schools like Smith and Hillcrest were there too, so we schoolboy patrolmen were really big time. Notice that there were no girls in this man's outfit.

"Well, Art would call the meeting to order and give us a pep talk about how important the job was that we were doing and saving lives, etc. Then for the coup de grace he led us down the alley to the Rialto Theater and we got in scot-free and got to sit in the balcony. (I can just imagine what we 30 or so boys sounded like coming in in the middle of a movie.) All this on a school night. Did our parents pick us up? Are you kidding! We rode our bikes home just like a posse returning home after catching the cattle rustlers."

Although I didn't understand the point in attending parochial school at Our Lady Star of the Sea, that should not be construed as religious prejudice. It is true that at age 6 or 7 I wittily taunted Bernard Glavin, who lived next door, as a Cat-Licker. But I was joined by Phyllis Johnson, herself a Catholic, so I think this was more a conflict of class than of religion. Among those who did attend the Catholic school were Mary Jane Hudson and Virginia Oass. Virginia says they competed for excellence and carefully counted each other's A's as the report cards were read to the class by Father Camerman. "I was crushed when Mary Jane was named valedictorian and I, salutatorian," Virginia remembers. "In the middle of her commencement speech she blanked out, looked stricken, and then began to cry. Needless to say, I stood behind her smiling from ear to ear, ecstatic." Virginia treated a fifth-grade classmate with greater deference after she reported witnessing a miracle one recess when she ducked into church. "The statue of Mary winked at her."

At Toni McHale's suggestion, I asked Dominican nuns who had taught at Star of the Sea to describe how their school functioned during WWII. Sister Catherine Mary responded in part:

"In the school . . . Wall-to-wall desks, no aisles to speak of, and no storage space for books or articles not in use. I've seen Christmas trees in closets and/or on top of a teacher's desk. Lunch was eaten in the classroom; PE consisted of stretching exercises, especially on rainy days, and medals should have been given to the staff who must have dreamed up games to entertain students on those rainy days.

"There was always a huge turnover of students each year, sometimes mid-term. Families of Navy officers and personnel would call long distance to ask, 'Is there room for my children at Star of the Sea School?' CCD classes, taught after school hours, evenings and every Saturday and Sunday, cared for the many children who found no room in the only Catholic school in Bremerton. Individual and small-group tutoring or in many cases music lessons helped to fill in the hours while children waited to go home with Dad or Mom who worked in the Yard. There were pianos in the convent music rooms, on the back porch at the convent, and one if not two pianos in the school basement. Familiar melodies could be heard from several pianos at the same time before recitals or special entertainments." Sister Catherine Mary said many were turned away from Mass after the city posted the seating capacity for the busy building.

Added Sister Catherine Mary, "For the Dominican Sisters who taught there for a good portion of this century, there will always remain happy memories of both the school and Bremerton, the city we all knew and loved."

Florence Sigrist Lindberg taught in the Bremerton public system, which, of course, also was jammed during the war. Without specifying in which school she taught, she wrote, "In 1944, I had 63 pupils in my room, but I was lucky, for I had a classroom. Some teachers had to conduct classes in the halls, or basements or lunchrooms, with only bookcases, screens or curtains as dividers. These pupils were from all types of environment, all degrees of preparation and grade levels, so we tried to place them, as nearly as possible, where they would be comfortable, both academically, socially and chronologically, not always easy nor satisfactory. At that time, I was teaching sixth grade, and each morning it was necessary to have each pupil empty all pockets, for often, I'd keep knives, switchblades, weapons of all kinds, and dangerous contents, until Friday P.M., when belongings would be sent home with the owners."

Lincoln Junior High was superior to Washington, the other public junior high, for the same reason that Central was better than the other elementary schools: It was the one I attended. Junior highs offered the seventh and eighth grades. Most pupils were 13 and 14, ages when they are mercurial, transitional, neither children nor adults. Teachers at Lincoln expected us to behave as adults, and were often disappointed. We moved in a group from classroom to classroom for various classes, kind of the way the big guys did in high school, and sometimes, *quelle horreur!* the teachers assigned homework. Despite the semi-adult trappings, our comportment in classrooms was, sad to say, often juvenile.

Each junior high grade at Lincoln was divided into three levels, supposedly based on ability to learn. School administrators perhaps had more felicitous nomenclature but I knew the class groupings only as top, middle and bottom. I confess that to this day I snap-judge old classmates' intelligence by the level to which they were then assigned, and such stereotyping is the evil of the system. The homeroom teacher for the top-level in the seventh-grade was Romaine Nicholson. She was competent — dramatic, sympathetic, resourceful — and she gently nudged us from elementary-school mentality into a larger world, although I'm not certain her sense of humor was highly developed. When it came time to choose a class motto, for example, I proposed "Life Begins at '40," the year we were to graduate from Lincoln. Miss Nicholson would have none of that. "It lacks dignity," she said. That was also her reaction when Joe Stottlebower, Don Haskell, Jim Hermanson, Bobby Murphy and I launched a newspaper we called the *Wetzel Blab*. When she remonstrated, we changed the name to the *Weekly Blab*. She did not comment again, perhaps hoping to cut her losses.

One edition of the *Blab* won the attention of the *Sun's* 'Round Towner, who reprinted one of the *Blab's* reviews of an operetta at Washington: "According to the reviewer the plot was as follows: 'The leader of a gypsy band is in prison. A wicked king has ascended the throne. The dethroned king is lost in the woods and his daughter comes to the gypsy camp. The wicked king gets his. The good king regains the throne. Everything is OK'."

Well, maybe we were short of space that week.

Miss Marguerite Whittle was our eighth-grade homeroom teacher. She drove a Model A coupe that today would be a classic. In her own way, Miss Whittle was herself a classic — growing bald, bless her heart, but a calm, astute, and sometimes witty teacher of English who struggled with modest success to teach us how to spell and parse sentences. Miss Ruth Klein, who taught literature, music and speech, was witty, too, and seemed to enjoy bantering with her pupils. A profile in the *Weekly Blab* said her hobbies were fishing and sewing; that her favorite actor and actresses were Leslie Howard and Norma Shearer, and "She went to UW and there got her B.A. degree, but she was born with her nice disposition." (I think that brought me an A). Some of the more mature boys said Miss Didrickson was sexy, perhaps because it was believed she dated sailors, and you know about women who did *that*. Nathan Cole was the principal. He taught shop — manual arts was the elegant euphemism — and mechanical drawing. As principal, he was the school disciplinarian. Someone once carved my name in the boys' lavatory and although Mr. Cole apparently believed me when I said I hadn't done it (I hadn't, so help me), he advised me nevertheless to "come down to the level of the other students." He was telling me, with acute accuracy, that I was conceited. (If he thought I was conceited then, he should have seen me in high school).

At Lincoln, boys were introduced to team sports; I don't remember any organized competition for girls. We played basketball on the tiny, slippery floor used for study hall and various other classes. High school kids also used it for their Friday night dances. We also played touch football. Jess Walgren was the coach. Cal Christensen was quarterback my first year there, and I succeeded him the next year. I don't remember many of the other positions, except Tommy McWilliams and Russell Goddard were in the lineup and Dave Poll played center. Joe Stottlebower and I played on the basketball team. The star was Russell Abad. He could do something the rest of us could not — consistently put the ball through the basket. Once when Joe and I were in high school, coach Ken Wills sent us back to Lincoln to referee a game. We had seen Emil Paluso officiate at the University of Washington so when calling fouls we imitated him by dramatically pointing at the offending player and yelling "Foul!" The notion that officiating should be unobtrusive hadn't occurred to us.

To be sure, Washington Junior High had something that Lincoln did not: a principal named Miss Mabel Plank. Whether that was positive or negative remains unclear. Washington students who contributed to this book mentioned her, without prompting, with surprising frequency. David Leathley said it politely: "A very formidable lady." Other former pupils, such as Ruth O'Grady, said simply, "Miss Plank had me completely terrified." In the written reactions of other former pupils, note the differing recollections of Miss Plank's finger:

Art McCarty: "Most kids were scared of her. She was tough but I think fair with the kids. She had no patience with repeat offenders. A favorite technique of hers was to push her stubby forefinger down behind your collar bone and squeeze. It was every effective. Of course, I never had it done to me!" Yeah, right, Art.

Mack Smith: "Miss Plank had a stub of a first finger on one hand which she could bury in a student's shoulder and get instant agreement on any issue; there was never any rebellion against authority that I can recall."

Dorothy Fick: "She wore her gray hair tied back in a bun and she had broken her pointer finger and thus had a cast on it. And for some reason during study hall she pointed that finger at Jerry Bradford and me. Jerry and I were always good friends and there was and still is a spark. When we made eye contact we both laughed . . . It was just sort of contagious. We got into a bit of trouble over that."

Betty Bromley: "I remember Mable Plank and how very frightened a lot of us were of her. She came to our class one time when I was reciting a poem and how I got through that I do not know because I was shaking."

Audrey Thompson: "She struck terror in all the kids and she ran a tight ship. In the eighth grade I was chosen to work in the library and then to assist her after school in her office. I discovered she really was a nice lady but she did demand respect. I got good grades and had been raised to be respectful and obedient so she thought I was OK."

Myron Richards: "There were boys and girls from Navy Yard City in that school. Navy Yard City had a reputation to uphold as the toughest place for a young person to be from. Even teachers were in fearful awe of Miss Plank (I later taught with one who had worked for her, and confirmed this) and there was very little problem with discipline among the students, as no one wanted to deal with the principal. Any inner city school in our nation today would love to have Miss Plank as principal."

Aileen Bellinger remembers happier times at Washington. After Sam Chollar transferred from his native Hawaii, "it snowed and the teacher let him run outside during class, because he'd never seen snow before and we all watched out the windows (that was fun and we were happy for him.)"

Mary Lou Flieder suggests our class at Lincoln needed some of Miss Plank's discipline. Mary Lou says we were the only class in the history of the school that was not permitted an outside outing or study project — because of our unruliness. Indeed, she says Paul Preus decided not to return to teaching after the war because of our rowdiness. I remember without pride that Joe Stottlebower and I brought Mrs. Ward, a new or perhaps substitute teacher, to tears with our antics in her mathematics class. Mary Lou may be accurate in her recollections but I confess I don't share them. I knew we were lively and spirited and sometimes had more fun in class than teachers thought acceptable. But I didn't realize we were out of hand.

We were still at Lincoln when a select group began going to Miss Margaret Tapping's School of Dance. (Actually, we were self-selected; Bremerton wasn't sophisticated enough to have anything but a self-appointed elite. But perhaps all elites are self-appointed.) Sessions were held Saturday evenings in the basement ballroom of the Elks' Temple. Girls who attended included Mary Lou Flieder, Susan Swanson, Shirley Sinclair, Helen Jean Stubblefield and Jackie Driscoll. Boys included Joe Stottlebower, Jorgen Nelson, Cal Christensen, Hans Sievertson, Bob Halverson and me. As a woman plunked on a piano, we learned to fox-trot, waltz, polka, schottische, rhumba and conga. The lessons led to frequent dance parties later in Jorgen Nelson's recreation room on Gregory Way. For the most part we dropped the esoteric Latin dances at these parties and concentrated on the steps we could dance to the music of Glenn Miller, Harry James, Tommy and Jimmy Dorsey, Benny Goodman, Duke Ellington and Count Basie, played on Jorgie's portable player from his 78-rpm records. These dances were not quite dates, because we didn't drive and we came and left in groups, but they were among our first boy-girl experiences. Jorgy's parents looked in on us infrequently during the dances but the testosterone was not yet fully flowing and there was no need for close chaperoning. (Later, more than one high school boy took to wearing a jockstrap to dances so his erections wouldn't be so apparent.)

It was at this point in my life that I made a very bad decision: I consciously decided not to learn how to jitterbug. Like most adolescents, I was developing artificial social attitudes and decided that the key to a sophisticated life was *Being Smooth*. This became my general standard, applied to as many parts of my life as possible without appearing completely insufferable. I watched with wry amusement — and, I was certain, with great sophistication — as my peers flung themselves through the undignified gyrations of jitterbugging. (Shirley Sinclair remembers Bill Gates tossing her over his shoulder and sliding her between his legs). By eschewing jitterbugging I did not realize I was forever eliminating a lively, sensuous experience that in later life might have been liberating.

I entered Bremerton High School on September 4, 1940. Among the classes for which I signed up as a freshman was German, confident that in that class I would find Katy Stingl, with whom I was seriously but secretly smitten. But the perfidious Katy took Spanish instead, leaving me to struggle with a language that I've spent parts of 50 years attempting to learn with little success. I remember two other freshmen classes particularly: World History, taught by the affable Alva Hugenin, who would read Snuffy Smith from the comic strips to us each day (Hugenin later became director of the apprenticeship program in the Yard), and band, taught by Mark Freshman.

Speaking of comic strips, the 10 most popular during the war, based on size of readership, according to Richard R. Lingeman[1], were 1, Joe Palooka. 2, Blondie. 3, Li'l Abner. 4, Little Orphan Annie. 5, Terry and the Pirates. 6, Dick Tracy. 7, Moon Mullins. 8, Gasoline Alley. 9, Bringing Up Father, and 10, The Gumps.

Playing in the band put me among sophisticated juniors and seniors (that's how they seemed to me, anyway) and permitted participation in various public performances. In October of 1940, for example, the band played at a Teachers' Institute in Seattle. Midway through the performance three of us marched down the middle aisle, dressed in uniforms of the Revolutionary War representing the "Spirit of '76," I playing "Yankee Doodle" on my piccolo. It brought down the house. I have been insatiable for applause ever since.

---

[1] Lingeman. Ibid.

That was the highlight of my dim musical career. I had taken flute lessons for a few years from Pete Barth; I came from a musical family (siblings Scott, violin; Edith, harp; Barrett, piano), and my father insisted on it. But I never became proficient and in band often was trying to play things beyond my ability. This led to faking — and also to an intense struggle with my father. A year or two earlier he had pleaded with me to join a Boy Scout orchestra led by Miles Blankenship's father. But I had been shocked to the core by the dirty stories the older kids told on one of Troop 511's overnight hikes and I flat-out refused to become a Scout. That meant I couldn't play in their orchestra. In retrospect, I'm sad that my prudishness robbed me of an opportunity to become a competent musician — or a Boy Scout, for that matter. If I had my life to live over again, music would play a bigger part.

I'm also simultaneously delighted and dismayed at how innocent an adolescent could be in those times. There was no sexual education in our family, absolutely none. Sister Edith remembers being told by Mother one day to play her harp particularly well at a public performance because Dad wasn't feeling well. Edith, 16 at the time, interpreted that to mean that Dad was having his period.

- **Chapter 11**

(Headlines from the Bremerton Sun in 1942)

USS Lexington Sunk . . .
Balloon Falls, Hits Lines and Chimney . . .
NY Workers' Pay Raised . . . Mercury Hits 98 . . .
Feminine Yard Workers Told to De-Glamorize . . .
Pacific Coast Dimout Becomes Effective . . .
Jarvis, Entire Crew Lost . . .
Speed Limit of 35mph Now Enforced . . .

≈

Glenn Miller Put Us In The Mood

Today's social historians must be forgiven if they conclude that Americans won World War II by dancing, particularly if they focus on Bremerton. My God, how we danced! There were sock hops at noon in the high school gym. There were mixers on Friday nights at Lincoln Junior High. There was modern dancing Friday nights at Perl's and square dancing there on Saturdays. There were dances at the Legion Hall and at DelMarco at Sixth and Callow. There were USO dances on Washington Avenue and Navy dances at Craven Center. Occasionally there was dancing in the streets, as at the end of the evening when a conga line snaked from Craven Center up Burwell, down Pacific and into the main gate of the Yard. There were special dances at 1 or 2 o'clock in the morning for swing-shift workers. There were noon dances on the decks of the various aircraft carriers in the Navy Yard. High school kids danced on the ferries coming home from basketball games in Seattle.

But America has long been a nation of dancers; my grandfather Selton Wetzel played Saturday-night gigs in the area before the turn of the century and a newspaper clipping from 1909 tells of "an old fashioned Virginia reel, danced on the smooth beach to excellent music furnished by Mr. Wetzel and his three sons . . ." Rosalind Gillie describes her mother as "a modern miss of the Roaring '20s. She danced the Black Bottom and the Charleston, and taught us the schottische: 1,2,3 hop; 1,2,3 hop; 1,2,3 hop. I remember dancing it on the way to Naval Avenue school when I was in the first grade."

Big-name bands came to Bremerton during the war and their performances were jammed.   They included Jack Teagarden, Tommy Dorsey, Louis Armstrong, Freddie Slack, Frankie Masters, Henry King, Bob Crosby, Henry Busey, and Lionel Hampton, described by the *Sun* as a "famous Negro swing band." An entertainment ad in the July 10, 1942, *Sun* lists such dancing domains as Island Lake Park, Kingston Grange Hall, Reynolds Park, "a popular spot for afternoon and evening dancing parties, the Tip Top Inn" and the Chicken Coop, "an atmosphere you can't find anywhere else, Sixth and Montgomery, established 1933." High school students could patronize the dance halls but not places that served wine or beer. Archaic state laws forbade liquor by the drink; the result was crude drinking from bottles in cars parked outside the dance halls.

This was the era when big-band music was at its most popular. Its best is still played 60 years later. *Metronome Magazine* named Glenn Miller the nation's most popular dance band in 1940 and 1941; Miller went into the Army Air Corps early in the war and Tommy Dorsey took his place as No. 1 in *Metronome's* poll. Benny Goodman was the most popular swing or jazz band, alternating with Duke Ellington from 1939 until 1945 when Woody Herman was the winner. Bing Crosby and Frank Sinatra dominated designation as most popular male vocalist from 1939 to 1945. Most popular female vocalists in those years were Ella Fitzgerald, Helen O'Connell, Helen Forrest, Jo Stafford, and Dinah Shore. *Metronome* voted the Andrews Sisters, Merry Macs and Pied Pipers as most popular vocal groups.

Tommy Dorsey in Bremerton
(Photo courtesy Shirley Sinclair.)

When Tommy Dorsey played in Bremerton, several Bremerton High boys decided he should be invited to play at the high school, too. Xie Olanie, Bill Gates and several others tracked Dorsey to Tacoma and then Seattle, where they waited for hours in the lobby of the Olympic Hotel for him to appear. When at last he did arrive, he was supported on each side by his — well, I suppose they had become, literally, sidemen.

Dorsey was so drunk he couldn't navigate by himself. The invitation to play at BHS was not soberly acknowledged.

"So popular was dancing that more than 2,000 war plants provided facilities on the premises for dancing during their off hours," wrote Richard Lingeman[1] He said that conservative parents bridled at the idea of their daughters fraternizing with strange servicemen, but patriotism forced them to swallow their snobbery. "For girls it was a flattering rush, this being surrounded by available young men in uniform, and they participated eagerly — to the disgruntlement of the local boys."

Irving Berlin's *God Bless America* was the most popular patriotic song of the war; WWII didn't come close to producing such popular WWI flag-wavers as *Over There*. Berlin's nostalgic *White Christmas* was probably the most popular song of the war. It was introduced in 1942 by Bing Crosby in the movie "Holiday Inn." It sold more than one million copies of sheet music and was atop the Hit Parade for nine weeks that year, repeating its popularity at Christmas in 1943 and 1944. "It was indeed a song in the wartime mood, a bit sad and yearning — an emotion with which both homesick soldiers and civilians could identify," wrote Lingeman.

Other popular wartime songs included Johnny Mercer's swinging *GI Jive, Coming In on a Wing and a Prayer, Praise the Lord and Pass the Ammunition, Somebody Else Is Taking My Place, Saturday Night Is the Loneliest Night of the Week* and *I'll Walk Alone*, which led the Hit Parade eight times in 1944. The most popular song of 1944, however, was *I'll Be Seeing You*.

When the patriotic passion of the war waned in 1944 and 1945, the "dream" songs became popular — *I'll Buy that Dream; My Dreams Are Gettin' Better All the Time; Linda; Laura*, and finally, *Dream*. "The last was unabashed fantasy; no longer did the dream provide consolation by supplying an absent or indifferent loved one, but in *Dream* it was total opiate," wrote Lingeman.

But the instrumentals — particularly Glenn Miller's *In the Mood, Tuxedo Junction, String of Pearls* and *Chattanooga Choo-Choo* — were as popular as the ballads and can still send wartime adolescents into paroxysms of nostalgia. So can Artie Shaw's *Frenesi* or *Begin the Beguine*, Tommy Dorsey's *Song of India, Opus One*, and the driving trumpet chase in *Well Git It*, Benny Goodman's *Sing, Sing, Sing*, Count Basie's *One O'Clock Jump*, Charlie Barnett's *Cherokee*, Duke Ellington's great theme, *Take the A Train*. It should be confessed that ricky-tick music played

---

[1] Lingeman. Ibid.

by Guy Lombardo or Sammy Kaye was popular, too, but over the years has properly been forgotten, with the exception of Lombardo's *Auld Lang Syne* on New Year's Eve.

Virginia Oass mentions many of the same big-band names. "I often recall how lucky Teddy Green, Edna Eastwood, Diana White, Dorothy Dolan, Audrienne Larson, Helen Jean Stubblefield, Noray Smith, Jeanie Schairer, Betty Schricker, Barbara Boller, many others and I were to be teenagers during that glorious period when Tommy and Jimmy Dorsey, Duke Ellington, Glenn Miller, Count Basie, Artie Shaw, Dizzy Gillespie, Harry James and Woody Herman set the country in motion with their sense of swing. And to feel we were aiding the war effort as we kicked up our heels! Moreover, we were literally surrounded by men — tall and short, slim and stocky, handsome and homely, sharp and dull, young and old, single and married, smooth and crude ones — but if they could dance, we were willing! Yet there was a flip side, too. At times we would spend the last hours of shore leave with a young serviceman ready to 'ship out' the following morning. Or we would be shocked when correspondence stopped abruptly only to learn the ship had been torpedoed with great loss of life. More than one budding romance was broken when a serviceman revealed he had a wife and sometimes even children."

Helen Jean Stubblefield remembers playing records at Brown's Music Store on Pacific Avenue. "Mr. Brown would slip some records from their jackets and we could take a stack back and play them before committing to purchase. Sometimes we packed those booths — but whew! no ventilation. My record-shopping pals seemed to be Norma Lee Dues and Jackie Driscoll, but that is where we met and visited with many others. We listened to Glenn Miller, Tommy and Jimmy Dorsey, Frank Sinatra, Kay Kaiser and Ishkabibble. Jo Stafford and Vaughn Monroe sang wonderful love songs and Ella Mae Morse could make anyone jump to her beat."

Dolores Gutoski moved to Westpark from Tacoma in the spring of 1941. There Judson "Buddy" Black introduced her to a gang that over the past half-century has been remarkably cohesive. Members included Milton Haylett, Doris and Elaine Gendron, Milton Blake, Chuck Cundiff, Beverly Bressler, Leo and Bob Westerman, Nadine Balsom, Shirley and Chuck Cain and Betty Prebula. "What a group we were," says Dolores. "Probably because we had all left the security of our hometowns, we tended to find great joy in each other's company. We went swimming at Kitsap Lake, hung around Haddon Hall and told great stories, rented nickelodeons and had our own dances. Never were we bored. Did we jitterbug? Did we ever! Buddy taught most of the girls the intricacies of jitterbugging. He was the best. But if you wanted to waltz, it was Milton Blake."

Robin Perrigo lived in Westpark, too, but she was taught to jitterbug by a former Chicago taxi driver at the USO Center at Second and Washington. She says the dances were carefully chaperoned. Furthermore, a Westpark bus driver would leave his normal route to deliver Robin to her doorstep. He wouldn't let other passengers off until Robin was safely inside her door. Jo Peterson also had a private

Shirley Sinclair and Bill Gates.
(Photo courtesy Shirley Sinclair.)

taxi service: The Bremerton Police Department. "The police who were at the dances used to take pity on us because we couldn't afford cabs. They would take me home to Westpark and then Spence (her boyfriend) across town to Sheridan Park. Possibly they didn't want us to get picked up for curfew (violation) by some other policeman that didn't know us. But I was the talk of the neighborhood to be brought home in the wee hours by a police car." The curfew, which at various times covered youths up to age 18, was a nuisance for teen-agers. Jo says she could never figure out how it was enforced because so many servicemen and Yard workers were not yet 18. "I used to carry a note in my purse signed by my mother that I was allowed to be out after 10 p.m.," Jo said.

Teddy Green described military dances she attended: "In 1942-43, when I was a senior, 25 young ladies were selected to entertain enlisted Navy personnel and military stationed at barrage balloons and anti-aircraft batteries. These ladies, juniors and seniors, were screened and very carefully chaperoned and there were very strict rules. We were available every Tuesday and Thursday and we would climb into trucks, sit on a board (no backs) and bounce in total darkness down a road which was basically two very rough ruts. I remember that the majority of the men were shorter than I, and I would quite often not be asked to dance. Some of the men were old enough to be our fathers. They would always bake a cake which was not like mother used to bake and we would be polite and eat it."

Peggy Faulkner, high school correspondent for the *Sun*, wrote a long feature story on Nov. 5, 1942, of attending a dance sponsored by the Bremerton Recreation Commission for an Army battery. Her horizons were expanded: "The orchestra gave out with everything from *You Made Me Love You* to *String of Pearls* so smoothies and jitterbugs alike were pleased. I danced with a former pianist with Gene Krupa which was quite a thrill and all the fellows were interesting and had different viewpoints, being from different sections of the country. Besides having a swell time dancing, the girls received a good lesson in geography and human nature. I found out for instance that my own hometown wasn't the center of the universe and that soldiers were human beings just like any of the fellows you and I grew up with and went to school with . . ."

Ruby Jewett had danced all her life — tap, ballet, ballroom — so she always found a boyfriend who could dance or else she taught him. "I also taught several friends. Jitterbug was our preference of the time. My husband and I still do it. Glenn Miller was our favorite band. Friday nights at Perl Maurers was a favorite with my friends. That's where I met my husband."

Mack Smith says, "Alberta Hill taught me the basic steps to the 'Lindy,' or jitterbug, which is still my favorite dance step. Favorite band was Glenn Miller." Mack says he took Alberta to his Senior Prom and "rode in the back seat of someone else's car to a roadhouse out on Hood Canal, and danced all night and had a wonderful time." (I dated Alberta, too, and I'm jealous that she didn't teach me to jitterbug. But she did croon in my ear, which Mack didn't mention.)

Dancing was an important part of dating — and romance. On his first leave at home from the Navy, Harry McIntyre went to a dance at the Civic Center. It left fond memories: "I danced with Shirley Eskridge. We kissed while we danced and we miscued with our feet. The kiss was aborted unceremoniously — but long remembered."

Dancing sometimes led beyond a simple kiss, as for Jo Peterson: "One day at the Women's USO I danced with a guy everyone called Junior and he said his name was 'Spence'. So every time I saw him leaving the Navy Yard or on the street I would say hi. One Sunday afternoon in September of 1944 Melba Tveten and I were in the drugstore on the corner of Pacific Avenue and Burwell when Spencer and his friend Mel came in and asked if we would take them to the Women's USO. So we went and danced all afternoon to juke box music. Spence is a very good dancer and we had a great time and ended up taking the foot ferry to Port Orchard and back. Of course I find out all I can about Spence. His name was Merle Spencer. He came from Sioux City, Iowa. He was recruited from there to come to PSNY when he was 16 years old in July of '43. From that day on we went together. In December '44 we became engaged and were married May 8, 1945, the day the war was over in Europe. We were both only 18 years old. From September on till we were married we spent our hours away from work mostly dancing. We used to dance on Saturday nights at the DelMarco on Callow Avenue. They had the regular dance and a swing shift dance that went until 4 a.m. We always went to Perl Maurer's on Friday night. During the week we could go to the Women's USO and every day in the Navy Yard we would meet at lunchtime and dance to the Navy bands on whatever aircraft carrier was in the dry-docks for repair. Occasionally we would take the ferry to Seattle and dance at the Trianon Ballroom. They would have big bands like Les Brown and I guess he was our favorite."

Dagney Smeback and Jim Taylor
(Photo courtesy Shirley Sinclair.)

Alice Jane Levin: "Jim Taylor was my first dancing partner and we sort of learned together and then he went on to greater things. Dates were school dances, Maurer's on Friday nights, maybe the American Legion on Saturday nights, movies and later the DelMarco Ballroom that attracted mostly young war workers, servicemen, and had a special Swing Shift Dance.

"I loved the formal dances. Actually we had a great many of them including the Navy Junior dances that made us feel so adult and sophisticated. I know people my age who have never been to a formal dance or owned a full-length gown and think I'm very lucky."

Mary Jane Hudson and Xie Olanie. He didn't jitterbug either.
(Photo courtesy Shirley Sinclair.)

The formal school dances — the Junior and Senior Proms, Varsity Ball, Crystal Ball, Navy Junior dances — also involved dance cards and corsages, usually gardenias, for the girls. Corsages raised the problem of where to wear them, particularly when the older girls wore strapless gowns. In such cases, the usual solution was to wear them on the wrist, a practice that disappointed me; I liked to imagine that someday I would summon the courage to help a girl pin the flowers to her bosom.

On May 11, 1943, the *Sun* described Bremerton High's Junior Prom. Wally Brown and his 12-piece orchestra played. The theme was "Hawaiian Nights."

> In the center was a large island centered with a pool, complete with goldfish and tropical flowers. The walls were covered with trite signs printed in Hawaiian lettering such as "No Smoking" and "Greetings." Firmly enclosed in a grass hut placed at one end of the auditorium was the orchestra.

> Chairman Jackie Driscoll was gowned in black and white net and came escorted by an alumnus, Les Eathorne. The majority of the formal dresses worn by the girls showed the influence of spring. Pamela Miller looked especially well in blue satin; petite Gail MacDougal appeared very "Gone With the Wind-ish" wearing a red velvet gown fashioned in the style of the Colonial period, the low neckline offset with eyelet ruffles. Also glimpsed hither and yon about the throng were Dagney Smebak in white with a multi-colored jersey bolero; in striking

constrast to her black hair, Lottie Maciukiewicz wore a white pique gown with eyelet embroidery.

Seen escorted by out-of-towners Bill Pearce and Doug Funk were Patti Serry and Teddy Green. Representing Seattle were Betty LaFave and Jackie Lutley, guests of Jim Henry and Wayne Lichter. Alice Jane Levin, escorted by Jack Bender, wore blue jersey and flower marquisette; Frances Korb wore yellow net; Lorraine Allison came wearing a blue cotton print; Lorraine Greenwalt escorted by student body prexy Xie Olanie wore teal net; Susan Swanson wore rust and green chiffon; Nadine Zieman, yellow satin and net; Rhoda Olsen, pink organdy; Phyllis Thornton, escorted by Lowell Wiley, was wearing pink net with an upswept hair-do; Joyce Leyden wore white and red net; Donna Scott unconsciously fit in with the theme wearing a Hawaiian print with a lei necklace. Shirley Eskridge wore blue net over satin and was accompanied by Frank Pease, and Mary Jane Hudson chose a red and black flowered taffeta formal.

As some girls grew older, they became more sophisticated and school dances lost their allure. Virginia Oass's sister Jo Ann introduced her to fraternity men and Navy officers who were, she says, "older and more interesting than my high school contemporaries." She pulled off the epitome of one-upmanship: "I did put in an appearance at the Senior Prom with my date, an ensign, and then went off to the Officers' Club." As Geraldine Petersen said, "To date an officer and go to the Officers' Club made me ecstatic." A friend wrote me after I had gone into the Army that LaVerne Gatlin was dating an ensign (she couldn't have been more than 15) and that so-and-so was drooling with envy.

Virginia Eddy grew up in paradise — at Doc Eddy's rustic Rose Point Resort on Hood Canal. The resort included a dance hall. The five children of Doc Eddy (Virginia was second from oldest) went in and out with the tide; all learned to dog-paddle by age 5. "People from all points came out here to picnic, swim or go row-boating, camp in a tent or rent an old-time cabin, equipped with wood range, beds, a table, and an outside privy, placed here and there. Basic, but everyone seemed to have a great time," Virginia remembers.

"Our living quarters were in a lodge-type building and half of it was a dance hall that sported hardwood floors, no less. Our piano would be moved out there for summertime music in the early days, but later, after electricity, a 'magic' juke box was acquired and the campers and us enjoyed Glenn Miller, the Dorseys, Artie

Shaw, the Andrews Sisters, on and on. With the beats and energy of these groups there was no way you could stand still! Summer nights brought many campers up off the beach and/or the campfires to dance or watch for a few hours. It was a wonderful time and atmosphere."

In her memoir written for this book, Adrienne Johnson captured the essence and variety of wartime dancing: The joy and freedom of movement, the sexiness, the romance, the formality, and the decorum. She wrote: "Hey, let me tell you about Craven Center. What a place! I loved to dance and that was the place to go. There was no charge and the music was the finest. There were some restrictions. The girls had to arrive and leave alone or in the company of other girls. There were MPs at the entrance who checked our purses for any alcohol, and they generally just screened the arrivals. The boys came in through an entrance from the Navy Yard, and left the same way. Thus they could attend the dance even though not on leave. They were all military — no civilians. There was a spacious, clean ladies lounge where we left our coats and purses, yes purses, and there was, as far as I know, never a theft of any kind. Then it was on to the ballroom area, a huge, high ceilinged arena filled with young people dancing to some of the best music in the country, best because most of the musicians were professionals, some heads of university music departments, teachers, performers. When the hall resounded with the great arrangements of *String of Pearls, Tuxedo Junction, Chattanooga Choo Choo, Sunrise Serenade,* we were transported and almost became part of the music. Henry Fonda (the famous film star) was there briefly one night but, gosh darn it, he didn't ask me to dance.

"On that fateful night of April 4, 1944, I had just entered the ballroom where I had promised to meet a Marine named Job Werner, whom I had danced with on a previous occasion. As I was glancing around trying to spot him in the crowd I heard, 'May I have this dance?' In front of me stood the handsomest man I had ever seen, rather tall, blond, blue eyes, and an intangible refinement in speech and manner. I hesitated. After all, my patriotic duty was to keep my promise to the Marine. But, oh well.

"Half way around the dance floor I caught the glowering eye of the Marine. Too late. My partner was a musician first class with the *USS Washington* band that was providing the music that evening. It turned out he was a high school instrumental music teacher from Wabasha, Minnesota, and first violinist with the Rochester Symphony Orchestra.

"The battleship, *Washington*, was in the Yard for repairs to her bow after a collision with the *USS Indiana* during a night maneuver without lights out in the Pacific. The repairs were accomplished quickly as a new bow was built and ready for installation when the Washington arrived in Bremerton. It left at the end of April shortly after Mr. Moen gave me an engagement ring on April 26, 1944. So I knew him only a few weeks of April and he spent 10 days of that time on a trip home to Minnesota to visit his family. He was gone back to the South Pacific during the next 14 months and recalls that there was a period of 80 days when they didn't even see land. He returned to Bremerton on June 23, 1945, and we were married one week later. We scarcely knew each other, and I think that was typical of the era."

Earlier, while in high school, Adrienne worked at the Commissioned Officers Club in the Yard. She remembers the Saturday night dinner dances as grand affairs. "Reservations would come pouring into the Club's office days before and the events were always attended to full capacity. The officers' ladies dressed in beautiful evening gowns, often with flowers in hair or on shoulders. The men were impeccably turned out in uniform. There were two dining rooms, one with carpeting, beautiful windows, French doors and all the amenities one can imagine. The other, more frequently used during the week, was less formal and generally used for breakfast and luncheon. On Saturday nights, however, both dining rooms were filled to capacity, the tables all with immaculate white cloths and napkins, candles and silver service shined with care — I should know — I helped shine it."

Another ballroom, called the DelMarco, was on the corner of Sixth and Callow. Adrienne recalls, "We didn't enjoy that so much as there was a different mix of people and the music wasn't as good. I mention this because a neighbor told about one occasion when he and some other young fellows wanted to go to the dance but one of them didn't have the price of admission. Girls didn't have to pay to get in so they decided to dress him up as a girl. He was a dark-eyed, round-faced boy and it was always dark inside the DelMarco.

"They wrapped his head in a turban, the kind Carmen Miranda wore, rolled up his pant legs and found a dress to cover up his clothes. The plan was for him to head right for the men's room and discard his dress and turban, but before he could get there a big fellow came up and asked for a dance. Poor Joe (the late Joe Stickney from Quilcene) lit out the door in a most unladylike manner and never went back there."

Duane Thompson wrote that he and Jimmy Taylor went to the DelMarco for swing-shift dancing and beer. "He and I sang in the alley and were jailed for keeping the war workers awake (we soon sobered up from our two beers and were released.)"

On another occasion Adrienne herself was at the same dance hall. She wrote: "Oh, yes, and I see that fresh young sailor at the DelMarco, bottle of beer in hand, approaching and slowly lowering himself before me until his knees almost touched the floor, then slowly rising with a long, low whistle and, 'Helloooooo, Baby, can I borrow your frame for this struggle'?"

Chapter 12

(Headlines from Bremerton Sun in 1943)

City Population now 45,000...
Shoe Sales Rationed...
7 Badly Burned in Balloon Explosion...
Meat, Butter, Cheese Rationed March 28...
Bomber Crashes Near Port Orchard...
Wynstra Elected School Superintendent...
Capsized Battleship *Oklahoma* Will Be Raised...

≈

For Parents, a Pain; For Kids, a Frolic

We had several days' warning that the weather was going crazy, although not from the press; weather reports in newspapers and on the radio were restricted because of the war. But on January 15, 1943, you didn't need a newspaper to know it had turned bitterly cold. Mother's diary noted, "We haven't had weather like this in years." The snow started three days later, followed by two glorious weeks of wretched weather — glorious for adolescents, wretched for adults. Past a certain age, loss of electrical power, collapsing or leaking roofs, impassable roads, closure of stores, inability to deliver milk, mail or groceries — those corollaries of snowstorms lose their charm.

"The January snowstorm of 1943 dumped 13.5 inches of snow on Bremerton in one day," remembers Gene Gurske, who worked at the Black Ball ferry terminal. "The ferry dock lost its power. The upper passenger ramp could not be operated, so the passengers loaded at the car ramp. The car ramp had to be raised and lowered manually. I could do it, but it took many turns to crank the winch. Everyone pitched in to push cars stuck in snow drifts in the parking lot. The Navy Yard commandant advised essential Navy Yard workers who lived in Seattle or outlying areas to sleep in the Navy Yard Administration Building for fear they could not make it home and return for their next shift."

Good advice. The *Sun*, despite wartime censorship, reported grim tales of stranded workers and widespread privation. Said the *Sun*:

> Reports of almost unbelievable conditions of suffering and hardship, mingled with acts of heroic rescues, were beginning to trickle into Bremerton today from outlying districts of Kitsap County and the Hood Canal area. Red Cross workers are preparing to go to outlying districts in Army trucks to haul provisions and bring in persons ill and stranded since Tuesday. Telephones are still out of order in outlying districts.
>
> Along the Canal many mothers with small children have been stranded since Tuesday, without milk. Physicians have been unable to reach them; they are without heat or electricity, their wells and private water systems frozen. It was learned that 50 Navy Yard workers including men and women hiked 30 miles to the Union area Tuesday night in the blizzard; others walked to their homes there and throughout other parts of the county from Bremerton . . .

Virginia Eddy was at home at Doc Eddy's, her father's resort on Hood Canal. "After hours of shoveling the snow off our dance-hall roof, Dad and brother Al had to call it quits. Between exhaustion and danger, they came down. Shortly after, the roof caved in with a resounding CRASH! We felt it highly possible that the living quarters might go also, so we gathered basic needs and traipsed through waist-deep snow up to our store by the road. It offered security, it was more compactly built, had a stove, etc. A frightened elderly couple joined us that night, fearful of staying in their cabin alone. So, with one double bed, blanket rolls, etc., a total of eight weary people slumbered. Navy Yard workers, otherwise trapped in town, ventured out here, worked their way to the beach for easier trudging, eventually to their Canal homes. Some were bedded down at places along the way."

The roof and walls of the ice-skating rink at Head of the Bay (now called Gorst) collapsed, too. The *Sun* estimated the damage at $15,000 and said the owners had no insurance.

Don Rolstad skiied on Ninth Street
between Chester and Veneta
(Photo courtesy Don Rolstad.)

A *Sun* headline said "Cold-Weather Damage Hits School-rooms in Silverdale." Added a subhead: "Frozen water pipes cause explosion; kitchen shattered in Bremerton Heights." By 6 p.m. on January 17 the temperature dropped to 21 and "before midnight had gone to 20. It dropped Sunday morning at 11 to 19 in official yard recordings." When the wind blew, it seemed much colder. The *Sun* also said a water shortage was acute. Reservoirs were nearly empty and pressure was lacking in water lines.

The day the snow started on January 18, Dolores Gutoski somehow missed the school bus home. "Not to worry, I thought, I'll just walk to Sixth and catch a city bus. Either they were too packed to stop or none came but, as the snow intensified, I realized that waiting was getting me nowhere. Sooo, being an indestructible teen-ager, I decided to walk home. I made it to Callow, but as I started up Kitsap Way, I really began to falter. Suddenly, this strong arm grabbed my arm and I heard a voice say, 'I think you might need some help.' It was George Tillett. Very few words passed between us. He kept a tight hold on me and off we went, one step after another. Frankly, I don't think I would have made it without him. We arrived at the entrance to Westpark and he said, 'Can you make it?' I nodded my head, he went one way and I kept going up Russell Road, finally reaching my home. I don't think I ever thanked him enough — and I certainly should have."

Getting home from school wasn't easy for Berenice Eicher, either. "About 10:30 a.m. it was decided to close the high school, and I walked over to Lincoln to meet Marion." Marion was her sister, a teacher at Lincoln. "The snow was already up to the bumpers of her car, and we could not move it. Somehow, probably by city bus, we made our way down to the out-of-town bus station, near the ferry terminal. We stood in the bus for several hours, then it finally got moving, and we got home at last. I think there was a fall of about two feet. After the snow stopped falling, it froze. That was what was so unusual . . . there were places I could walk on top of the snow. The schools closed for a week. As I recall, we had one day back at school, then the rains came, all the snow melted, everything flooded and the schools were closed for another week."

Jim Braman was attending the University of Washington, which closed because of the storm. Jim came home for a few days. "By the time I boarded the ferry the weather had cleared and a strong, cold north wind swept down the Sound. It was the roughest crossing I ever experienced. The ferry hugged the shore to Alki Point and then turned north toward Bainbridge to minimize its rolling. Even then, dishes were crashing to the floor in the eating area. I went down the stairs to the auto deck to see what was going on and found that water was flowing through it from waves breaking over the bow. Looking out from near the bottom of the stairs the waves were so high that I couldn't see shore anywhere. Frankly, I was glad to get to Bremerton, where I found snow almost three feet deep in our front yard and piled even higher where it had been scraped from Pacific Avenue onto sidewalks. There were a lot of stories of people making valiant efforts in walking many miles to get to work in the Yard."

The Army pitched in to help. "I remember," wrote Jay Hendricks, "when the Army had to pull the transit buses over their routes to pick up and deliver the shipyard workers to and from their jobs." Adds Frances Johnson, "I remember that some of the soldiers gave Mama a ride home in a Jeep because the buses weren't running and she was trying to carry groceries home from Sixth and Callow." But Aileen Bellinger managed to walk home safely from her job at Olberg's Drug at Fourth and Pacific, one of Bremerton's most popular social centers. "I remember walking down the middle of Pacific Avenue in the snow that night, almost to my knees. There must have been some cars out with chains because there were ruts that we walked in. I walked home — not at all afraid — which I did a lot." (The irrepressible Virginia Oass remembers her sister also remarking that the snow was so deep it came up to her knees. Her sister's companion, a 6-foot-6-inch Navy lieutenant, responded gravely that it all depended on where your knees were.)

Patricia Henning and her family experienced the best and worst of the storm. They lived in Illahee near the Navy wharf. "We had 18 inches of snow, which made transportation impossible up Illahee Hill so we were really in sad shape. Our lights were off for a whole week. There was no food at our store

***Big Snow of January, 1943, here on the newly
widened Navy Yard Highway to Gorst.***
(Photo courtesy Harry Harkness.)

and we were running out of coal for the furnace. My Mom cooked
in the fireplace and on top of a round space heater.

"My sister chose this time to go into labor with her first child.
There was no car and no one to take her to the hospital so her
husband called the Navy Yard and they sent out a motor launch,
bundled her up and off she went. The ambulance met the launch
in the Navy Yard and she went to the hospital and she gave birth
to a baby girl, Alice Leona Emerson (Gaudette), who lives in Port
Orchard, has three kids and three grandchildren.

"Since we were running out of supplies my Dad (a naval officer) brought one of the Navy tugs over from Pier 91 loaded with
food, fuel and other essentials, which we used to help others.

"My oldest sister Alice lived in Gilberton and had three wee
ones. Her husband, Bob Hilstad, was a fireman and he couldn't
get home to his family so my Dad managed to borrow a car and he
went out and brought them to our house. Bob was able to get
home about three days into the storm and brought food too so we
made out OK.

"My Mom was so great. She said this was 'roughing it' and we
were just like pioneers.

"One night a bunch of kids decided to go out in the snow and
build snowmen or whatever. We gathered at the dock and decided to build a barricade across the road so if a car came they
would smash into it. We built it about three feet tall and about
one foot wide. Then we waited for a car to come. Pretty soon a
car did come and it plowed through our barricade like it was
made of marshmallows. What a let-down!"

Harold Engebretson worked in the Navy Yard for the organization that operated cafeterias and vending machines. After the storm hit, "the vending machine staff was sent to work in the cafeteria. It was the worst work day of my life. We were put to work washing dishes and pots and pans. If I ever needed motivation to finish college and get into professional work, that provided it." (I doubt if Harold needed that nudge, but he did indeed become a professional. He became an executive whiz at Rockwell International for 25 years in inertial guidance systems.)

While the adults strived desperately to cope, we kids frolicked in an unexpected, unscheduled holiday that lasted almost two weeks. We had snowball fights of global scope with impregnable forts and mounds of packed snowballs in such quantity the Naval Ammunition Depot was envious. In one skirmish, Jeanie Schairer, Betty Crawford and Virginia Oass engaged the Marine guards at the Naval Avenue gate. "The guards out-numbered, out-threw and out-lasted us," Virginia said. "We were literally numb when we finally retreated to change our soggy clothes and shake the snow from under our sweaters." In another skirmish, I foolishly threw a snowball at Hal Worland, across High Street near Pop's Inn. The snowball that came whizzing back struck me fair in the face and gave me the blackest eye I've ever had. The lesson: Never initiate a fight with an upperclassman who has a sound throwing arm. In yet another skirmish, my sister-in-law Anna Mae Wetzel engaged the soldiers at the barrage balloon across the street. Mother's diary notes: "Edie went out to defend Anna Mae against the snowballs from across the street and got into a furious battle, which was very one-sided. One of the soldiers came over after the fray and shoveled off the steps and walk." An entry the day before said: "Edie and Anna Mae went out coasting and had plenty of help from the soldiers across the way. They made several trips down the hill flat on top of a soldier who was flat on top of the sled."

Betty Loftus lived on the east side of Phinney Bay. She says it was terrific there during the 1943 storm. "No power for 10 days, groceries on the sled until the stores ran out, and full moon all night sledding down our driveway. It started at the top of a hill, curved and turned a few times until it reached the beach — about two blocks. Each night when we finished, each sledder carried water to re-ice it — maybe the fastest run outside the Olympics. It was a month after the snow was gone before my Dad could drive up the driveway. We slept a lot during the day because it was cold, but nighttime brought sledders from everywhere. Mother was in her glory making cocoa, fudge and popcorn

Inside the shipyard, workers dumped tons of snow into a drydock.
((Puget Sound Naval History Collection, Kitsap Regional Library.)

~

on a little trash burner we had not yet removed from the kitchen. We were battered and bruised, but what fun!"

Westpark was without electricity, too, "and many homes were without heating oil," recalls Dolores Gutoski. "The gang discovered that if we all congregated at one home, sat on the floor with blankets over our shoulders and held candles, we could stay relatively warm. So that is what we did...and we told marvelous tales. We also built (the boys did) a big sled that held six or so people. It had one problem — no steering device. We would just fly down hills and then roll over. How did we survive all this?"

Gordon Lecair mentions another peril: "Pulling sleds with the '32 Ford V8 and others riding in the rumble seat." But, he notes accurately, "Traffic wasn't so bad in those days."

On many hills, Burwell and Gregory Way among them, traffic was non-existent. Although the *Sun* said the city did not have authority to close off streets for sledding, that didn't prevent unofficial closures. As the *Sun* suggested, "Clubs like Lettermen's or Boys' Club can make special requests for motorists not to use a certain street. The club could appoint monitors to police the hill."

I don't remember anything so formal as monitors policing the hills, and daredevils on Flexible Fliers, bobsleds, dishpans and skis flew down Burwell, from High Street all the way to Craven Center.

I had become enamored of snow a few years earlier. The first thing I would check as I awoke in wintertime was the possibility of snow. Most of the time, I was disappointed. During the winter of 1943, I was in heaven. In some of my children's books, such as *Jolly Good Times at Hackensack* (really!), or *Hans Brinker, Or The Silver Skates*, children who lived in cold climates elsewhere frolicked in the cold and snow. I wanted to do the same. The winter of 1943 gave me my first real opportunity to do so. For many of us in our teens, it may have been the most enjoyable experience of our lifetime.

Reading my Mother's diaries, I realize in retrospect the hardships imposed on adults by the storm. Her entry for January 21 summarized the adult-kid dichotomy: "Cold continues. No school and no milk deliveries....The roof started to leak in the Burroughs room (they were renters) and later in ours. The darn thing kept dripping all night . . . The two Scotts (my father and brother) got up on the roof again. Frank is enjoying the snow for they coast on Burwell and ski out at the cemetery." The same point is made later when she writes of being awakened by a sick granddaughter. "Saw red when I heard Clark (Dunn) and Frank just going to bed as it was 3 o'clock." When Clark and I went to a basketball game in Seattle that night we were under orders to get in early. I was happy to get off with only an admonition.

By February 3, Mother was clearly tired of the storm. "Our snow is going so slowly and there are still large snow banks on the streets and in the backyard. It has been two weeks since the snow started and it has been years since we have had snow on the ground for this long." By then I may have been tired of the snow, too, although I don't remember that I was. All that I remember of the '43 blizzard are the good times: The unexpected, unscheduled vacation from school, skimming down Burwell on Blaine Gordon's long bobsled, skiing cross-country in the moonlight to Alberta Hill's house, dances in Jorgen Nelson's rec room. No doubt it was a pain for adults. But for this junior at Bremerton High School, it was pure pleasure.

Chapter 13

(Headlines from Bremerton Sun in 1943)

Population Estimated at 62,000 . . .
Contract Awarded on New
Million Dollar High School . . .
Nearly 200 Daily Being Hired by NY . . .
Beer Drinkers Going Thirsty . . .
Theaters, Churches Closed To Check Spread of Polio . . .
Boys Must Register for Draft on 18th Birthday. . .
County Dim-out Restrictions Eased . . .

≈

Kilroy Was Here; So Was Eleanor

By the end of 1942, America's enormous industrial strength, the strength that would win the war, was gaining momentum. The Allies had 25 million men under arms and overwhelming numbers of planes and tanks were rolling off the assembly lines. The U.S. Army alone had grown from 2 million to 7 million (it eventually would reach 14 million). The American arms industry had grown from 2 million to 10 million workers. In November of 1942, U.S. troops invaded North Africa. Naval strength was growing despite losses in the Pacific; Professor Bridgman notes that on December 7 of 1942 the U.S. launched the *Bunker Hill*, one of the great Essex-class carriers, and the *Belleau Wood*, an attack carrier, as well as the mighty *New Jersey*, a battleship. It was apparent the huge war machine was in full operation.

Bremerton was on a roll, too. Workers at the Puget Sound Navy Yard already had repaired and sent into action two ghosts of Pearl Harbor, the *USS Tennessee* and *Maryland*, in the spring of 1942. A few weeks later, on May 1, another ghost arrived in Bremerton — the *USS Nevada*.

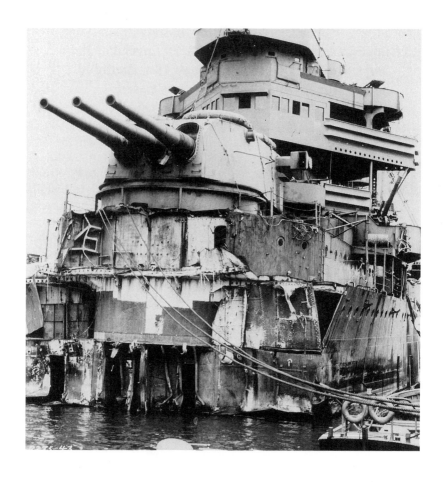

*A well-kept secret was the arrival of the battle-damaged cruiser
New Orleans, in need of, among other things, a new bow when it
arrived in May 1943.   Both an empty drydock
and bow were waiting for her.*
(Photo courtesy Larry Jacobsen.)

Seven months and 700,000 man-days of work later, the *Nevada* was returned to sea duty, eventually to pound German installations during the invasion of France in 1944. And in February the *Saratoga* limped back to PSNY only two months after extensive overhaul, seriously damaged by an enemy torpedo. (Professor Bridgman jokes that the *Saratoga* spent most of the war in Bremerton.) The need for carriers in the Pacific was urgent, so repair of the *Sara* at PSNY was given top priority. Later in 1942, the *Tennessee* returned to Bremerton for nine months of extensive modernization. Construction and repair of other ships continued.

The struggle with Germany and Japan preoccupied the entire nation, in few places more than Bremerton, where the war effort was all-encompassing. Teen-agers were deeply involved. Many were uprooted from other parts of the country when their parents took jobs in the Yard (by January of 1943 the city's population had soared threefold to 45,000.) They lived in houses that often were inferior to their comfortable residences back home. They attended high school in four-hour shifts and many held war-connected jobs. They bought war stamps and helped with salvage drives, and they volunteered as air-raid wardens and messengers.

The war was omnipresent in the classrooms at BHS, too — seldom more intensely than during a week-long rally to sell war stamps and bonds in April of 1943. Leader of the rally was the indefatigable Shirleye Sinclair (she later returned to the customary spelling of Shirley, but she was usually called Sindy anyhow), president of the Pep Club. Energetic? How about this: She would play in the band at basketball games, then at halftime hurriedly change and perform with the tumbling team. Then she would return to the clarinet section. She won five letters in various sports, was singles champion in badminton and both singles and doubles (with Mary Lou Flieder) in tennis.

The week was dedicated to General Jimmy Doolittle, who had led the famous air raid on Tokyo the year before. There were rallies, band concerts, skits and a Doolittle Victory Hop at the Civic Recreation Center. Students nearly doubled the goal of $5,000 by purchasing $9,039.33 in bonds and stamps. (That was a lot of money; multiply by 10 to approximate how much it would be today.) Students who bought bonds worth $18.75 were given rides in an Army jeep. A Victory booth set up in the halls sold $1,000 in bonds and stamps. The class of Mrs. Blanche Stineman won the "Hitler blackout poster" contest with the purchase of $557.73 in war stamps. Geraldine Petersen remembers that Miss Dunlap's Latin class memorized the phrase, *"Stampatis dies hodie est":* Today is stamp day. Robin Perrigo was so caught up in the spirit of the drive that she cashed in Puget Sound Power & Light stock that her grandparents had given her in the mid-'30s.

Shirley Sinclair wrote a dedication for the BHS Bond Rally Week that captures the high-minded attitude of students:

"To this and every other activity similar to it; to all organizations or groups who congregate together to unanimously and determinedly uphold the rights of a nation; who struggle and sacrifice to retain the principles of a steadfast democracy, which have been struggled for by our ancestors and their ancestors before them.

"To these and other patriotic contributors, goes the everlasting satisfaction and inward glowing pride that comes from the succuming (sic) to the natural tendency to be a part of something bigger than ourselves; to them goes the warmth and flow from the realization that they, in their small way, have done their bit towards the birth of a new era; a dream in the hearts of the American people: a Free World!!"

Well, of course, more than 50 years later, it sounds a little breathless. But it captures the gung-ho patriotism of the students during the war.

So do the nose-thumbing lyrics sung at a school assembly by the trio of Mary Jane Hudson, June Etten, and Shirley Eskridge. Their uniforms reflected the war: white knee-high boots; white skirts, white shirts and dark tie, naval jacket with braid on the left shoulder, white Sam Brown belts, and Navy officer's white hats. To the tune of *Der Fuehrer's Face* they sang:

The trio of Shirley Eskridge, June Etten, and Mary Jane Hudson sang at many BHS functions.
(Photo courtesy Shirley Sinclair.)

When the President said
"We'll put those Nips in place,"
Tojo leered — sneered —
right in FDR's face.
Then Doolittle stepped up
and he bombed that place.
So we cheered — Rah! — jeered —
right in Tojo's face.
Doolittle calls for men and ships,
To help him bomb again the Nips

And we gladly answer "Yes!"
We'll back him up — we'll end this mess.
We won't complain, we'll go without
— 100 percent of our goal without a doubt.
We will send him ships and men,
our cause we're sure to win.
From this world, these tyrants we will route.

Then, amid hoots of laughter, onto the auditorium stage
pranced teachers Dwight Scheyer, Orville Johnson, Fred Graham
and Willard Trepus, dressed like little girls. It isn't clear just why
they were in drag, except for the fun of it. Anyway, in song, they
urged students to buy bonds ("You'll be craving and slaving to
help to kill a Nip," went the words to one tune, lyrics-writer fortunately unknown.)

The trio returned and to the music of *There's a Star-Spangled
Banner Waving Somewhere*, sang:

If you buy more bonds and stamps every payday
If you save and sacrifice, our cause to win
Buy a bond and trust your old Uncle Sammy
There's none better on this earth you can trust in.

Stage directions offered these dramatic instructions as the
program ended: Trumpet plays Taps (muted) backstage. Trio sa-
lutes; blue spot on flag — lights dim.

In the audience, spines tingled, fists clinched; we'll fix those
Japs!

Highlight of the week, however, was the surprise appearance
of Mrs. Eleanor Roosevelt, the peripatetic wife of President
Roosevelt. She had visited the Navy Yard and Naval Hospital six
months earlier and she was back to visit the hospital again. Mrs.
Roosevelt's daughter Anna and grandchildren Eleanor and Cur-

tis, nicknamed Sistie and Buzz, lived in Seattle where Anna's husband, John Boettiger, was publisher of the *Post-Intelligencer*. That might explain the frequency of Mrs. Roosevelt's visits, except that she traveled the world so extensively it had became legend. Her impromptu visit to the high school was arranged through Rear Adm. S.A. Taffinder, commandant of PSNY, and Rear Adm. C.S Gillette, yard manager and step-father of Diane Gillette, a student at BHS.

Shirley Sinclair introduced Mrs. Roosevelt. The prepared introduction, preserved in Shirley's scrapbook, went like this:

"Mrs. Roosevelt, as a representative of the Pep Club, I would like to thank you for being with us during stamp rally week. And to further express our appreciation for your very gracious aid in boosting our bond sales, I would like to present you with this small token, as a reminder to you that our high school and others like it all over the nation are doing their part to help win this war. Members of the faculty and students, I wish to present our guest — Mrs. Eleanor Roosevelt."

Instead of reading *"Mrs. Eleanor Roosevelt,"* however, Shirley, naturally flustered, introduced her as *"Mrs. Theodore Roosevelt."*

We've had fun teasing Shirley about that introduction for the past half-century. At the Class of '44's fiftieth reunion I kidded her yet again about it. She muttered something like, "I just wish everyone would forget about it." But she took the joshing in good grace nevertheless.

Mrs. Roosevelt didn't flinch; she seemed not even slightly perturbed by being introduced as the wife of her uncle. She waited for the titters to die and then asked the students, who had arisen and were applauding, "Would you all like to sit down?" Betty Loftus remembers, "Bremerton High was known to be rude, noisy and discourteous to speakers. Instead of scowling and fuming, Mrs. Roosevelt smiled and waited patiently until we quieted and then spoke beautifully. I don't remember a thing she said, but I remember being spellbound, as was the entire audience. Everything I had ever read about her seemed true that day — she really cast a spell."

Mrs. Roosevelt was often described as unattractive. Not to BHS students. Remembers Mary Jane Hudson: "I met her at the microphone with our school guestbook. I was so thrilled that when she smiled at me, I thought she was *beautiful!* "

Eleanor Roosevelt visited Bremerton, PSNY and the Naval Hospital several months previous to her speech at the high school. Here with Captain Daniel Hunt, a Navy nurse and a USS Lexington seaman.
(Clipping courtesy Marjorie Lamb.)

~

Bernice Welch met Mrs. Roosevelt before the assembly at a reception in the Navy Yard, where she worked for the commandant. Bernice said, "I thought she was the homeliest woman in the world — but quickly became aware she was the most beautiful woman I had ever seen."

LaVerne Jacobson was an officer in the Girl's Club and part of the welcoming committee for Mrs. Roosevelt. "It was an experience I will never forget," she says. "When I met her backstage at BHS auditorium she was so personable and unaffected, yet had a certain 'presence' about her that seemed to denote intelligence and dignity. I was *very* impressed. She seemed to be sincerely interested in our school and personal activities."

Geraldine Petersen says Mrs. Roosevelt's visit is still vivid. "Though she could not be called a beauty, she was intelligent, educated and a forerunner to women's lib. My country school" (Geraldine transferred from Utah) "could never have had such a notable visitation."

David Leathley had graduated from high school by the time Mrs. Roosevelt visited. But, he wrote, "I recall my sister Ellen and Dorothy Williams had greeted Mrs. Roosevelt and shaken hands. We were told that night that they were never going to wash those hands!"

Virginia Eddy remembers wishing her mother, a fan of Mrs. Roosevelt's, could have been there. "I don't remember too much what she said," Virginia wrote, "only being very impressed."

Recalling my own encounter, if so it may be called, makes me wince. I was a hall monitor and stood alone, unsmiling, as Mrs. Roosevelt passed, prominently wearing on my sweater the campaign pin of the 1940 Republican candidate for president, Wendell Willkie. Mrs. Roosevelt glanced my way; whether she noticed the Willkie pin I do not know. I can only hope not.

Florence Dunlap, the Latin teacher, was escorting Mrs. Roosevelt. As they passed, I heard her accurately tell Mrs. Roosevelt that everything that happened in Bremerton was determined by the ferry schedules. But with 28 departures for Seattle daily, Mrs. Roosevelt didn't have to wait long; she caught the 12:20 p.m. ferry with a minimum of foofaraw, escorted not by big brass but by the commandant's aide, Lt. Comdr. J.L. Walker. For lunch, Mrs. Roosevelt and her secretary, Malvina Thompson, ate sandwiches from a paper sack on the ferry.

The *Sun's* account of Mrs. Roosevelt's visit said in part:

> From Mrs. Roosevelt's talk, every student was made to understand that this war is his war just as much as his parent's war. By her descriptions of children in war-torn countries, she painted a picture of what the American youth must do as his part in the war effort — mainly to make an all-out effort in the purchase of war bonds and stamps, work toward maintaining the American home as it has always been, and studying now to prepare to lead the government of the future.
>
> "Your government is a government in a democracy. It will be in your hands what you do with the future of the world," she concluded.

Mrs. Roosevelt's primary reason for revisiting Bremerton was to talk with patients at the Naval Hospital. But perhaps part of the reason she agreed to visit BHS was a conversation — an argument, really — she had with FDR at Hyde Park, the Roosevelt family estate in New York State's Hudson Valley, shortly before his third inauguration in 1941. It was reported in the *New Yorker* magazine on August 15, 1994, by Doris Kearns Goodwin[1], who drew the article from her book:

[1] Goodwin, Doris Kearns. *No Ordinary Time: Franklin and Eleanor Roosevelt.* New York: Simon & Schuster. 1994.

According to Joe Lash, who was present and recorded the scene in his diary, Eleanor, in the course of the dinner conversation, raised the troubling question of housing for people working in the defense program. During her last trip to the West Coast, she had seen the effects of over-crowding in Bremerton, Washington, where the Navy Yard and the shipbuilding industry had attracted thousands of workers from all over the country — part of the first wave of what became the greatest internal immigration in American history. In Bremerton, she had noted, every habitable shack or shed had been rented, scores of families were crowded into unsanitary trailer camps, and two thousand children were without schools. "I think we are going to have to be a nuisance about these questions if we are going to be fair to people all over this country," she had said.

Mrs. Roosevelt's statement to the President about housing in Bremerton was entirely true. It was not true, however, that 2,000 children were without schools. In returning to Bremerton, Mrs. Roosevelt perhaps remembered the discussion with FDR, and wanted to learn if Bremerton students were still without schools.

I suspect the source of the misinformation — this is speculation — was Warren Magnuson, who at that time represented the First Congressional District, including Bremerton. A doctoral dissertion in the Kitsap County Library by Carolyn L. Ferguson quotes Magnuson as saying, "In my town of Bremerton the children are given red and blue slips. Those that have red slips go to school on one day and those that have blue slips go another day." Ferguson called Magnuson's statement "sad and entirely untrue." She is correct.

Schools in Bremerton were, as we have seen, dreadfully crowded, and we did go to school in shifts. But no one was "without schools." Maggie made the statement when he was pursuing federal funds for school buildings. No one was better at bringing home federal dollars; as Jack Kennedy once said of him, "He stands up on the floor of the Senate in the late afternoon and mumbles a few words, and Grand Coulee Dam is built." So maybe Magnuson stretched the truth a little; the federal money was needed — and he got it.

On April 9, 1943, Mrs. Roosevelt tidied up after her visit by writing a thank-you note on simple "White House/Washington" letterhead.

Dear Club Members:

You were all very kind to think of me when I was in your community and I am appreciative. Thank you for the lovely pin, which I am delighted to have.

With all good wishes, I am

Sincerely yours,

Eleanor Roosevelt

The above is a copy of the original note that rests, appropriately, in Shirley Sinclair's scrapbook.

- **Chapter 14**

**Polio Threat Discounted . . . Bidu Sayao To Sing Here . . .
Many HS Seniors Receive Awards at Assembly . . .
Dance to Follow Graduation Rites . . .
Test Tube Babies Born in England . . .
David Soter Will Appear in Recital . . . 9,752 US Casualties
on Saipan . . . USS Bremerton to be Launched**

We Shall Overcome — But Not Very Soon

The relocation of Japanese-Americans from the West Coast in 1942 brought hardly a peep of protest from their neighbors. There were several reasons. One was that the sneak attack on Pearl Harbor a few weeks earlier had demonstrated the unexpected power of the Imperial Japanese Navy. Many Americans lived in genuine fear of an assault on the mainland and they remembered that fifth-columnists, such as the Quislings of Norway, helped bring down their countries. Another reason was that West Coast newspapers had bombarded subscribers for generations with bigoted warnings of a "Yellow Peril" they said threatened American racial purity. Caucasians in America routinely discriminated against Chinese laborers and in earlier times sometimes ran them out of town. Japanese who migrated to the United States, Issei, were not permitted to become citizens or in some states to own real property.

So it was not a surprise when, on February 19, 1942, President Roosevelt signed Executive Order 9066, which permitted the secretary of war to designate military areas from which certain people could be excluded. The order was aimed directly at the 112,000 Japanese-Americans living on the West Coast. About 47,000 were Issei; about 77,000 were U.S. citizens. Three-quarters were 25 or younger; 30,000 were school children.

At first, relocation was voluntary and about 9,000 Japanese-Americans moved from the war zone to wherever they could find jobs.

But on March 30, 1942, the 300 Japanese-Americans who lived on Bainbridge Island, many of whose families had arrived in the 1880s, were packed off. A headline in the *Sun* said, "Jap Population of Bainbridge Moved Out in Four Hours". A subhead said, "Army Directs Evacuation; Residents of Island Will Go to California." The story describes a poignant scene:

> Bainbridge is the site of a naval radio station and is on the main water route from Puget Sound Navy Yard to Seattle. Army trucks rolled out to Japanese homes promptly at 9 a.m. Families dressed in their Sunday best were waiting on their porches, all luggage and personal belongings were packed, tagged, and waiting to be moved. Some of the luggage bore small American flags. Groups were gathered by families and neighbors and taken to a ferry dock. A few young Japanese-Americans had been appointed to guide the soldiers and trucks to the strawberry and pea ranches. At the ferry dock the Japanese were assembled on a hillside in small groups, each under the guard of one or two soldiers in full equipment. White boys and girls played hooky from school to bid their Japanese friends good-bye. Filipinos who took over many of the farms of their former employers came down to bid them farewell. Trucks, a ferry, and a train were involved in the movement of the Japanese who will be taken to a reception center at Manzanar, California, aboard special railroad cars.

The Japanese-Americans from Bainbridge Island were among the first to be relocated. Why were they moved first? John de Graaf suggested in a 1985 television documentary, *Visible Target*, that the U.S. government wanted to determine the reaction of both Caucasians and Japanese-Americans to the general internment. If there had been an outcry, he speculated, the evacuation might have been called off. Sadly, there was no such protest. In six weeks, a general roundup of Japanese-Americans started along the West Coast. By June, more than 100,000 had been moved to hastily constructed internment camps, in the interior West, Midwest and Arkansas.

Two who did protest were Walt and Millie Woodward, publishers of the weekly *Bainbridge Review*. Recounting the events in 1985, Walt Woodward still spoke vigorously. "It was a violation of the Bill of Rights," he said indignantly. The Woodwards were called "Jap lovers" and their paper lost advertising and circulation. But they persisted in their support. They printed a weekly column from the camps, providing comforting assurance to the Japanese-Americans that they had a home to which they could return. But theirs was a lonely voice in the crowd.

A contemporary report (1942) in the *National Geographic* painted a ridiculously bright picture of life in the camps:

> Compare the safe, pleasant life of these internees with the cruelty and privations which, we read, are imposed on some American and British prisons in Japanese custody.
>
> In the big kitchen here I saw piles of flour, vegetables, fresh meat and fruits, canned goods, tea, coffee, sugar, ham, bacon, eggs, cereals — everything you might find in first-class restaurants . . .
>
> By day these 'prisoners' play games, go to school, read or write. I saw many sending 25-word messages, through the Red Cross, via Geneva, to friends or relatives in Japan.
>
> Their own camp newspaper is issued, in English. Their Boy Scouts drill to their own brass-band music, and with appropriate ceremony they raise and lower — the American flag! Each night a dance is held or indoor tennis is played . . .
>
> We walked out, past a baseball game where most shouting was in English . . . Up and down, outside the barbed wire, American soldiers with rifles on shoulders strolled back and forth. Now and then a soldier would wink, and get back answering grins from a group of sport-clad Jap maidens who were flapping their skirts and flashing bare legs as they practiced jitterbugging.

The absurdity of that report was in comparing the Japanese-Americans to prisoners of war. Most of those interned were American citizens, held captive by their own government.

Although life was not easy in the camps, it is misleading and unfair to characterize them as "concentration" camps, as do some latter-day hand-wringers, because that makes what happened under the Nazis in Germany seem trivial. Furthermore, it was possible under some circumstances, admittedly stringent, to leave the camps. During 1943, the War Relocation Authority granted some 17,000 such leaves and by the end of 1944, a total of 35,000 had been issued, most of them to younger Nisei, many of whom served valiantly in the military services. At the same time, 8,700

Japanese-Americans either refused to give up their allegiance to the emperor of Japan or somehow qualified their answer to a loyalty questionnaire. Richard Polenberg[1] wrote that "These included one of every four male Nisei of draft age, who did not believe that their one right as American citizens should be that of military service." Later, some 8,000 Japanese-Americans chose to leave for Japan, whether from anger at their mistreatment or from continuing loyalty to Japan cannot be determined. There probably were some of each frame of mind.

The exclusion order was rescinded in December of 1944. It remains a shameful chapter in U.S. history, the result of panic, prejudice and hysteria. DeGraff's TV narration said of the relocation, "It was too painful to talk about — but too important to forget."

Still, fear of an attack on the West Coast, and particularly on Bremerton, was palpable. An attack on the mainland would not have been a greater surprise than was the Japanese bombing at Pearl Harbor. I regret the internment, but understand it.

Aside from the Japanese-American families on Bainbridge, most of Kitsap County was lily-white prior to the war. There were a few Filipinos, mostly mess boys in the Navy, a handful of Chinese, and, to mix faith with race, about a dozen Jewish families in Bremerton.

The Jewish family I knew best were the Polls, but there also were the Sorianos, Naons, Cohens, Kahns, Shifrens, Friedmans, and no doubt others. There were too few for a synagogue, so families went to Seattle to observe the Jewish high holidays. The Polls brought in an instructor once or twice a week from Seattle to teach sons David and Bob the Hebrew needed for their bar mitzvahs. When the war started and Army units moved into Bremerton, a number of Jewish soldiers came with them. Harry Poll, younger than Dave and Bob, thus learned his Hebrew from a soldier from the Bronx, stationed with a barrage balloon unit at Central School. The Polls opened their home to many Jewish soldiers and a half-dozen or more weddings took place there and lasting friendships were formed.

Many years later, Harry Poll recalled, his father Itzak planned a visit to New York City. He asked Harry to get the New York telephone directory and give him the number for Max Kaplan. "There are probably six million Max Kaplans living in New York City," Harry told him. "There's no way I could ever find the right one." That disgusted Itzak. "So you can't do so lit-

---

[1] Polenberg, Richard. *War and Society: The United States, 1941-1945.* Philadelphia: Lippincott, 1972.

tle for your father?" he said. "OK, thanks, Mr. Big Shot." Later, when he got to his New York hotel room, Itzak got out the telephone directory and dialed the first Max Kaplan listing that caught his eye. "Hello, Max Kaplan?" he said. "My name is Itzak Poll and I live in Bremerton, Washington . . . "

"Itzy!" came back the happy shout.

Nationally, every law school and probably medical schools, too, had quotas for Jews, and so did many private clubs. (That produced Groucho Marx's famous line about not wanting to join any club that would have him.) There was little overt discrimination in Bremerton, however, because at first there were so few minorities to discriminate against. My brother Barrett, who wore horn-rimmed glasses and whose complexion is moderately swarthy, was widely known by the nickname "Kike." The name was given, I think, in complete innocence and was taken without offense. Even my mother would call him that occasionally.

The 1940 census reported only 17 blacks living in Bremerton. Seattle's black population was small, too — only one percent, or about 3,800. The national population in 1940 was 131,669,275, of which 12,865,518 were black, some in the East but mostly in the South. (Jo Peterson wrote of growing up in the Midwest. "I had only seen one black person face to face when we lived in North Dakota and that was a man who came through town on the bum during harvest time. Two years in a row we went down to the bum camp and stared at him.") But the war created a hungry demand for war workers and during the early '40s almost 1.5 million Southern blacks migrated to the North and West. Los Angeles's black population grew from 75,000 to 135,000; San Francisco's from 4,800 to 20,000; Vancouver, Washington's from 4 to 4,000. By 1943, Seattle's black population had doubled, although blacks were not hired at many major industries until 1942, and then only under pressure (a headline in the *Sun* on April 2, 1942, said "Boeing Unions Lift Ban on Negroes".)

Fifty years later, it's hard to remember the extent of segregation in the United States. Black citizens, about ten percent of the population, for practical purposes had no vote. Periodic lynchings reminded blacks not to get uppity by claiming their civil rights. When the U.S. entered the war, there were 97,000 blacks in segregated units of the Army. That grew to 700,000 in 1944, but units were still segregated and there were only a few combat units. The Air Corps agreed to train black pilots at Tuskegee in an inferior program. In the Navy, blacks could serve at sea only as mess stewards. The Navy started accepting blacks for general labor service in April of 1942; after James Forrestal became secretary of the navy in May of 1944, integration proceeded more rapidly. When the Army ordered training camps desegregated, the order was often disobeyed, particularly in the South.

Up to WWII, Bremerton was almost completely white and many of us remember the community's racial outlook as benign. Truth is, however, that the city's outlook was no freer of bigotry than was the nation's. Accommodations in Bremerton weren't segregated because there was no one to segregate. Reflecting the practice of newspapers everywhere, the *Sun* commonly used racial identifications regardless of relevancy, often in crime stories but also for Lionel Hampton when his band visited; for Satchel Paige, when he came to pitch; for the Kansas City Monarchs ("Negro Club Plays Here Wednesday.")

An Amos-and-Andy story from the 'Round Towner column in the *Sun* of January 15, 1944, demonstrates the acceptability of racial prejudice:

> Adm. C. S. Gillette, PSNY industrial manager, has a wealth of interesting yarns from true life that he's observed in the Navy Yard. For instance, the case of the Negro worker who, for cause, was discharged and had his badge taken up. This Negro had done some "headline" newspaper reading and felt that he understood something of the current manpower ruling. Next morning, not satisfied that he had been discharged and sensing his "rights," he appeared at the Yard gate, minus badge. "Where's your badge?" queried the Marine. "Ah ain't got one," replied the colored boy. "Well, you can't come in here without a badge." "Wot, you talkin," the man shot back. "Ise gotta get in. Ise frozen on my job." "That might be," chortled the Marine, "but lemme tell you somethin, sonny. You've been defrosted."

Once the war began, local recruiters enlisted black workers in substantial numbers for the Navy Yard. With that, segregation began. In 1943, says a summary report in the Civic Unity Community files at the University of Washington Library, "the Bremerton Housing Authority, contrary to advice from Federal Public Housing Authority, established an all-Negro project at Sinclair Heights, Bremerton."

Furthermore, says the report, "We must recognize that attitudes of the community are closely related to housing and that the attitude of the Bremerton Housing Authority is truly representative of the city of Bremerton. The city has taken no steps to remove discriminatory signs from restaurant windows nor to provide adequate recreational facilities for the Negro group. The

Mayor of Bremerton is not interested in trying to approach the problem intelligently and there seems to be an idea that 'if the Negroes are treated too well, they will remain after the war.' The Mayor has gone on record as believing that the all-Negro project, in spite of its isolated location, should be the Negro center for all Negroes, including servicemen, in the area.

"Since Sinclair Heights reached full occupancy, Negroes have not been accepted at Bremerton projects but have all been referred to Port Orchard . . . Although the Bremerton Housing Authority has claimed that Negroes were permitted in ALL projects, a recent study reveals that only two of remaining projects have Negro tenants, and there only 1 percent Negro. Furthermore, as Negroes have vacated these two projects, they have been replaced by whites."

The report noted that when Negro families were moved into another project, View Ridge, white families protested. Attached to the report was a petition said to have been signed by almost 1,000 workers. The petition asked for segregation with an implied threat: "It is to the interest of the government to keep skilled mechanics in the Yard, rather than have them leave because they are forced to live with colored people." The attitude of those who signed is summed up in the petition: "We have the kindest feeling toward the colored people, but object to living side by side with them."

Everett Humble of the Housing Authority alibied to federal authorities in 1943 that his agency was accustomed to dealing with higher-type blacks from local or western areas. But "the present influx of Negro workers (is) from the eastern and southern states. Racial differences in the living standards, racial relations, and psychology of Negroes has already become apparent to us." Later in the same letter he wrote, "The Negro families housed in our housing projects are probably of a higher type than the present Negro immigrant."

A subsequent report dated January 22, 1944, said, "The Roxy Theater is segregating Negros (sic), seating them in the rear of the theater, and one private theater refused to admit Negros." No one knew of an inter-relations committee supposedly started by a group of businessmen, said the report. "The only plan under way at present is the remodeling of a building by a Mr. Bremer, where he will operate a restaurant for Negros. This is purely a business venture, not promoted by an altruistic motive. The Negros have insisted that the restaurant serve white trade as well and Mr. Bremer agreed as otherwise Negro groups would not patronize the place." Beer was to be served in the restaurant and the report quotes the mayor, "Hum" Kean, "I want to help those poor devils.

They need a place where they can sit and have a glass of beer." The report gives the American Legion credit for making its hall available for black dances but notes disparagingly that when city police conducted a gambling raid in Sinclair Heights, 22 policemen participated, almost two-thirds of the force.

In January of 1944, the Bremerton Housing Authority ran 6,246 family units, 233 of which were occupied by blacks. Of 986 dormitory units, only 25 were occupied by blacks because single blacks were housed in Navy Yard dormitories. The Housing Authority of Port Orchard ran 5,554 family units, occupied by 118 black families, and 380 dormitories, occupied by 50 single blacks. "The pattern is partially controlled segregation, but the recreational facilities, nurseries, and schools are used by whites and Negroes."

The breakdown of black families by project in Bremerton was 170 Sinclair Heights; 23 at Qualheim, Westpark addition; 10 at View Ridge, and 30 at Sheridan.

Lack of vigorous action by the housing authorities led to ugly incidents. After a few black families were moved into Orchard Heights, two families were forced to leave, the first because white teenagers threw rocks whenever the black woman went outside for coal. The second family left after two cars of white men drove by their house and threw stones and pieces of pipe. A protest meeting at East Port Orchard on March 17, 1945, was attended by 250 people. One official said a tenant suggested they "try a petition first and if that doesn't work we will take matters in our hands like they do in the South where I come from." At subsequent meetings the tenants discussed Jim Crow buses and segregated recreation.

The *Sun* reported little of this. But on May 1, 1944, it ran this story:

> The formal opening of the Casino, Bremerton's exclusive Negro club at 820 Burwell, will be a gala affair and at 8 o'clock this evening "open house" will be in order. The Casino, located in a new building constructed by the Bremer Estate, is complete with a cafe and tavern, the cafe on one side of the building and the tavern on the other. Each division will accommodate approximately 90 persons in surroundings of refinement and rich appointments. The Casino supplies eating and recreational facilities for the hundreds of Negro people now living in the city. It is equipped with a banquet room on the balcony where approximately 150 people may be seated. A barber shop, kitchen and other facilities in the building are the most modern obtainable and the entire interior and exte-

rior of the Casino is one of beauty and pleasing to the eye. The manager is Bill Williams, well known former maintenance supervisor for Bremers for the past 16 years, assisted by his wife Willette. The Williamses have a daughter, Almeda, 13, who attends school here. They live at 523 Sixth Street.

If there is a villain to this loss-of-Eden story, it probably is the Navy. Sinclair Heights was made an all-Negro project because the Navy naturally feared anything that could disrupt swift repair of war-damaged ships. Lt. William Howell, housing coordinator for the Navy Yard, "claimed to have made a careful study of the situation and he was certain that Negroes preferred segregation," said a report. Some blacks had argued for segregated housing, too. And, as noted, the Navy segregated its own housing units.

Prejudice was not limited to housing. In 1993, Adele Ferguson wrote that during the war Kitsap County bristled with signs in stores and restaurants that said, "We reserve the right to refuse service to anyone." Virginia Oass told of her mother's anger when she saw a sign in a Chinese restaurant, of all places, that said, "We do not cater to blacks." Adele Ferguson wrote of how Lillian Walker, then secretary of the Bremerton chapter of the National Association for the Advancement of Colored People, confronted the Triangle Cafe on the corner of Front Street and Washington Avenue when she was refused service. A meeting among the owner of the Triangle, the NAACP, and a local minister quickly worked out an agreement that the restaurant would serve blacks. The Triangle was the first restaurant in the county to make such an agreement, Ferguson said.

Individual Yard workmen were prejudiced, too. Berenice Eicher says she saw her first really blatant act of bigotry in the blueprint room at the Navy Yard. "A Negro girl applied for a position in the blueprint room and a Texas woman announced that if the Negro got the job, she was quitting. This put my boss on the spot, because the Texan was a good worker and he didn't want to lose her, yet he wasn't allowed to discriminate. I think he talked the Negro girl out of applying; anyway she didn't join us."

But we should beware imposing today's standards on yesterday's history. Bremerton was no worse and, in fact, better than much of the rest of the nation. A terrible race riot in Detroit on June 21, 1943, for example, took the lives of 25 blacks, 9 whites, and injured 800. Servicemen in Los Angeles persecuted pachucos, Mexican-American youths who could be identified by their zoot suits.

Longtime Bremerton residents blamed the bigotry on newcomers from the South. But beware of stereotyping. Berenice Eicher reported that she met a good friend in the blueprint room in the Yard: Mary Dean Payton, from Hot Springs, Arkansas. "She was surely an atypical white Southerner, for she was strongly pro-union, and when I asked her about it once, said she thought Negroes were just as good as anybody else."

There were immediate bright sides to the mass migration. William M. Tuttle, Jr.[2] cites one in his book. Calvin Campbell came to Bremerton when his father took a job at PSNY. They moved from Tullahoma, Tennessee, when Calvin was 7. Calvin remembered that a white boy, a recent arrival from Alabama, called him a nigger. "A white friend beat the hell out of the Alabama kid." Calvin's father, a graduate of Tuskegee, welcomed other new black arrivals to Bremerton by asking them to dinner. Later, Calvin said that moving to Bremerton had been beneficial for him "as everybody had something in common . . . and there was not a lot of room or time for racial tensions . . ."

Despite the race riots, unsettling migrations, spread of segregation, and failure of supposedly enlightened communities to respond positively to racism, it's probably true that more progress toward racial equality was made during the five years of the war than during the entire period since the Civil War. In fact, the modern Civil Rights era probably started during WWII with James Farmer's first sit-ins and the threat of A. Philip Randolph to lead a Civil Rights march in Washington. Expectations of blacks were heightened as they found better paying jobs and saw the possibility of brighter futures. The link between the migration of the war years and the Civil Rights movement of the '60s is beyond the scope of this book. But I suspect it exists.

It is pleasant solace to remember that Andrew F. Brimmer lived in Bremerton during the war, coming with his parents from Louisiana. He became a Ph.D. economist and author and government official. His entry in the *International Who's Who* for 1970 notes that he was born in Newelltown, Louisiana. He studied at the University of Washington, University of Delhi in India, and Harvard. He was one of the first blacks to serve as a member of the Federal Reserve Board, the influential government agency.

More famous is Quincy Jones, who spent part of his adolescence in Bremerton. He was born in Chicago in 1933 and came to Bremerton with his family when his father, a carpenter, took work in Bremerton during the war. Quincy attended Bremerton

---

[2] Tuttle. Ibid.

schools for about four years but graduated from Garfield High School in Seattle.

Ron Gillespie, who directed music programs for the Bremerton school district said Quincy was "very likable". Quincy played the trumpet, an instrument he's given up after two nearly fatal cerebral aneurysms. His fourth wife is actress Nastassja Kinski. He's the father of six children.

Quincy has been nominated for seven Oscars including three for "The Color Purple." He's scored more than 35 films. He won an Emmy for his TV score of "Roots" and also produced the charity blockbuster "We Are the World".

He won the prestigious Jean Hersholt Humanitarian Award, presented by Oprah Winfrey, at the 1995 Academy Awards. "It's nice to feel important," he said then. "I think it's more important to feel nice."

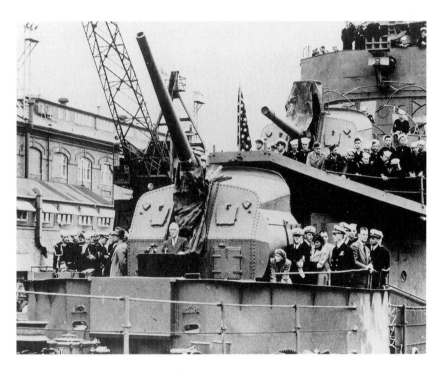

***President Franklin D. Roosevelt spoke from a podium mounted on
deck of the USS Cummings on August 12, 1944, delivering a
nation-wide radio broadcast.***

(Photo courtesy Larry Jacobsen.)

~

Chapter 15

(Headlines from Bremerton Sun in 1944)

5 Nabbed at Shel-Bac Pay $150 Fines . . .
Two-Cent Stamp To Become War Casualty. . .
Swing, Graveyard Pay Scale Raised . . .
Scarlet Fever Still Prevalent . . .
Infant Succumbs to Polio . . .
Colored Folk Plan Mother's Day Event . . .
Roosevelt Field To Get Lights, Paint . . .

≈

By God, If It Ain't Old Frank

Franklin Delano Roosevelt visited Bremerton during WWII, not once but twice. He already knew the Navy Yard well. In April of 1914, when he was assistant secretary of the Navy, he traveled up the Pacific Coast inspecting naval bases. He was in Bremerton soon after President Woodrow Wilson threatened to invade Mexico. That possibility excited FDR, who dreamed of making his reputation in somewhat the same way Theodore Roosevelt, his wife's uncle and his own distant cousin, had advanced his career during the Spanish-American War in 1898. Franklin Roosevelt made several bellicose statements and, hoping to oversee the operation, wired the Navy Department to determine plans for action on the west coast of Mexico. Instead, the secretary of Navy, Josephus Daniels, suggested Roosevelt would be of greater help in Washington and should return as planned. FDR, somewhat chastened, headed for the Capitol; en route he learned to his disappointment that President Wilson had accepted an offer of arbitration.

While in Bremerton in 1914, FDR spent two days inspecting the Yard and the Naval Magazine Depot (the ammunition depot) and attended a lunch given by the Commercial Club. Cost was 75 cents a plate. A newspaper account said, "Only men will attend, Mrs. Roosevelt being entertained by the ladies of the Navy Yard."

Already hoping to become president one day, Roosevelt promised more work for the Yard. He said the next drydock for the Pacific Coast would be built in Bremerton. He also said he would recommend construction of two tugs. "I am going back to Washington and try to arrange to send you enough work to tide this Yard over until next spring when the fleet will come through the Canal," he said. "Then there will be plenty of work to be done." His timetable for opening the Panama Canal was slightly inaccurate. The Canal was opened to shipping only four months later, creating new opportunities for PSNY as the Atlantic and Pacific fleets became less discrete. Roosevelt remained assistant secretary of the navy for more than seven years. Part of his responsibility was oversight of the Navy's civilian employees. So he had a long association with, and affinity for, Navy Yard workers.

Like the battleships sunk at Pearl Harbor but rejuvenated in Bremerton, President Roosevelt returned to Bremerton on September 22, 1942, as a ghost. He was on a two-week secret tour of defense plants and military bases, traveling aboard a 10-car private train. His first stop was at a Chrysler tank plant in Detroit. When his Packard rolled into the huge plant, a worker looked up and said, "By God, if it ain't old Frank." Roosevelt enjoyed surprising people wherever he traveled — across Wisconsin, Minnesota, North Dakota, Montana, and Idaho before making a whirlwind inspection of Fort Lewis, near Tacoma. Bart Ripp of the *Morning News Tribune* in Tacoma wrote in 1994 about 10,000 troops at Fort Lewis waiting to see FDR:

> A Lincoln limousine, flags flying, approached the parade grounds. The troops craned to see the president. A black Ford drove up behind the soldiers and the windows rolled down. Roosevelt, all smiles, waved his hat from the Ford.

A caravan of 16 cars left Tacoma and boarded the ferry *Defiance* and crossed the Tacoma Narrows, where the Narrows Bridge, the infamous Galloping Gertie, had blown down during a storm almost two years before. Because of wartime secrecy, newspapers were unable to report the President's tour until October 1. Then the *Sun* published this account:

> It was learned with little surprise today what most Bremertonians already knew . . .that President Roosevelt paid a "secret" visit to the city and Puget Sound Navy Yard 10 days ago. The President came here on Tuesday, Sept. 22, but at the request of the White House, as a

special wartime safeguard, disclosure of his trip had been withheld by the press and radio until he returned today to Washington, D.C. Thousands of Navy Yard employees saw the President when he visited the Navy Yard and spoke briefly there and hundreds of Bremertonians caught a fleeting glimpse of the nation's leader as he left the Navy Yard enroute to the Bremerton-Seattle ferry.

Word of his visit was a closely guarded secret until an hour or two before he arrived. But once the "secret" was out, it spread like wildfire. President Roosevelt entered Bremerton from the west side about 10 minutes past noon that day coming in on the Head of the Bay highway from Tacoma via Gig Harbor and Port Orchard. His route was closely guarded and his party drove along Cambrian to Farragut and then into the Navy Yard through the Charleston gate. Half an hour prior to his arrival in the west end, crowds began to gather along Front Street between Pacific and Washington. Marine guards, aided by city police and state patrolmen, diverted auto traffic from Front Street and kept the hundreds of persons standing by on the sidewalks. The Front Street crowds caught one glimpse of the President's party as it drove through the Navy Yard prior to the chief executive's brief remarks. He spoke from his open automobile in the Navy Yard with the microphone placed in the car.

He introduced the thousands of PSNY workers into the newspaper world of "off the record" explaining that "I'm not really here because I am taking this trip under Navy orders and that means that my cruise is not published in the papers."

"So just remember that for about 10 days, you haven't seen me," he added as the several thousand workers listening to him roared with laughter over the "secret." Mr. Roosevelt lunched at the home of Rear Adm. S.A. Taffinder, PSNY commandant, while the hundreds of Front Street watchers waited patiently for him to come by. Even the Marine guards in the Front Street vicinity were not aware of why they were on duty. Until the word went thoroughly about the crowd, there were remarks such as "Must be some Navy Department big shot coming to town." Other citizens who knew what was in the air, passed it off jokingly with such remarks as, "Oh, it's just the fourth assistant postmaster."

Many persons believed that the guards and obvious precautionary steps were but a "camouflage" and that the

President would arrive and depart from the Navy Yard aboard a naval vessel which would berth at one of the Navy Yard piers. But at about 2:15 p.m. the President, with his party, left the yard via the Washington Avenue gate, taking the shortest possible route from the government plant to the ferry terminal.

As he rode by in his open car, President Roosevelt waved his hat and smiled at the crowd. There was loud applause, but the multitude respectfully refrained from boisterous cheering. Advance Secret Service agents had cleared the way for the President's safety. Commercial trucks reportedly were ordered out of the Navy Yard by 11 o'clock in the morning.

Windows at the YMCA building at Front and Washington, directly overlooking the President's path, were closed. Doorways of buildings in the vicinity likewise were shut and only authorized persons were allowed in the ferry terminal on the city dock and in other buildings below Washington Avenue. Marines on the streets were armed with tommy guns; city police, in the streets and on the roofs of nearby buildings, carried shotguns; Secret Service men, their identity unknown, mingled in the crowd.

The President returned to Seattle via ferry with naval vessels providing an escort in the channel. In his visit to the potentially dangerous Pacific Coast theater of war operations, President Roosevelt found increasing evidence that "the people of the whole region are in this war to win it, and to win it just as fast as we can," a White House announcement said today.

His admittedly mounting confidence in the American war effort stemmed from visits to Fort Lewis, the highly active Navy Yard here and the Boeing aircraft plant. In touring this area, the President saw countless preparations for attack that might come at any time from the Pacific.

Precautions and defense installations rarely seen in the East were visible on every side as the chief executive and his party went from Fort Lewis to the Navy Yard and later, the Boeing plant. At the Army post, which is geared for instantaneous action to repel an enemy attack on the Northwest, the President reviewed crack infantry and field artillery troops, some just back from desert maneuvers and thoroughly seasoned by sand and heat. At Bremerton he saw "wounded ships and wounded men" being prepared for service again, and at Boeing he inspected a new, secret bomber that is much larger than a Flying Fortress. . .which should be bad news for Axis forces everywhere.

The complete text of his remarks:
I can only say a word or two to you. The first is that I am not really here because I am taking this trip under Navy orders and that means that my cruise is not published in the papers. So just remember that for about 10 days, you haven't seen me. I have been looking things over, coming across the country, and all I can tell you is that I am more and more convinced that the people of the whole nation are in this war to win it, and win it just as fast as we can. I am proud of what I have seen: the officers and men, the workmen here in this old Navy Yard, which I used to know in the old days. The golf course that I played on during the World War is now covered with machine shops and other buildings. I am glad to see Bremerton again and I am very happy in knowing all that you are doing. I have seen wounded ships and wounded men and we are bringing them back and making them new. I am on my way almost immediately to take in other places and other yards and other camps and when I get back to Washington maybe if they will let me talk I will say something about what I have seen and how fine the effort of all of you is throughout the nation. Thanks.

The President had dinner that night in Seattle at the home of his daughter Anna, then continued to Portland, where the next day he saw the SS *Joseph N. Teal* launched at the Kaiser shipyard. He also visited the Alcoa plant in Vancouver. Before returning to the White House, he continued through California, New Mexico, Texas, Louisiana, Mississippi, Alabama, Georgia, South Carolina, North Carolina and Virginia. The only members of the press with him were representatives of the Associated Press, United Press, and International News Service. They withheld their stories until the journey was completed.

Many Bremerton teen-agers saw the President during his secret visit. Remembers Mack Smith: "I was working in the Navy Yard for an outside contractor, filling candy machines during the summer, when FDR came riding through in a convertible with the top down, smoking a cigarette with that long cigarette holder that he always used. I was close enough to get a good view of him smiling his trademark smile and acting as though everything was right with the world."

Young Gene Gurske worked at the Black Ball ferry terminal when he wasn't attending high school. The Secret Service sent him and other workers across the street from the wharf to a tavern while awaiting the President's departure. "There were security men on the streets and on top of the buildings," Gene remembers. "They cleared the dock parking lot, the streets, and the sidewalks. The President's entourage came from the Navy Yard, down past the YMCA, and into the terminal through the exit ramp. President Roosevelt had a 'private' ferryboat ride to Seattle." It probably was Gene's first visit to a tavern.

I was among the small crowd that watched the caravan sweep past the intersection at First and Washington. I don't remember how I heard the President was coming. It was the only time I ever saw him. I remember the wave and smile and I was impressed. FDR had been president for most of my life. Seeing him was like seeing royalty — which, we Republicans frequently alleged, he considered himself to be.

Adrienne Johnson remembers a curious sidelight to FDR's visit. "I was inside the Yard and the President's motorcade appeared. It was moving along the street just inside the fence between State Street gate and the Naval Avenue gate, going toward the hospital area. There came a long, open car with a row of men, obviously Secret Service, lining both running boards, facing out, and hanging on behind themselves, and sure enough, sitting in the back of the limousine was a man with the familiar face of the President, complete with jutting chin, smile, long cigarette holder. They passed quickly and while I was still staring after them a duplicate scene appeared, a second limousine with Secret Service and President. It was a clever security trick."

From such sightings are mystery novels constructed. No doubt the Secret Service was concerned for the President's safety; that was demonstrated by the way he surprised the troops at Fort Lewis by sneaking up from the rear in a small car while to their front a big limousine distracted the soldiers. Fleeting sightings also are deceptive; a Tacoma man told the News Tribune he had seen Joseph Stalin riding with FDR.

President Roosevelt returned to Bremerton on August 12, 1944. This time his visit was widely publicized. It was clear proof that victories in the Pacific had made the West Coast secure; unlike his secret visit in 1942, it was unnecessary to conceal his presence. The White House announced the night before his arrival that FDR would broadcast a war progress report to the nation over all major networks from a ship at the Puget Sound

Navy Yard. It was his first speech since he had accepted the Democratic presidential nomination, his fourth, on July 20 at the Marine base in San Diego. News accounts said the President's decision to speak from the Bremerton yard underlined his announced intention to campaign not in the usual sense but by going about his duties as an active wartime commander in chief. A sidebar account in the *Sun* gives details:

Accommodations Were Slim
Fala Wags Tail and Steals Show
Yard Workers See President
By Charles H. Bird
Bremerton Sun Staff Writer

The rumor that President Roosevelt might visit the Puget Sound Navy Yard has been confirmed. He came, he was seen, he spoke.

Lack of information as to just how and when he would arrive put officials of the Yard somewhat on the spot in planning for his reception. First a platform with a ramp, strong enough for the President's official car to be driven on, was hastily erected. Later, advice arrived that he was coming on a ship and would not come ashore, so an entirely different plan had to be quickly worked out. The results showed that quite a few officers, men and workers missed most of their sleep Friday night to whip things into shape.

Mr. Roosevelt came sailing up the Sound on a fighting ship. It was warped into one of the big drydocks and tied up where workers and guests could gather around fairly close. Near the gangplank, seats were provided for officers and their guests. Everybody else had to stand behind ropes patrolled by gimlet-eyed guards. Secret Service men were stationed every few feet, facing the crowd, and never missing a motion, even when an innocent hand dived into a pocket or purse for a cigarette.

ALL OVER PAINT

Members of the press were met at the main gate and escorted into an office where painters were just putting on the last of a fresh coat. There were no chairs and several elbows and shoulders took some of the fresh paint with them. Cmdr. D.J. Sass, personnel officer, rescued the writers from this rendezvous and took them to his office, where they could be more comfortable while waiting for Lt. Bob Thurston of the public relations office to escort them to the dock. Everyone else had apparently arrived first so Lt. Thurston led a serpentine sortie through the massed audience to a less crowded plot of standing room between the bandstand and the Teletype tower, facing the President, who was sitting on the gundeck of the ship.

Mr. Roosevelt wore a battered brown hat which looked as if it would not be complete without a festoon of fish-hooks. Below that he wore a blue-gray business suit, and a light blue shirt and a darker blue tie. He pushed the hat up in front and down in back, so it wouldn't shade his face against the photographers and newsreel cameras which were mounted on another tower, grinding steadily.

HIGH PRESS PERCH

A ladder led steeply to the Teletype tower, where both men and women worked like beavers on those mysterious machines that flash important events to the world almost as fast as they happen. It must have been quite a trick for the girls to get back to terra firma from their commanding perch.

The Navy Yard band played live tunes to entertain the crowd until time for Mr. Roosevelt to begin his world-wide broadcast . . .When the President rose and got set behind his bank of microphones on the gundeck, he took off his funny hat and the crowd applauded. He looked much better bare-headed. His face was tanned and he looked quite robust. While he was speaking, a sailor stood near the rail, sketching his picture and several other sailors kibitzed over his shoulder.

FALA STEALS SHOW

After the broadcast, the Navy Yard band rose and put inspiration and cymbals into the national anthem.

Anna Roosevelt Boettiger had been sitting in her father's chair while he was talking, taking care of Fala, the president's beloved Scottie and constant companion. Anna picked up Fala and put him up over her shoulder to see the crowd. That drew the only cheers from the thousands of workers. Fala perked up his ears, wagged his stubby tail and laughed down at his master.

After a drink of water, the President fished in his pockets for a cigarette. But he must have lost or forgotten his famous long holder, for he smoked it "unmuzzled" just like any swing shifter. The crew of the cruiser (sic) filed smartly up the gangplank for duty. Helmeted wharfmen released the new manila lines and the fighting ship slowly backed out of the drydock. The President waved farewell once more to Bremerton.

HIGH TRIBUTE
PAID P.S.N.Y.
BY PRESIDENT
(By United Press)

Warning that "the word and honor of Japan cannot be trusted," President Roosevelt told the nation on his return from his Pacific tour that a network of forward Pacific bases in the years to come was essential to the safety of the U.S.

The President spoke from the deck of a destroyer in the Puget Sound Navy Yard shortly after he returned from Alaskan waters where he viewed the bases at Adak and Kodiak after his visit to Pearl Harbor for conferences with Gen. Douglas MacArthur and Admiral Chester Nimitz.

WILL NOT PREDICT

Mr. Roosevelt said the war in the Pacific was "well in hand" but told his nationwide radio audience he could not tell, if he knew, when that war or the one in Europe would be over.

The President said this nation had no desire for any possession of others of the United Nations but that he was confident "the United Nations who are working so well with us in the winning of the war will be glad to join with us in protection against aggression and in machinery to prevent aggression."

In a special tribute to Bremerton workers at the Puget Sound Navy Yard, Mr. Roosevelt said he would never forget the outstanding contribution made to victory by these "home-front fighters."

MAGNIFICENT JOB

"I will never forget," said the President, "how you people worked night and day to reclaim, repair and rebuild that sunken fleet after Pearl Harbor and send those battered ships out, better, stronger and more dangerous to the enemy to win victory out of that first temporary defeat. I can tell you now that the battleship *Nevada*, put back into service through your magnificent efforts, played an important role in the invasion of Normandy."

Berenice Eicher provides the perspective of a Yard worker. "I remember there was a grandstand built on one side of the dry-dock for the dignitaries, officers' wives, etc.; we plebeians stood on the other side.   To my delight, when the destroyer came in, President Roosevelt was on our side of the deck; I had a lovely view. He was seated, with an overcoat and hat on. His daughter, Anna Boettiger, was with him.   Someone called out, 'Where's Fala?' and Anna held the terrier up. It was all very jolly. Various dignitaries came on board, then after 15 minutes or so, President Roosevelt stood at a podium on the deck and gave a speech. I cannot remember a word of it.   Then the destroyer left the drydock and went away."

My Mother, Republican to the core, provided her own partisan perspective. By then, I was at Buckley Field. She wrote: "If you were in Denver Saturday night I don't suppose you heard the President speaking from Bremerton. The Yard personnel worked for days getting ready for FDR. A ramp was built to the Griffins' house — into the Administration building and a stage was built on the dock — the windows were nailed shut in the front of the shops — then the old fuddy-duddy didn't get off the cruiser. It was quite a convoy that brought him in — three destroyers and a cruiser.   I'm afraid this political tour of his is going to be a boomerang, for everyone was very disgusted both with his speech and the fanfare also crossing up the Yard's plans."

There was more to this speech than was apparent. His best addresses were usually written by playwright Robert Sherwood or the most experienced of his speech writers, Samuel I. Rosenman. This one, however, he composed himself as he cruised down the inland passage from Alaska to Bremerton. After he dictated the speech to a Navy lieutenant who accompanied him, FDR hardly glanced at the manuscript until an hour or two before he arrived in Bremerton. It was intended to reassure the public, in a folksy way, about progress of the war. But it was flat and rambling, says a biographer, Frank Freidel, without the polish that Sherwood or Rosenman would have given it.   Other factors affected his delivery: The President decided to stand for his speech, although he had not worn his leg braces for a year. They did not fit well, cut into his legs, and pained him. Furthermore, Freidel says the slope of the deck (FDR stood in front of the number one gun mount of the *USS Cummings*) made it difficult for him to stand. Adding to his difficulties, a wind ruffled the pages of his manuscript.

A far more serious problem was not revealed until long afterward. A young Navy heart specialist, Lt. Comdr. Howard G. Bruenn, says the President suffered a heart attack while speaking, the first and only angina attack in FDR's life.

"The excruciating pain in his chest extended up into both of his shoulders, and only slowly, after 15 minutes, subsided," Freidel has written. "Yet, he went on talking as though nothing was afflicting him. It was a spartan performance. He apparently told no one but his doctor what he had undergone while speaking. An

An enlargement of the photo of FDR on page 148 was taken while he may have been suffering his first heart attack.
(Photo courtesy Larry Jacobsen.)

hour later, Bruenn took an electrocardiogram and checked his white blood count. There were no abnormalities." Hypertensive heart disease was diagnosed. The President's personal physician, Adm. McIntire, was informed. But the President, who seemed to pay little interest in his health, apparently was not.

Because of unflattering photos taken of Roosevelt as he spoke at the Navy Yard, rumors circulated during the 1944 presidential campaign that he was in poor health. It is true that pictures made his face looked sharp and drawn. But that was because under doctor's orders he had already lost 15 pounds. Ironically, his effort to improve his health had caused him to look old, tired and ill.

The tides of war did indeed now favor the Allies. Campaigning as commander-in-chief of the armed forces, Roosevelt was re-elected in November for his fourth term, this time defeating Thomas E. Dewey. FDR never returned to Bremerton; after his re-election, he lived only five more months.

***Jim Taylor typifies what the
well-dressed student wore
during WWII.***
(Photo courtesy Audrey Thompson.)

- **Chapter 16**

(Headlines from Bremerton Sun in Winter of 1944)

**Cupid Should Do Better Than '43. . .
Ballet Thrills Audience at Civic Center. . .
Railroad To City Assured. . . Local Draft Quota Steep. . .
New Hospital Fully Opened. . .
US War Dead Totals 32,662. . .
Population Estimated at 71,000. . .
County's 3-year Population Gain 113%, US Figures. . .
New Working Hours in Navy Yard. . .
Jennifer Jones, Paul Lucas Receive Filmdom's Oscars. . .**

≈

God Loved Us All

The defining extra-curricular events at Bremerton High during the war were sports contests, formal dances, the Senior Sneak, class and student body elections, and the annual Vodvil. Superficially, that's not much different from peacetime. But from 1942 to 1945, the war colored everything.

"The war was there about us," remembers Patti Serry. "We bought savings stamps and saved tin foil and walked a lot." Eventually, the intensity of the war faded a little — but the barrage balloons, anti-aircraft units and smudge pots were still there, and so were the war-scarred ships and crews arriving from the Pacific.

The addresses given by graduating students at the 1944 commencement reflect how the war and its leaders dominated attention. Jewell Griffith spoke on Generalissimo Chiang Kai-shek and China; Bob Halverson on ex-president Eduard Benes and Czechoslovakia; David Soter on General Charles de Gaulle and the New France, the Third Republic; Patti Serry on Prime Minister Winston Churchill and the British Commonwealth; Bob Presser on Marshal Tito (Josip Broz) and Yugoslavia, and Esther Miller on Premier Josef Stalin and Russia.

Bremerton High's annual yearbook, the *Cat Log*, showcased teens' lives during this period. Youthful experiences were divided between serious, somber, and sometimes tragic events and the exuberant fun that kids manage, almost always, to embrace.

Although production of the 1942 *Cat Log* was under way before Pearl Harbor, editor Joan Gunnar made the pages reflect the war. Pete Burmaster, president of the student body, wrote in the yearbook of organizing Student Defense Committees for Air Raids and buying defense bonds with profits from athletic contests. It's particularly poignant to see Pete's photo and read his report. Forever young: As an infantry officer, he died in the assault on Okinawa in 1945, only a few months before the end of the war.

A full-page photo near the front of the 1942 yearbook shows Cal Christensen selling war stamps to Luann Travis. Opposite, another fullpage photo shows students standing with their faces to an inner classroom wall where they are less likely to be injured if a bomb hits outside; an unidentified boy grins at the camera from beneath a table. The yearbook message from the principal, H.D. Sorenson, said he felt certain that students would be willing to make "sacrifices great and small in order that our priceless democracy may survive to the end of time." His prose was usually more subdued.

Even more than in 1942, the 1943 *Cat Log* is steeped in the war. On the cover is a Navy ship and anchor. The editor, Lorraine Greenwalt, dedicated the yearbook to Larry Ramm and Art Broetje, teachers in the service. On the same page are listed other teachers already in the armed forces: Mark Freshman, Robert Flumerfelt, Paul Preus, Tom Sheldrake, Vernon Jackson, Patricia Skinner, Jean Strassman, Robert Anderson and Garnet Kaiyala. The inside cover shows a soldier, sailor and Marine marching shoulder to shoulder. On the opposite page are women in the military: an Army WAC, Navy WAVE, and a nurse. The message from the principal is somber. "The immediate future does not present a very pleasant prospect," Mr. Sorenson conceded. (Even 50 years later, respect compels me to precede the name of this kind and gentle man, always accommodating and sympathetic, with the honorific.) He noted that hundreds of BHS grads were already serving in the armed forces, and some already had been killed. "Practically every member of this class will in some measure contribute his services to the war effort either at or behind the war front," he said. Photos sprinkled through the yearbook show a variety of war-connected activities: a big pile of scrap metal, collected during a salvage drive; gifts for servicemen, mostly books; kids riding in a Jeep, a reward for purchasing war bonds. Xie Olanie said in his message as president of the student body that school activities had to be geared to war-time conditions in a war-time community. In his handwritten note to me over his picture he said, sardonically, "You lucky boy, you have another year of civilian life." Immediately after graduation, Xie joined the 10th Mountain Division and later fought as an infantryman in Italy. Frank Wright, president of the senior class, summed up his class's future: "Now comes graduation and we step forth into the welcoming arms of Uncle Sam." He was soon in a Navy training program.

The war affected the 1944 *Cat Log* too — but in a different way. This is acknowledged by Mr. Sorenson, who wrote of obstacles in producing the yearbook. He was referring to the shortage of manpower and materials faced by the editor, Alice Jane Levin, and her staff. Because of the shortages, quality of the yearbook suffered. Photo captions under some pictures are in typescript, in other places in regular type. Pasted-up headlines are crooked. These are production problems, not the responsibility of the high school staff. The inside cover focuses on the war — it shows ships, planes, tanks, a soldier with a bayonet — but the conflict seems somehow to be fading away. The informal photos do not focus on the war, as they had in the '42 and '43 editions. Instead, they show teen-agers frolicking — at dances, picnics, initiations, school plays. I cannot explain why but dress had become more formal; more boys are wearing ties and jackets in group photos, for instance.

Mr. Sorenson mentions something else that signals the start of an end of an era: "The class of 1944 is historical in that it is the last class to graduate in this building." He was not quite right. Construction delays meant only partial occupancy of a new high school in the spring of 1945, and full occupancy not until September of 1945. So to the class of '45 goes the distinction of being the last class to graduate at the old BHS building. Still, Mr. Sorenson probably was correct when he wrote that the class of 1944 has "been more subjected to the results of the war than any other class."

The *Cat Log* of 1945 is distinguished by its handsome, dignified cover that gives no hint there's a war on. The inside covers depict the once and future high schools: The old (1908) building jointly financed by the Charleston and Bremerton school districts before they combined; the BHS then in use, and the exterior of the new high school, soon to be occupied. On Page 2 is a full-page sketch and brief eulogy of President Roosevelt. The editor, the exuberant Georgie Eckroat, must have been hard-pressed to get that into the yearbook, because FDR died on April 12, 1945, surely near the annual's publishing deadline. Appropriately, the yearbook is dedicated to Mr. Sorenson, a fact that has no connection, I guarantee, with this modest man's statement that "This annual excels those preceding it." He must have liked this class, for he pointed out in his annual message that the Class of '45 was unique in attending split shifts for all four years of high school but still exemplified, "this year more than ever, the philosophy of the school: Education in democracy and democracy in education."

The lay-out of the '45 *Cat Log* is airy and eye-appealing but details presented in earlier annuals are lacking. There's no indication, for example, of how the football and basketball teams fared, and the war is scarcely mentioned. Although the war in Europe ended a month before the '45ers graduated and the conflict with Japan ended two months after their graduation, the draft continued and most of the boys soon went into the armed services.

Looking through the '45 annual, I am surprised at how few of the students I knew. That suggests a truism: Underclassmen pay close attention to the older classes, but very little to the younger students who follow.

One of the most popular high school activities during WWII was production of annual shows called Vodvils. (I don't know why it was spelled that way). They were produced by the high school Chamber of Commerce and were significant events, the brainchild of Larry Ramm, an energetic and progressive teacher of mathematics who also was second vice principal. He left soon after the war began to become a lieutenant in the Navy. The Vodvils were really a series of songs, dances, and skits loosely stitched together with a theme that was as adult as students could devise without forcing the administration to intercede.

The theme of the 1941 Vodvil was television. Wes Wager was the announcer for Station BHS. The overture was played by the orchestra from the *USS Maryland*. Bill Daulph was general manager and Betty McCaslin was business manager. The show included "Rhythm Varieties" a series of dance acts; "Radio City Music Hall," played by the high school band; "Spot Feature," including xylophone solos; "Pan American Fiesta," "Navy Life," "Hollywood Stars" and a finale of drum majorettes, acrobatics and a drum major. The show included everything that TV has produced over the past half-century since, only the Vodvil presentation was better.

In 1942, the theme was "Night Club." General manager was Luann Travis. Harry Fletcher was business manager. Big wheels made up the executive board: Cal Christensen, Bill Gates, Mary Jane Hudson, Lois Black, Helen Jertson, Dale Burkland. It probably was the most professional high school production I have ever seen, mostly because the music was provided by an outstanding Navy orchestra, said by the *Cat Log* to be from the *USS Saratoga*. I may have particularly liked this Vodvil because I was cast as a drunk and was thrown out of the night club. In getting the boot I made so much noise yelling and tripping down a flight of stairs that I was rewarded with thunderous applause. Of course, every act was rewarded with thunderous applause.

Cal Christensen told me a half-century after the fact that I may not have been the only student acting tipsy. As Cal recalls it, the bartenders were putting liquor in what were supposed to be soft drinks. "Larry Ramm thought he detected a tap dancer acting a little looped," Cal said, without explaining how anyone could tell when a tap dancer was looped. Larry Ramm telephoned Cal to ask with concern how they could prevent Mr. Sorenson from learning about it. Apparently the bartenders were warned, and service the second night was non-alcoholic. Cal says Denton De-Long confessed at a reunion many years later that he had spiked some drinks. That may or may not be true; I sat at the bar during part of both shows and I didn't see (or taste) any liquor. However, Duane Thompson reports that after a typhoon ravaged Okinawa in October of 1945, Denton, in the Seabees and "ever the promoter, salvaged a ship's bridge and converted it into a bar — alcohol/juices/ and a little five-card." We rest our case.

And here's another secret: Cal was told by Vodvil stage-hands of a peephole up in the rafters that overlooked the showers in the girls' gym. How it got there and who used it Cal does not know. Cal was told that few of the girls took showers after their physical education classes and that nothing much was revealed. But it's testimony that in high school the testesterone is flowing crazily and it's a wonder the boys survive. Or the girls, for that matter.

Next year, the synopsis in the program for Vodvil 1943 says the three scenes are set in the Gay '90s, Roaring '20s and Frivolous '40s. The '40s were anything but frivolous, but stereotyping a decade is a daunting task, particularly when you are in the middle of it. Here's how the *Sun* reviewed the show:

> "Vodvil of 1943" presented by the Bremerton High School Chamber of Commerce last night enjoyed a successful premier in the school auditorum and will be played for the last time tonight. Written, produced and directed by Patti Serry, it is a three-act hodge-podge packed with laughs. "Slips" of the performers are more than offset by the characterizations portrayed and costume effects furnishing the theme. The show opens with a beer garden

setting harking back to the gay '90s, complete with barber shop quartet, the villain, the heroine, a barmaid who sings "Tell Them That You Saw Me" and a bloomer chorus.

Bill Gates was supposed to be the narrator, but for reasons he couldn't recall 50 years later he resigned and his place was taken by Cathy Anderson. Instead, Bill acted as master of ceremonies. My recollection is that the original setting for the third act was not an ice-cream parlor but a beer garden and that Bill politely but firmly decried the school administration's intervention in forcing the change. Whether that was a factor in Bill's resignation I do not know.

Although this Vodvil didn't have a professional Navy band, the Swingsters were unusually talented for a high-school group — particularly Benny Carlson on saxophone and Stan Mathiason on trombone. (Stan was killed two years later, just before the end of the war, an 18-year-old Army infantryman in the Pacific.) Other standouts were Danny Wing, in a patter act; Phil Thornton, the hero of the second act; Jack Hayes, who played the stride piano; Juanita Gary, a talented singer and dancer, and David Soter, who later had a distinguished career as a first violinist with the Seattle Symphony.

The "slip" mentioned in the *Sun's* account may have referred to a duet sung by Jim Hermanson and me. Although the program says we sang "Five Foot Two," my memory says it was "Shortnin' Bread" — so it must have been "Five Foot Two." Whatever, we forgot the words and had to fake it for awhile. I was impressed by Jim's singing nevertheless; when he talked he stuttered, but he sang flawlessly. Jim, a friend since the seventh grade, chose to ignore my suggestion that thereafter he should sing his conversations.

Phil Thornton was general manager of the 1944 Vodvil and Lincoln Perry was business manager. Again, big wheels were on the executive committee: Marvin Cohen, Dolores Gutoski, Alice Jane Levin, George Meyer, Bob Halverson, Donna Rae Scott, Joyce Leyden, Pat Bryant. Both acts were set in a Washington, D.C., hotel, the first in the morning and the second in the evening. I didn't see this Vodvil; by then, I was in uniform so I can't report on its merits. Some of the stars from earlier shows performed again: Thornton, Dan Wing, Stan Mathiason, David Soter, the Music Maids (Mary Jane Hudson, Kay O'Neil and Shirley Eskridge) among them. The *Sun* said proceeds would go toward purchase of an organ for the auditorium of the new high school.

(The auditorium was never built because of war shortages of materials. I don't know where the money went.)

Only two weeks later, students staged a patriotic operetta, "Hat's Off." Sam Chollar and Kay O'Neill sang the leads. "Some 125 students will take part in the brilliant musical show, the first operetta by the high school in several years," said the *Sun*. "Its patriotic theme is laid in the Revolutionary days." A photo was displayed on the *Sun's* front page; it was unusual for school activities to win such prominent newspaper display.

Did participation in the Vodvils interfere with school work? In some cases, indeed it did. A letter to me from Joan Evanson reported that Lincoln Perry had been suspended from school for cutting classes to work on the 1944 Vodvil. He was reinstated four days later. Linc clearly took Vodvils seriously. He was gone the next year, a member of the Army Air Force. On April 27, 1945, he wrote in his diary, "Vodvil is tonite. Damnit. Wish I was there. Went to see Snow White and 7 Dwarfs to get my mind away from it." He apparently brought Grumpy back to the barracks with him.

For Dolores Gutoski, the Vodvil reminded her of most embarrassing moment. "I was asked by Patti Serry to be on the Chamber of Commerce, to work on the Vodvil," she wrote. "I knew that this group contained two suave, sophisticated upper classmen. I was truly petrified to attend my first meeting. I sat there awed as these two suave, sophisticated men tossed jokes back and forth. Then Patti said something about needing to know our homeroom numbers so she could contact us. I went blank. Of course, I knew *where* my homeroom was but there was no number on the door. Suddenly, it was my turn to speak . . . and I couldn't. All eyes were on me. Nothing would come. Now, when I pictured the room, there wasn't even a door. I quietly mumbled, 'I can't remember.' There was a second of silence...and then, the two suave, sophisticated upperclassmen roared with laughter. They almost fell out of their chairs. How could this little underclassmen not know her homeroom number? Oh, I could die . . . better yet, I wanted them to."

Later, I wrote Dolores to express my disappointment that she had not identified the two suave, sophisticated upperclassmen who had laughed at her so uproarously. She said of me, using the third person: "He didn't recognize himself . . . and Bill Gates. I can't believe that! Wow . . . just goes to show you how *his* memory is holding up."

Fifty years later, Dolores gets the last word.

Tucked away in Audrey Thompson's scrapbook is a tiny handbook produced by the Girls' Club for the throng of new students of

1943-1944. It gives the names of teachers and student body offi-
cers, lists clubs, activities, school songs, and even includes a map.
In the style of "don't put beans in your ears," it also lists Student
Council Offenses:

1. Do not run in the halls.
2. Do not skip assemblies.
3. Do not throw paper in the halls.
4. Habitual tardiness to classes.
5. Do not throw articles in study or throughout
   school building.
6. Do not wear street shoes on the gym floor.
7. Do not cause disturbance on the
   school campus.
8. Do not damage school property.
9. Do not leave lockers open.
10. Do not light matches in the school building.
11. Do not leave rubbish on campus.
12. Do not fail to serve a former council sentence.
13. Do not enter school building in the shift you
    are not attending class.

A half-century later, when school administrations are right-
fully concerned about handguns and drive-by shootings, the ad-
monitions seem almost quaint.

The handbook also reminds students, under the heading of
Clothes, that BHS isn't a movie colony or a public picnic grounds.
"It's the grin on your face that makes the shine on your shoes
sparkle.   Most high school students wear sweaters, skirts or
slacks or cords, and oxford or moccasins. Chic cotton dresses are
sensible in the early fall or spring, and for you boys, remember
that neckties are always a welcome sight."

The handbook also says, "Swearing is a sign of ignorance and
only crude, uncouth men would ever swear in the presence of a
lady. No girl should ever hesitate, when necessary, to put a boy
in his place."

Under the heading of *The Real Girl*, the handbook says,
"Every girl wants to be popular, and she can be, through self-per-
severance. She must have high standards of living and a spirit of
loyalty. Honesty to herself, her school and her friends, interest
and attentiveness in any of her activities, and a resentment of
pettiness, 'cattiness,' and self-assertion are a few important factors in gaining her goal."

The real boy, on the other hand, "is the boy who is congenial,
cheerful and courteous and a friend of all. In school he is conscientious and works with a purpose, yet not constantly pouring (sic)

over books. He participates in school activities. He gives his best to whatever he undertakes. He is considerate of his co-workers, thoughtful of his neighbors, and loyal to his friends. Behind his qualities is a strong character, built on a firm foundation of sound body and mind. He is the boy who hits the line hard, and doesn't shirk his task."

That could have come directly from the books about plucky Dink Stover.

The handbook's description of students' clothes was accurate but incomplete. Ed Bejeault wrote, "Most of the boys wore slacks and sweaters. Some wore shirts (white) and ties with slacks and sports coats. I don't think there was any specific dress code and my dress was far more casual. I usually wore a clean pair of cords and a bright-colored tee shirt with a long-sleeved shirt over it, but unbuttoned all the way to show off the tee shirt and I would leave the shirt tails hanging out...I was one of the uncouth ones. For shoes, I usually wore my high-topped Converse tennis shoes."

His recollection of wearing clean cords is not congruent with the memories of others. "Boys' cords were never washed," it was agreed by alums at a slumber party at Fort Worden in 1994. "Guys would gang up on anyone who wore clean cords, yanking them off and getting them muddy. Customarily they had writing all over them." Mine did, and, to my mother's horror, were often so dirty they could stand up unassisted. We wrote not only on our cords but on the cover of our notebooks, too; mine said, "Bored of Education." Patricia Henning's said, "Open All Night," "Hubba

When brother Barrett went off to the Army,
youngest brother Frank inherited his
wardrobe. Here the Wetzels gather in 1943: Frank,
Scott, Edith, Barrett.
(Frank Wetzel photo.)

~

Hubba Ding Ding, honey you got everything," and "Take me, I'm Yours, Sweet Thing." A busy notebook.

When my brother Barrett went into the Army, I inherited his wardrobe — not by bequest; it was confiscated, without his permission. As a result, I was a dapper dresser in high school, if I do say so myself. (This also helped me play out the conceit of my senior year, in which I decided to pretend I was visiting from college.) A letter from my mother after I entered the Army gives the dimension of a combined wardrobe: "Sent two suits, overcoat and about six pair of slacks to the cleaners to be cleaned and demothed and sealed in cedar bags. I also sent your yell sweater and the blue letterman's sweater. Then I washed eight other sweaters and sprayed them and packed them in your trunk." I remember everybody wore ski sweaters; the girls wore plaid skirts, white anklets, saddle shoes or wooden shoes. Often they also wore a single-strand neckless. A fad were slave bracelets, worn on the ankle. The wooden shoes, made in Portland, didn't require rationing stamps but were slippery on snow or ice. Stylish boys wore key chains that hooked to their belt and led to a pants pocket, the style probably borrowed from the zoot-suiters of Los Angeles.

Alice Jane Levin remembered that when Frank Sinatra was the rage, members of the Girls' Club decided every Friday would be bow-tie day. So the boys said that if the girls wore bow ties, they would wear their pajamas. "What an array of stripes and plaids and wild colors," she remarked.

Don Rolstad said he helped one fad in high school. A group of boys and girls bought hip-length green slickers, then decorated them with adhesive tape. Most prominent were diagonal stripes: One stripe if you were a wolf (someone who is unattached and on the prowl), two stripes if you were going steady, three stripes if you were engaged. "I do not remember anyone having three stripes," Rolstad said. The cognoscente put aluminum tax tokens on the ends of the jacket's drawstrings; Don Fry also remembered that the tax tokens, which had a hole in the center, were put on shoelaces so they made noise as kids walked. The jackets intrigued the columnist who wrote the column 'Round Towner in the *Sun*. With some hyperbole, he wrote:

> The significance of some of the tape markings on the jackets in this current teenage mania had us stumped. The kids also are using the markings on their cars, so fearful that some clandestine high school fraternity had sprung up, we investigated. Cornering a couple of prepsters, we learned as follows: One stripe indicates that the

boy or girl is, as we would phrase it, "available" for dating. But the HS young 'uns explain that one strip stands for AWOL:, meaning explicity "a wolf on the loose".... Two stripes means he or she is going steady and other admirers must keep their distance. Two and a half stripes, we learned, shows that your steady is out of town and that's got us puzzled. In the case of a girl, we don't know whether she is inviting new dates with no need for worry because her steady won't know about it, or is warning others to stay away because her boyfriend might come home and start a mess of trouble. Three stripes means you're engaged and three and a half gives the word that your betrothed is out of town. Four stripes shows you've taken the plunge into matrimony and then stars are added for each child. There actually are about 20 four-stripers in the HS, we are told. Ah, to be young again.

Patti Serry described students' apparel in letters to a cousin serving with the Army in France. "He said he read my letters out loud to his whole platoon and they remembered plaid skirts and sweaters and dates and Tangee lipstick and school and sunshine and it made them happy." Patti's letters could do that; after I entered the Army I received them regularly and they made me happy, too.

Patricia Henning "remembers becoming an expert at putting on leg makeup because we couldn't buy hosiery. I also drew a seamline on the backs of my legs. I remember some of the sailors we danced with would get mad because when we danced slow, close dances, we'd get leg makeup on their bell-bottoms." Some women painted the back seam with burned-out matches; I think women missed silk or nylon stockings as much as any rationed item. Patricia also said, "All high school girls went to Woolworths to buy Blue Waltz or Irresistible perfume. That was the only kind that kids could afford." But Patricia said clothes played a role in the dark side of high school life, too. "I was very unhappy at BHS," she wrote. "It was very

What students do best:
Hang out.
(Photo courtesy Audrey Thompson.)

clannish; there was a lot of snobbery and looking down at kids that didn't have the saddle shoes, clothes from Bremer's (the local department store), etc. There was a very clear separation between shipyard workers' kids and Navy kids."

Geraldine Petersen said, "Those colorful boys' striped socks that we used to wear were knockouts. There were no polyesters or Levis. We wore wool sweaters and pleated skirts. Remember the sailor knit caps that we embroidered with our names and the letters, BHS?"

After the war started, the government banned double-breasted suits and cuffs on pants; the elimination of the useless cuffs was such a good idea that few could understand why they reappeared after the war. Patch pockets were prohibited, too. The purpose was to conserve cloth.

A rite of spring was election of student body officers. Jim Braman remembers: "A group of friends talked me into running for student body office in the 1941 elections. Several of us formed a slate, with Warren Stone running for president, me standing for vice president, Lois Black for secretary, and Marjorie Kleisath for treasurer. Of course, slates didn't mean anything since votes were for individuals, but we urged everyone to 'Vote the SBBK Way!' It was a real campaign! We pulled a coup and signed up early for the school's display window. We built a model of a suspension bridge with the slogan, 'Bridge the gap between the double shifts with the SBBK ticket' or something similar. We had our pictures and other propaganda in this very visible display area. I talked my friends at the Bremerton Ice Creamery (I always did and still do like ice cream!) into creating a sundae called the SB-BK Special. It was black raspberry and darn good. We plastered the school with signs, including a huge 'Jim Braman V-P' all the way from one wing of the front of the balcony in the auditorium to the other. The dad of one fellow on our campaign ran the Bremerton Cruisers baseball ball-park concession and had hundreds of bags of peanuts in the shell left from the previous season. They were rather stale but we freshened them up a bit by storing them beside our furnace, and passed them out after school one day to pupils leaving the building, with the plea, 'Vote for Braman.' What we didn't anticipate was that some people would go back inside to eat the peanuts and got shells all over the hallway floors. Principal Sorenson called us in to clean up the mess . . . I really don't think my rival (and friend) Joe Steele was behind the mess although the thought crossed my mind!

"SBBK had 50 percent success: Marjorie and I were elected, but highly popular Eddie Burmaster was elected president and Joan Gunnar secretary. (We surmised that Lois Black didn't win because she was so popular with boys that no girl would vote for her!) The four officers got along very well in planning school activities and had a good year in spite of the double shift. Eddie conducted all school assemblies for one shift (morning, as I recall) and I did the honors for the other shift. Appearing before this large group of contemporaries was a good experience for me and helped in later life."

In the same election, Shirley Samson was named president of Girls' Club and Art McCarty was chosen president of Boys' Club.

The next year, two of the school's best and brightest ran against each other: Bill Gates and Xie Olanie. They were warm friends and remained so long after. I honestly cannot recall for whom I voted. Both were bright and energetic, and they demonstrated their capabilities by success in later life. My instant post-election analysis, 50 years later, is that Xie was elected because as a track star he won the athletes' votes; Bill was late developing physically and did not attain his full height (about 6-5) until after high school, so he didn't play basketball or turn out for other sports. But there was skulduggery, only now publicly revealed. Dave Poll says when he collected the votes in his classroom he switched the votes from Bill to Xie. The changes were not enough to change the result, Dave says, and he told both Bill and Xie a half-dozen or so years later, apparently when the three were sharing a house while attending the UW.

Elected with Xie, presumably without any vote-tampering, were Jack Bender, vice president; Mary Jane Hudson, secretary, and Margaret Shannon, treasurer. June Etten was president of Girls' Club and Walt Jack was president of Boys' Club.

I well remember the election for 1944, because I was a candidate. Let Don Rolstad give his version of the campaign first:

"One of the highlights in high school was being the campaign manager for Terry Crawford and his three co-candidates. The opposition had four gigantic colored portraits made and put them on display. We raised questions about them because of the expense. They said that they had them made for Mother's Day. We outfoxed them by placing a sheet with poems about each of our candidates on every desk in the school the morning of the election. Needless to say, we won.

"During the campaign we indulged in some very dangerous undertakings. We climbed up above the skylight in the auditorium and crawled out on the narrow wooden frames over the skylight glass to hang up banners for our candidates. We were lucky no one slipped onto the glass as we would have had a long fall to the auditorium seats."

I remembered nothing that Don described, so I wrote him: "I was taken aback to learn that Terry Crawford won election as student body president because 'poems about each of the candidates on his slate were placed on every desk in the school the morning of the election.' I had always supposed Terry won because the other two candidates, Lincoln Perry and I, drew from the same group of students and split the vote. (The loss was one of the best things that ever happened to me; I would have been a terrible president, and winning the election would have swollen an ego already the size of the *USS Saratoga.*")

Don wrote back: "In the 1943 student body elections we calculated that Linc would win hands down with you second and Terry running in third. Somehow we had to tap into both your potential votes to obtain enough votes to win. The distribution of the sheets on the day of the election is what put Terry and the others in office, so we believed."

Uh, well, how to put this politely? To assert Terry won because of poems left on students' desks is absurd. Terry split the vote and won because he was quiet and unassuming while Linc and I paraded around school like preening peacocks. Maybe Don was just being discreet in not pointing that out. Anyway, Terry was a good choice.

Running with me were John Gordon for vice president, Audrey Thompson for secretary, and Patti Serry for treasurer. A pamphlet we distributed in the halls listed our aims: "1. Furtherment of War Effort to the utmost. 2. Coordination of Shifts." Candidates gave memorized speeches at morning and afternoon assemblies. Audrey Thompson has a copy of hers. She said in part: "In all sincerity and genuine truthfulness, I promise that I shall do all within my power to achieve perfection in my duties." Perfection! There's a campaign promise to be taken seriously.

Audrey's nomination speech was given by Esther Miller, whose droll humor still shines through in her remarks in Audrey's behalf. Esther noted matter-of-factly that Audrey had been born, which did not seem to startle the audience, and added the clincher: "Equally important is the fact that Audrey is human, which adds much to any candidate's character." Given those attributes, it's hard to see how she lost.

But students elected Terry's straight ticket: Robert Presser, vice president; Katie Stingl, secretary, and Shirley Eskridge, treasurer. Esther Miller was elected president of Girls' Club and Jorgen Nelson was named president of Boys' Club. Running on Lincoln's ticket were Norman Stone, vice president; Jackie Driscoll, secretary, and Alice Jane Levin, treasurer.

(Clockwise from upper left):
Patti Serry, Easter 1944
(Photo, Patti Serry).
**Mary Lou Flieder, Shirley
Sinclair, Susan Swanson,
Pat Bryant** *(Photo Shirley
Sinclair.)*
 Audrey Thompson *(Audrey
Thompson.)*
Rainbow Choir:
*(Back)***Shirley Brandelein,
Doris Saunders, Esther
Miller, Helen Hackleman,
Audrey Thompson.** *(Front)*
**Katie Stingl, Shirley Pellenz,
Alice Jane Levin.** *(Audrey
Thompson)*
**Don Haskell, Olympic
Mountains** *(Shirley Sinclair.)*

Later, Linc was elected president of the senior class, so he retained his position as Big Man on Campus. He has officiated at so many class reunions since that we enjoy kidding him about being elected not class president but Pope.

The following year, George Meyer defeated Marv Cohen for student body president. Pierce Parker was elected vice president; Joan Evanson, secretary; and Janet DuPuis, treasurer. President of Girls' Club was Dorothy Goulding and president of Boys' Club was Jack Dunn. No doubt that election was fraught with heart-stopping drama, too. If so, I don't know about it because I wasn't around, and none of the contributors to this book thought to mention it.

Another rite of spring at BHS was the Senior Sneak, when graduating students cut classes for a day to have a picnic at a park or resort, sometimes but not always with the approval of the administration. Jim Braman was chairman of the sneak in 1942. He remembers: "I was chairman of a committee to plan the Senior Sneak, a great tradition at the time. On this day, the entire senior class just didn't show up at class and instead had a big party somewhere.

"We did this thing in 1942 at the North Kitsap park at Lofall (now a state park). One big issue was what we should have to eat. 'There's a war on, you know' feeling was very strong and faculty advisers felt we shouldn't have the barbecued chickens we had planned on. However, the chickens were available, not rationed, and we went ahead anyway. Basically, all I remember about the day was a lot of food, a lot of games, a lot of horsing around. I don't remember serious drinking but I didn't drink anyway and may have been naive. However, the event was deemed a success and as chairman I got thanked by being hauled down to the shore of Hood Canal and tossed out into the cold water. What the heck, it was a great day."

Jim wasn't the only one thrown into Hood Canal that day. Myron Richards says, "We threw vice principal George Martin into the water, and I always felt sorry about that."

A nice thing about the sneaks is that they were less threatening socially than dances or movie dates. Harold Engebretson describes himself in high school as "very shy and scared to death of girls...As testimony to how shy I was, I offer the following: At our 50th reunion, I met Mary Jane Hudson, now Glaser, for the first time since 1943. The first thing she said was, 'Are you still as shy and nice as you were?' All I could say was "no". (I wrote Harold that a better and more accurate answer would have been, "Not as shy, perhaps, but certainly as nice.") Anyway, Harold took the popular Pat Remmen to the sneak at Lake Wilderness near Seattle in 1943 — pretty daring for a shy boy.

Naughty Robin Perrigo went to Lake Wilderness in 1943, too — and she was only a junior. "I'm not sure what the consequences would be today but I was expelled from school for two weeks and had to have my Dad come to the school for a conference — then I could return to class. I wonder how a student would be disciplined today." Certainly not by being kicked out of school for two weeks; that would be reserved for burning down the building.

It's not clear, even 50 years later, why Robin was disciplined so severely. Duane Thompson said he went to an earlier Senior Sneak as a junior, with Ray Lombard, Lowell Wiley and others. His penalty was to work as a janitor for George Martin, the vice principal.

Under the headline "Boy — Did We Snuck!" an item in the school paper, *The Lair,* gives an idea of what happened at the sneaks:

> Reaching Lake Wilderness, our class teachers (and the uninvited juniors) split up, some going for horseback riding, others headed for the motor, row, bicycle and paddle boats, while still others looked over the grounds, or went swimming. Ah, yes, swimming — you might ask Edward McCrea how the water was; he went in a little unexpectedly — so did the canoe cushion (but it floated!)
>
> While the percentage of us were blistering our noses, or bringing out the freckles, Mr. Martin, June Etten, Lorraine Greenwalt, Dolores Fatland, Wally Thoemke, Barbara Eskridge, Floreine Laes and Dorothy Olsen were sweating away at tennis.
>
> Even Marilyne White did a pretty good job of "laying herself out." Aleen Mynheir had a blister on her heel, Johnny Lindberg sprained his arm, and if Denny Force, Grant Fry, Jack Keck, Buddy Greenwood, Harry Harkness and a few more sliding to every stop on their better parts weren't black and blue the next day, they must have been too tired to know the difference.
>
> After the skate everyone was so tired and hungry they made for the nearest bread baskets. In fact, we saw Harold Crosswaite and Miss Dunlap heading on a dead run for Miss Hoffman's and Mrs. Derick's spread of food. Miss Dunlap was far in the lead, however.

Information about the sneak in 1944 came from girls still in school who wrote me at the University of Idaho. Maxine Forrest, who on May 23 of that year wrote from her Comp class immediately after taking a 100-word spelling test and getting all the words correct (we give you all the news), noted that the Senior Sneak would be that week.

"I think most of the school is going," she wrote. "The school isn't giving one this year. The kids are going to skip and go." On June 19, Audrey Thompson elaborated. She said the class had indeed planned to go on an unauthorized sneak but found that members of the Lettermen's Club (boys who had played on the high school's varsity teams) were taking cases of beer and many students decided not to go.

"We were rather disgusted because we felt that if they hadn't planned it for just a drunken brawl, then everyone could have gone and had a really swell time."

One who did go was Patti Serry, and for doing so she was hauled before principal Harry Sorenson and vice principal George Martin.   They told her she had been indiscreet to attend. "Imagine I was," acknowledge Patti in her letter, "for everyone was drunk, male and female alike, but Mitzi, and Joyce, and me." The administrators said attendance by a school leader was inappropriate. "I said, quote, 'I had never thought of myself as a student leader, and I will lead my own life'," which prompted angry expostulations from them.

The overriding fear of the school administration was that the kids would drink beer at the sneaks, smash up their cars — and themselves. As was demonstrated in 1944, they had justification for their fears. Harry Harkness, a true bon vivant, wrote about beer-drinking: "Sure, we did a little on the Senior Sneak and after the commencement ceremony. Raced, in my brother Dave's convertible, with Al Kean. Almost got in an accident that graduation night. We both had a car full and had had a beer or two."

As further evidence their fears were well founded, comes now Harry McIntyre, telling about some of the cars he owned in high school. He says he paid $550 for a 1937 Plymouth convertible, "which six weeks later I wrecked on the way to the lettermen's picnic at Lake Wilderness. Ron Jones didn't want to be passed so he swerved into me as I tried to go around him. I hit a telephone pole and flew off a 15-foot bank onto railroad tracks. My friend Clyde Wilson stuck his face through the windshield and I bent my steering wheel flat with the side of my head. We went on to the picnic after a trip to an infirmary in Renton. Clyde looked like a mummy from his neck up and I looked normal unless you ran your hand over my head and noticed one side was swollen — sort of squared-off."

Harry says it for us all: "God surely must have loved me because I didn't kill myself or anyone with those cars."

- Chapter 17

(From the Bremerton Sun of 1943)

**Boys Must Register for Draft on 18th Birthday . . .
Bond Sales Top Quota by $300,000 . . .
County's Dimout Restrictions Eased . . .
Gas Coupon Value Reduced to 3 Gallons . . .
Polio Claims Life of Child . . .
Jap Sub Packs Reported Off Coast . . .
8,000 More Workers Still Needed Here**

Yes, We Have No Bananas or Much of Anything Else

By the end of 1943, the United States had overtaken Japan's advantage in naval power. Four U.S. carriers — the *Lexington, Yorktown, Wasp* and *Hornet* — had been sunk, but shipyards on the East Coast were rapidly launching replacements. The ships were the magnificent, 27,000-ton *Essex*-class carriers, capable of speeds of 30 knots or faster. They carried 90 Hellcats, a new plane designed specifically to destroy the Zeros, the best Japanese fighter. In quick succession during 1943 came the *Essex*, the new *Lexington*, the new *Yorktown*, *Bunker Hill, Intrepid*, the new *Wasp* and the new *Hornet*. By then, notes Professor Bridgman, we had eight large carriers plus nine smaller carriers of the *Independence* class, plus the surviving *Enterprise* and *Saratoga*, for a total of 19 large carriers. The Japanese had seven, of which only two were really effective ships. Furthermore, Navy aviators were now equipped with first-rate planes. The famous Corsair, called "Whistling Death" by the Japanese, had structural problems that made it difficult to land on carriers, but that was corrected and in 1944 it became a carrier-based plane. Also came the Helldiver, a dive bomber, and, at last, an effective torpedo plane, the Avenger. Of earlier models

Professor Bridgman joked, "We had very poor torpedo planes. It made very little difference; we had very poor torpedoes."

Other vital military equipment was being introduced, too, including improved radar that permitted carriers to track planes out 50 or 60 miles and vector them into incoming hostile planes. Also introduced in 1943 was the VT shell that detonated within a designated number of yards of enemy planes. It was 10 or 15 times more effective than conventional anti-aircraft shells.

In 1942 the Navy broke the Japanese naval code, JN25, and the battle of Midway was largely determined by the Navy's ability to read a percentage of the Japanese messages. The Japanese changed the code but briefly continued using the old one. The overlap permitted Navy intelligence to cross-reference the two and eventually decipher the new code. Then came an interesting message: Admiral Yamamoto, the commander-in-chief of the Japanese Navy, was on a tour of inspection. His precise itinerary was transmitted. A large number of American planes was sent to ambush Yamamoto's plane. One of the fighters was flown by Ray Hall, the former Bremerton High basketball player. Yamamoto's plane was shot down and he was killed. Professor Bridgman said it wasn't revealed until well after the war how the American planes happened to be in precisely the right place. That the Japanese naval code had been cracked was a carefully guarded secret, of course.

If the planes that shot down Yamamoto were in the right place, in August of 1943 an American PT boat was in the wrong place and got sliced in two by a Japanese ship. The skipper was John F. Kennedy, who exhorted his crew to swim four hours to a nearby island, where they were picked up a few days later.

It wasn't as dramatic at home, but the entire nation was mobilizing as seldom before in support of the war. Professor Bridgman noted that American productivity was awesome. He quoted the *New York Times*:

> A mighty revolution (is) in progress. American industry is beating the plowshares of peacetime — the autos, the electric refrigerators, the toasters and washing machines — into the swords of total war, planes, tanks and high-explosive bombs. It's a revolution that can have but one end: The doom of Nazidom. American industry did not ask for this job of total conversion to production of the tools of war; it did not want it any more than America wanted the war, any more than Americans wanted to change their cars for tanks. In many instances it was even slow to take up the task. But now the colossus is at

work and the results of this gigantic effort are discernible in every manufacturing city in the land. You can see the planes and tanks and deadly bombs and you can grasp the inexorable promise of hundreds upon hundreds of thousands more ready to pour from the production lines. The Nazi propagandists may laugh and cheer and whistle in the wind, snorting fantastic lies just as long as it suits them to do but the wave of American industrial might built by the great free effort of a free and angry people is going to mount a terrible deluge that will pour forth and flood the anguished scenes of brutality and oppression that are now upon the earth.

Such overcharged rhetoric was common during the war, even in the usually staid *New York Times*. It's also worth noting that the identified enemy is the Nazis, not the Japanese. On the East Coast, Germany was the identified foe. On the West Coast, particularly in the early days of the war when attack seemed imminent, the war with Germany seemed more distant. National market research in 1943 showed, moreover, that Japan was a stronger emotional symbol than Germany. The American public thought Japanese were "ungodly, subhuman, beastly, sneaky, and treacherous," wrote William M. Tuttle Jr.[1].

As the nation mobilized, shortages appeared. The first item in short supply was silk, which became scarce when the government imposed an embargo on the Japanese product. Nylon started to take its place, but then was diverted to parachutes (each parachute took 36 pair of nylon stockings.) The first table item to become scarce was sugar and in May of 1942 it was rationed. Wrote Walter Winchell, the columnist: "Roses are red, Violets are blue. Sugar is sweet. Remember?"

Housewives were issued ration books that contained coupons for a 52-week supply. Ronald H. Bailey[2] wrote: "Soon the housewife's proverbially cluttered handbag was stuffed with books of ration stamps — red for meat, butter and fats, blue for canned foods such as peas or beans. To prevent hoarding, the stamps were coded so that they would be redeemable only for a specified period, usually a month. Meat rationing was further complicated by the fact that each cut required a different number of red stamps." To make it even more complicated, the value of the stamps varied; a pound of lamb chops might be worth one stamp one week and three stamps the next. "On average, how-

---

[1] Tuttle. Ibid.
[2] Bailey. Ibid.

ever," wrote Bailey, "each person was allowed two pounds of meat a week."

Not only did housewives have to juggle ration cards and points, they had to change menus to take into account shortages of meat, sugar, vegetables and other staples. They also had to adjust shopping schedules to get scarce items whenever they appeared — and this often meant standing in lines. Many planted Victory Gardens, canned the produce from the gardens, and segregated and saved tin cans and other products for the various salvage drives.

Gasoline rationing was complicated. A motorist who drove only for pleasure received an A sticker for his car, good for one stamp that was worth three to five gallons per week. Commuters received a B sticker worth varying number of stamps, depending on how far they drove to work. C stickers were for unlimited amounts, but the paperwork in getting and keeping a C sticker was substantial. The rationing process was cumbersome; each month, three billion postage-sized stamps changed hands. It was administered by the Office of Price Administration, comprised of local volunteers and 60,000 fulltime employees.

Richard Lingeman[3] said: "As the war drew on, nearly every item Americans ate, wore, used or lived in was rationed or otherwise regulated." There was even a shortage of alarm clocks; Lingeman wrote that the theft of clocks became such a problem in rooming houses that many workers took theirs to work. In connection with the shortages, Florence Fraser remembers, "Oh, yes, the lines to get into anything. If you saw a line, you asked what was selling and if it was something you wanted or needed you got in line, mainly if it was stockings. Never had enough of them as they did get runs in them."

Sometimes bosses sent their secretaries to stand in lines for scarce items. After completing high school, Adrienne Johnson took a job as secretary to Alex Ottevaere, then business manager of the *Sun*. "One afternoon, Mr. Ottevaere came rushing up to my desk, shoved some money at me and said to get to Bremers as fast as I could. His wife had just phoned to say the store had a shipment of stockings. When I got there the line was already half-way around the block and they ran out of merchandise before I got near the place. Most of us gave up trying and just painted our legs stocking color. Sisters and others sometimes tried to help by drawing seams down the back — very time consuming and a real mess."

---

[3] Lingeman. Ibid.

An item in the *Sun* in March of 1945 tells how quickly lines could form:

> A line of happy shoppers with beaming faces stretched half a block along Pacific Avenue this morning from the Navy Yard Produce Market to the National Bank of Commerce. "They've got bananas!" was the answer to curious questioners. Up front, two fast salesmen were ripping open crates and cutting bunches from stems, weighing and sacking the greenish yellow tropical tubes, faster than this can be read. But the line didn't seem to get any shorter, for as fast as one satisfied customer departed, two more scurried into the banana line up at the Fourth Street corner.

It was a time more of shortages than sacrifices —and rationing had an underlying egalitarian thrust. The rich and poor shared alike; money no longer was the sole criterion in acquisition of food and other goods. Yes, there was a black market, but author Lingeman thought the term "black market" was rather romantic. "Actually, the black market was not a clandestine place like a speakeasy or brothel, through whose doors slunk furtive citizens . . . A good deal of the black marketeers were, in fact, 'legitimate' businessmen who connived in numerous ways to evade price and rationing regulations."

The shortages sometimes caused unanticipated problems. In February of 1942, the *Sun* said rubber would no longer be used in girdles, garters or other apparel that normally used elastic, such as suspenders, garters, and underclothing. "Of course, as a male you wouldn't know this," wrote Florence Fraser, "but the women's underpants didn't have elastic in them, either a button (which always came off) or they tied. Oh, what fun." One of the innumerable salvage drives was for anything made of rubber. Ed Bejeault was so caught up in the drive that he swiped the rubber mat from his mother's bath scales to throw in the collection at the corner gas station. Later, he wrote, he took "any table-sized radio I could find or pick up to give to the war-effort, because there were 10 or 12 pounds of aluminum in them. Later, I wised up and sold them as scrap for about 10 cents a pound."

In May of 1942, some 60,000 Kitsap County residents registered at schools for War Ration Book No. 1. The book contained 28 numbered stamps used first for sugar rationing and later for other commodities that were rationed as shortages developed.

Page 1

Consumer Instruction Sheet

WHY CANNED FRUITS, VEGETABLES, AND SOUPS ARE RATIONED

Every week we are sending shiploads of canned goods to feed our fighting men and our fighting allies in Africa, Britain, and the Pacific islands. We must see that they get all the food they need.

We at home will share all that is left. Point Rationing will be used to guarantee you and everyone a fair share of America's supply of canned and processed fruits and vegetables, soups and juices.

─── HOW they are rationed ───

1. Every eligible man, woman, child, and baby in the United States is being given War Ration Book Two. (This book will not be used for sugar or coffee.)

RATION BOOKS FOR ALL

2. The BLUE stamps are for any kind of
   Canned or Bottled Fruits and Vegetables
   Canned or Bottled Juices and Soups
   Frozen Fruits and Vegetables
   Dried Fruits

   (The red stamps will be used later for meat.)

3. The stamps in this book are POINT stamps. The NUMBER on each stamp shows you how many POINTS that stamp is worth.

A 5

NUMBER SHOWS POINTS

4. The LETTERS show you WHEN to use the stamps. The year will be divided into rationing periods. You can use all BLUE stamps marked A, B, and C in the *first* rationing period. A, B, and C stamps cannot be used after the first rationing period ends.

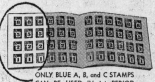

ONLY BLUE A, B, and C STAMPS CAN BE USED IN 1st PERIOD

5. You must use the BLUE stamps when you buy ANY KIND of the rationed processed foods. See the official list, showing every kind of rationed processed food, at your grocers. Different kinds of these foods will take different numbers of points. For example, a can of beans may take a different number of points from a can of peas.

RATIONED FOODS

JARS	DRIED	FROZEN	BOTTLED	CANNED
Fruits Vegetables Soups Juices	Fruits	Fruits Vegetables	Juices Soups Catsup Chili Sauce	Fruits Vegetables Soups Juices Baby Foods

(See Complete Official List at Your Grocers)

6. Of course, the more of anything you buy the more points it will take. For example, a large can of peas takes more points than a small can.

7. The Government will set the points for each kind and size and send out an Official Table of Point Values which your grocer must put up where you can see it. The Government will keep careful watch of the supply of these processed foods and make changes in point values from time to time, probably not oftener than once a month. The Government will announce these changes when it makes them and they will be put up in the stores.

OFFICIAL POINT LIST

8. The number of points for each kind of processed food will be THE SAME in ALL STORES and in all parts of the country.

WATCH THE OFFICIAL TABLE OF POINT VALUES

Turn this sheet over and see how to use your Book.

The county's entire quota for new tires that month was only 24. Students in the mathematics and commercial classes in county high schools were involved later in helping residents complete their complicated applications for their fuel oil supplies.

By 1943, rationing was well established. On February 8 of that year, the *Sun* told of the rationing of shoes; only three pair per year could be purchased, and their colors were limited. With the exception of heavy-duty rubber footgear, shoes were the first item of apparel to be rationed, but the nineteenth overall. Other rationed goods included sugar, coffee, gasoline, autos, tires and tubes, typewriters, fuel oil, and bicycles. All canned goods were added in March of 1943 and meat, butter, and cheese the month after. In Oregon and Washington, motorists were limited to four gallons of gasoline per week, effective in June; gasoline had been rationed earlier on the East Coast at only two gallons per week, and pleasure driving was banned there entirely. Bremerton schools forbade use of buses for athletic trips and the federal government imposed a highway speed limit of 35 miles per hour. The state rationed hard liquor: One quart per week, to be purchased every two weeks.

Adrienne Johnson tells a story about liquor that affirms the image of newspaper reporters as hard-drinking reprobates. "Alcohol was in short supply to civilians, and in great demand. Rumor had it that the black market was doing a thriving business but I haven't the slightest idea where the reporter had gotten his that day. He came in with a brown paper bag tucked lovingly under his arm, set the package on the desk, looking smug. Other reporters cast knowing glances at him. Then with a grand gesture he removed his raincoat and accidently knocked the package to the floor where the bottle inside shattered. You can imagine the scene, some of the reporters even pretending to get down on all fours and lick it up off the floor. We were all treated to the pungent odor of alcohol for a long time that day."

Unlike the mandatory rationing, Victory Gardens were strictly voluntary. Based on their experience during World War I, people assumed there would be a shortage of vegetables. So, with little encouragement from the Department of Agriculture, by April of 1942 at least 6 million gardens were being cultivated. In 1943, more than 8 million tons of produce were grown on 20 million individual plots. They appeared everywhere — on parking strips, empty lots, parks and playing fields. Collectively, they amounted to 7 million acres. It was estimated that Victory Gardens provided 30 percent to 40 percent of the nation's vegetables. So bountiful were the crops that sometimes they created shortages; the *Sun* said in 1942 that gunny sacks and cloth bags were

Page 2

Use Your OLD Ration Book for SUGAR and COFFEE

HOW TO USE YOUR NEW RATION BOOK
TO BUY CANNED OR BOTTLED FRUITS, VEGETABLES, SOUPS, AND JUICES;
FROZEN FRUITS AND VEGETABLES; DRIED FRUITS

1. The Government has set the day when this rationing will start. On or after that day, take your War Ration Book Two with you when you go to buy any kind of these processed foods.

14 POINTS

YOU GIVE MANY POINTS FOR SCARCE FOODS

8 POINTS

YOU GIVE LESS POINTS FOR FOODS THAT ARE NOT SO SCARCE

2. Before you buy, find out how many points to give for the kind of processed foods you want. *Prices do not set the points.* The Government will set different points for each kind and size no matter what the price. Your grocer will put up the official list of points where you can see it. It will also be in the newspapers. *The points will not change just because the prices do.*

3. When you buy, take the right amount of blue stamps out of the book. Do this in front of your grocer or delivery man and hand them to him. The grocer *must* collect a ration stamp, or stamps, for all the rationed processed foods he sells. Every rationed processed food will take points as well as money.

SHOW YOUR BOOK PLEASE

4. Do not use more stamps than you need to make up the right amount. For example, if the food you buy calls for 13 points it is better to tear out an 8-point and a 5-point stamp than two 5-point stamps and a 2- and a 1-point stamp. Save your smaller point stamps for low-point foods. You can take the stamps from *more than one book* belonging to your household if you need to.

8 → 8
5 → 5
13 Points

5. Every person in your household, including children of any age, has a total of 48 points to use for all these processed foods for one ration period. This means that you may use ALL the blue stamps marked A, B, and C from all the books during the first period. You may use as many of the blue A, B, and C stamps as you wish at one time. When they are used up you will not be able to buy any more of these processed foods till the next stamps are good. The Government will announce the date when the next stamps are good.

USE THE BLUE STAMPS WITH A-B-C ON THEM

6. Use your household's points carefully so that you will not run out of stamps. And buy with care to make your points come out even, because the grocer will not be able to give you change in stamps. Use high-point stamps first, if you can.

IMPORTANT

You may use ALL the books of the household to buy processed foods for the household. Anyone who can take the ration books to the store to do the buying for you or your household.

A FAIR SHARE FOR ALL

We cannot afford to waste food or give some people more than their fair share. . . . That is why canned fruits and vegetables are rationed and that is why meat is going to be rationed. Rationing of some foods is the best and fairest way to be sure that every American gets enough to eat.

BE SURE TO READ OTHER SIDE

☆ U. S. GOVERNMENT PRINTING OFFICE : 1943 16—33240-1

U. S. Office of Price Administration Washington, D. C.   January 1943 sorely needed to avert serious loss of Washington state's "food for victory" crops.

Many Kitsap County residents had gardens long before the war, and no doubt were pleased when they became a symbol of patriotism. Wrote Aileen Bellinger, "My dad always had a garden, even in the hard-pan of Navy Yard City and later they were called Victory Gardens and we had some really good carrots and corn. He worked many years, always on swing shift, and liked being able to work on his garden during the day."

So expansive were some local gardeners that they created territorial problems. Said the *Sun* in 1945, "Since the advent of Victory Gardens, city commissioners have looked the other way, as it were, when folks put out their tomato plants and onions in their parking strips. Strictly speaking, the strips are city property, but no objection has been raised so long as fences were small, inoffensive affairs of temporary nature designed chiefly to keep the neighborhood dogs away from the spinach. But now come several East Side residents who have built permanent fences right out into unimproved streets as far as 20 feet beyond their property lines. The city fears that the practice may be spreading and it must stop. Polite but firm letters from the city attorney's office will be received by offending gardeners. After that, if cooperation is not forthcoming, well, it takes a mighty heavy fence post to stand up against a bulldozer."

The rationing system fluctuated as goods became scarce or plentiful. A story in the *Sun* in December of 1944 illustrates the shifting needs, and the steps taken by the Office of Price Administration:

> Blue points again are needed for most canned vegetables, and red points for meat that has been point-free for many months. Would-be hoarders were caught unawares by the suddenness of the OPA's move, which was advanced at least 24 hours due to premature circulation of reports that OPA was going to broaden the food rationing program. All ration-free vegetables are now back on the list. Beginning Sunday, 85 percent of all now-rationed free meats will go back on the ration list. All red and blue ration stamps validated before Dec. 1 are no longer valid. All sugar stamps except No. 34 are no longer valid. A new sugar stamp will be issued Feb. 1 but will be good for five pounds over a three-month period instead of the present two and a half months. Butter is up from 20 to 24 points.

POINT BUDGET GUIDE

USE BLUE TICKETS ONLY—A, B, C, NUMBERS 1-2-5-8 for MARCH

An added Exclusive Service from your LOCAL INDEPENDENT GROCER
Showing you how to get the utmost in value from your points.

POINT VALUES OF THE SIZES YOU BUY MOST FREQUENTLY

ITEM	No. of Container	Wt.	Point Value	ITEM	No. of Container	Wt.	Point Value
BABY FOODS	—	4½-oz.	1	BEANS Green & Wax	No.2	1-lb. 3-oz.	14
SOUPS Dried and Dehydrated		4-oz.	4	CARROTS	No.2	1-lb. 4-oz.	14
SOUPS	No. 1	10½-oz.	6	CORN	No.2	1-lb. 4-oz.	14
CATSUP & CHILI SAUCE ½ Pt.		8-oz.	6	GRAPE JUICE Qt. equals 2 lbs.	—	Qts.	15
CATSUP & CHILI SAUCE	—	14-oz.	8	LIMA BEANS	No.2	1-lb. 4-oz.	16
GRAPE JUICE	—	16-oz.	8	PEAS	No.2	1-lb. 4-oz.	16
GRAPEFRUIT JUICE	No.2	1-lb.-2-oz.	8	TOMATOES	No.2	1-lb. 3-oz.	16
DRY BEANS Dried and Dehydrated		1-lb.	8	PINEAPPLE	No.2	1-lb. 4-oz.	16
PEAS and LENTILS DRIED		1-lb.	8	RAISINS & PRUNES DRIED		15-16-oz.	20
TOMATO JUICE	No.300	13½-oz.	8	SPINACH	No.2½	1-lb. 14-oz.	21
APPLESAUCE	No.2	1-lb. 4-oz.	10	PEACHES	No.2½	1-lb. 13-oz.	21
BEETS	No.2	1-lb. 4-oz.	10	PEARS	No.2½	1-lb. 13-oz.	21
PINEAPPLE JUICE	No.2	1-lb. 2-oz.	11	GRAPEFRUIT JUICE	46-oz.	2-lb. 14-oz.	23
SPINACH	No.1 tall	1-lb.	11	TOMATOES	No.2½	1-lb. 13-oz.	24
TOMATO JUICE	No.2	1-lb. 2-oz.	11	APRICOTS	No.2½	1-lb. 14-oz.	24
PEAS	No.303	1-lb.	13	PINEAPPLE	No.2½	1-lb. 14-oz.	24
BERRIES	No.2	1-lb. 4-oz.	14	PINEAPPLE JUICE	46-oz.	2-lbs. 14-oz.	32
CHERRIES	No.2	1-lb. 3-oz.	14	TOMATO JUICE	46-oz.	2-lbs. 14-oz.	32
ASPARAGUS	No.2	1-lb. 4-oz.	14	DRIED PRUNES	—	2 lbs.	38

R & H Super Market

BREMERTON   PHONE 2868

James R. Warren[4] reported that even with rationing sudden shortages appeared, then vanished, without warning. Sliced bread was banned for the duration. "For several months in 1942 and 1943, butcher shops in many cities were without meat . . . Furthermore, members of the armed services on leave in Seattle consumed from 35 to 40 percent of all restaurant output." Sometimes precious items became plentiful again; the rationing of coffee ended in July of 1943, for example.

Salvage drives were mounted in efforts to ameliorate shortages. The *Sun* reported in December of 1943 that local housewives had salvaged 18 tons of tin cans in a month. "Salvage of tin cans are still essential to the war effort," said the *Sun*. "Housewives should take their cans to their nearest grocery store from which they are picked up and taken to salvage." Even beer caps were saved; Seattle brewers directed their truck drivers to collect the caps for shipment to manufacturers, where they were processed and used again. Students joined the salvage drives with a vengeance. Even wire coat hangers were recycled.

Women were delegated a disproportionate share of the burden of coping with rationing and salvaging. For the 26 percent of American women who were holding jobs, the burden was heavy indeed.

Teen-agers were probably more affected by gasoline rationing than other restricted items. Stealing gasoline by siphoning was so prevalent that Alice Jane Levin complained that her dates always tasted like gasoline. And, as noted earlier, three of five Westpark girls at a slumber party in 1994 admitted they had siphoned gasoline from cars not their own.

Dorothy Fick said, "Rationing brings to my mind my chore of adding the little yellow coloring pellet to the margarine. One had to break it, then stir and mix, and stir and mix. It was quite a job to get it all blended in." She mentioned the various stamps needed for shoes and gas and meat and added: "Somehow it seems when we needed extra tickets they would occasionally turn up."

LaVerne Jacobson remembers "the ration stamp books we fussed over for food, gasoline, even shoes. I recall having to give up my shoe coupons to my sisters because they always needed them more than I did (at least this was the general consensus)." That somehow reminds me of Cinderella and her selfish sisters, but LaVerne insists she didn't resent giving up her shoe stamps. Alice Jane Levin wrote, "I remember the rationing, of course, saving fats and tin cans and waiting for hours for sugar stamps

---

4 Warren. Ibid.

because Mom made so much jam and canned so much fruit. My Dad had always kept meticulous records of this and we had no trouble getting the sugar, but I did use all of my shoe stamps for school shoes and had to buy unrationed shoes for graduation. The heel fell off of one just as I stepped up to accept my diploma."

Robin Perrigo, who loved athletics, told of using an entire year's shoe ration — for a pair of bowling shoes.

Aileen Bellinger said, "My grandmother was a depression survivor who taught me to save a dime a week. Our family shook our heads at her because she had a basement pantry and she had up to four each (Aileen didn't specify in what quantity) of coffee, sugar, shortening, and I forget other things, and — she really believed this — she said she wanted to get a little ahead before the hoarders started. I didn't drink coffee but when I was 17 and it was a rationed item I started liking coffee. My mother and dad had used my coffee coupons and all of a sudden I wanted to use them for myself. Bad timing!

"We took the rationing in stride, though. Everyone was in the same boat. I think people really pulled together — make car trips count, keep blinds down at night, recycle before there was recycling, barrage balloons, lines at theaters and no silk stockings (nylon came along and was great at first but you couldn't really get that till after the war). So mostly it was rayon stockings and they were terrible, even if you could get those."

Adrienne Johnson remembers that doctors and dentists not called into the services were left to fight a nearly hopeless battle in providing care in Bremerton. "We had the Schutt Clinic, and down on Callow, Dr. L.E. Foster had his clinic. I went in there one day because I had been having pains in my chest and trouble breathing. I came in about 8 a.m., waited until late in the afternoon and never did get a chance to see the doctor. The waiting room was jammed all day. Years later, I happened to read an article describing the problem I'd had. It was a widespread complaint during the war years, and the author suggested it was caused by stress brought on by the war. That could be, because the problem disappeared when the war was over and I was never bothered by it again. Once I simply had to see a dentist and the only time I could get an appointment was at 10 p.m. with Dr. Lamberton. He was just gray with fatigue when my turn finally came. These doctors were real soldiers and heroes, in my opinion."

LaVerne Jacobson worked in the dentists' office of Drs. Swanson and Christensen and also remembers the pressures in providing treatment. "We were one of only a very few dentist offices left in town, and as we grew from 20,000 to 90,000 or so, our services were at a premium. In our particular office, we had Navy dentists who were temporarily stationed at the Naval Hospital or aboard the various large ships come and 'moonlight' for us. They worked in the evenings. Likewise, we were open until at least 9 each night. After 5:30 each day, I usually worked with three to five of these dentists as their receptionist, assistant, X-ray technician and bookkeeper. I received 35 cents an hour."

From the early days of the war, Virginia Oass remembers the Army trucks rumbling by, the barrage balloons going up, the war workers streaming in. "This soon created severe shortages of everything, including housing and household supplies, clothing and gasoline, hospital beds and spaces in schools, restaurants, theaters, buses, churches, and stores. The net result was that long lines became the norm and virtually everyone was forced to live with inconvenience and hardship. It was sobering, particularly in the early months, when war news was always depressing, we were losing ground on land and at sea, and many families in our midst were parted from loved ones. Gold stars, indicating loss of a family member in service to one's country, started appearing in windows about town . . . Remarkably, a feeling of solidarity seemed to emerge, a spirit that we were all in it together, that we could do it."

Gordon Lecair with his
1938 Ford V-8 "60".
(Photo courtesy Gordon Lecair.)

Chapter 18

(Headlines from Bremerton Sun in Summer of 1944)

City Quietly Greets D-Day . . .
Largest Class Will Graduate at High School . . .
9,752 US Casualties on Saipan . . .
USS *Bremerton* Launched . . .
Bremertonians Do Big Job on Paper, Tin Can Salvage . . .
Temperature Hits 98 Here . . .
Allies Shaping Major Push on Berlin . . .

≈

It's OK to be Sophomoric When You're a Sophomore

Bremerton kids who were young during the '30s and '40s found fun in a great variety of places, usually not connected with school. Sometimes the pleasure was as simple as playing catch with a friend, as Art McCarty did with Bob Romberg or George Strong on the parking strip of Callow Avenue. "It was great fun to wave at the cars and especially the girls in the back seats of their parents' car," says Art. "We used to talk about how some day there would be a way to shift gears without using the clutch. Then out came Hudson with a shift on the steering column — amazing!" If America has had a love affair with autos, teens have had an obsession. More about that later.

Art recalls the playground programs developed in the '30s by the federal WPA, the Works Progress Administration. He played baseball at a field just south of the old Harrison Hospital on Marion Avenue, where the director was named Maggard. Dave Leathley remembers some of the players for the team, called the Hockeymore (derivation unknown) Athletics: the Blakey brothers, Tom, Bob and Dick; Lindy and Rex Brown; Bob and Coy Love, Dudley and Lee Stoltz, Bob Quimby and others. At the high school Bowl playfield, the director was named (or, more likely, nicknamed) Bunny Wolf. We fielded a dreadful softball team; at shortstop I once made three errors in a single inning.

Duane Thompson says his "drinking uncle," Ted Jensen, advised him to keep playing as long as possible, because most of life is spent working. "Sound advice," wrote Tommy, "but the war overwhelmed normal considerations."

Still, there were simple pleasures, as Dave Leathley remembers: "Summer times in Bremerton were a lot of work in our vegetable garden, weeding and watering of course but also lots of fun. The woods came right down to our back yard and there were trails through them that we played on and, of course, there were wonderful huckleberries to pick in season for Mom's pies. We also had apple, plum, prune, and pear trees to gather fruit from."

The easy access to the wilderness of the Olympic Peninsula from Bremerton was assumed. So were areas closer to our homes: Often small but still pristine, where kids could pretend they were in the forest primeval but remained within calling range of their mothers. Vacant lots were an essential part of kids' fun, too. Next door to Helen Jean Stubblefield, living on Park Avenue just two doors from Smith Elementary School, was a vacant lot with two huge maple trees that Billy and Jimmy Box, Dick and Jackie Edwards, among others, happily climbed. Helen Jean's first business venture was a partnership with the Box boys that irresistibly advertised "Fresh Mom Made Lemonade." I suspect it was the lemonade, not the moms, that was fresh. The little Park Avenue jitney would stop so the driver and passengers could refresh themselves. Mothers closed down the stand after the kids, without permission, added homemade root beer to their bill of fare.

Later, Helen Jean moved farther down Park Avenue, not far from the city dump on Warren, which was filled later and became Roosevelt Field. Still later it became the Sons of Norway Center. Children salvaged items too good to throw away — environmentalists from an early age. "A gang of us combined our efforts to retrieve, down our hill and into our backyard, a wonderful old bathtub," says Helen Jean. "My parents were less than pleased."

Later, the Stubblefields moved to a rental on Highland Avenue, where her neighbors were Bob and John Berkey, Bill and Bob Conn, Billy Gates and Franklin Wright. "Tarzan and Jane and Cops and Robbers were acceptable play unless my Mother imported girls for me to play with. This house had a cellar door to slide down, and an apple tree to climb. We did not have a rain barrel but the popular song of that time, I was sure, was written just for me." Nearby, Mrs. Chaffee's teen-age son would sit in the front window working a Morse code key, learning how to be a telegraph operator. He also had a crystal radio set that Helen Jean says was a wonderment.

On Gregory Way where I lived, spring was the favorite time of year. We knew that spring had arrived when there was enough daylight after dinner to go back outside to play. But, you might ask, doesn't that depend on what time you eat dinner? Certainly not. In Bremerton in the '30s, *everyone* ate dinner at 6 o'clock. While the length of dinner varied somewhat from household to household, the variation was slight, depending on how long the mother-boy debate lasted about eating the over-cooked vegetables. In even the most genteel households on Gregory Way, pre-pubescent boys could complete their repast, slip their napkins into their rings, excuse themselves and dart out the backdoor in 35 to 38 minutes, regardless of whether he had completed music practice.

Then we scurried down to Anoka Avenue and a utility pole that served as home base for most of our games. For reasons that remain unclear, we preferred Washington's Poke to hide-and-seek, which was considered plebeian. Occasionally, it is true, we would also play kick-the-can or run-sheep-run. Later in the year, we played softball. The sound of a bat whapping the ball, then clattering to the pavement as the hitter digs for first base is a sequence in my memory as inevitable as thunder following lightning.

Kids often misunderstand words and phrases they use in games. We, for instance, shouted, "Oly, Oly, Olsen free!" to signal that everyone still hiding during Washington's Poke was granted freedom from capture and could come home. If any of us had wondered who was Oly Olsen, and I think none of us did, we would have assumed he was one of the many Scandinavians who lived in the Northwest. It came as something of a start, ranking short, however, of finding that Santa was a myth, to learn that we actually had been shouting, "All the outs in, free!"

When it became too dark to continue the game, we would sprawl on the grass and confer and wrestle and punch and shove and yell and whisper until the unmistakable signal came to head home:

"JORRRRR—GEN!"

The name started in the middle range and then soared toward higher register.

It was Jorgen Nelson's mother, bless her; she had vocal chords that would have been envied by an opera diva. She would step to her front porch and without so much as a scale or two to warm up, cut loose. We kids would imitate her — good-natured Jorgen took it in stride — but we were unable to achieve half the decibels of

What the well-dressed students wore: Jorgen Nelson, Frank Wetzel, John Gordon. (Photo courtesy Audrey Thompson.)

Mrs. Nelson. The summons affected us all, for our parents, although inside, maybe even in the shower, heard the call, too. It was understood tacitly that when she called it was time for everyone to shag home. Few sailors had a more effective Lorelei. And every spring since childhood, when the days lengthen long enough to go outside after dinner, I hear the call:

"JORRRRR—GEN!"

Patricia Henning tells about growing up in Illahee. "A fun thing was our 'cow-pie' football on Schutt's Point. Dr. Schutt owned a big beautiful house right at the foot of the big hill and all the beach-front property across the street. It was a sandy beach surrounding a pasture where the doctor kept some cows. In the summer we would go there and throw cow-pies at each other and while most were dried up there were always a few that weren't. It wasn't a pleasant game but it was fun.

"One day, some of the sailors off the barge (moored nearby) came over and joined us, including my future husband. One of my brothers got him right on the head. I've never seen anyone so mad as he was and the madder he got the more we laughed. It was hilarious."

As the youngsters grew older, pursuit of fun became less spontaneous. Many joined the Boy or Girl Scouts. Audrey Thompson says Yvonne Nelson's mother was her Girl Scout leader. Members included Yvonne, Mary Lou Flieder, Susan Swanson, Helen Hackleman, Mary Lou Parker, and Shirley Sinclair. "We went on camp-outs, earned our badges, and met weekly. Mrs. Nelson gave a lot of time to us. Yvonne, David Soter and I were also avid stamp collectors and would meet weekly to go over our collections."

Audrey Thompson's schedule, meticulously preserved, was surely busier than most. Still, it illustrates the activities in which many of her cohorts participated. About the time she became a high school freshman, Audrey joined the Rainbow Girls, open to girls 13 to 20, connected with the Masonic orders (her father was a Mason and her mother an Eastern Star.) "Most of my other girl friends also joined," Audrey wrote. "We were so impressed by the older girls in office, such as Margaret Jolley, Fern Eathorne, Shirley Samson, etc. What lovely girls and role models these were for us to emulate. We worked on committees for various dances and eventually worked our way up through the chairs in the next few years. I was Musician, playing the piano, for the rituals and Helen Hackleman was the choir director. I was now good friends with Esther Miller, who, in September of 1942, was general chairman of the Rainbow Back-to-School Dance and I was in charge of music. I secured and made all the arrangements for Bill Winder's Orchestra to play. The committee met several times and we had great fun at these meetings." Helen Jean Stubblefield says the Bremerton Rainbow Assembly was the largest in the state; in 1944, when she was worthy adviser, there were 350 members. The equivalent organization for boys was DeMolay.

Audrey Thompson's 1942 Date Book (bless pack-rats!) shows basketball tournaments in Tacoma and Seattle, school concerts, Varsity Ball, Spring Swing, committee meetings and Vodvil, Chamber of Commerce dance, Junior Prom, Rainbow Mother-Daughter Banquet and Rainbow Installation. Audrey worked that summer at Dolly's Hair Salon on Fifth Street. That summer the owner held a dinner at Rau's on Hood Canal. There Audrey drank her first cocktail and got a little giggly. Audrey's fall schedule was busy, too: Tolo Week, where girls take the initiative and ask boys for dates, as well as more meetings and dances and football games. On November 23, 1942, Tommy Dorsey brought his orchestra to Bremerton and Bob Landon took her. More about the Landon-Thompson liaison later.

In 1943, Audrey attended more proms and dances, and

worked hard on the Vodvil. As we have seen, she ran for student body secretary and that summer worked in the Navy Yard as a clerk-typist, the third generation of her family to be employed there. The pay was $1,260 per year.

"About this time I was asked to join the first Bethel in Manette of another Masonic organization for girls, Job's Daughters," says Audrey. "Cleo Fellows was the first Honored Queen and I became the second. Other girls were

Audrey Thompson
(Photo courtesy Audrey Thompson)

Wanda Schenck, Pauline Pidduck, Geraldine Calder, Patti Serry, Edna Eastwood, Corinne Bullard, etc." (It's hard not to lampoon those titles. Did they have a Dishonored Queen, an Unworthy Adviser? If not, a pity; the organization might have been more fun.)

By the middle of Audrey's senior year, many of her male classmates were gone, often into Navy or Army programs in which they could continue their schooling. So many had volunteered, in fact, that although Audrey was general chairman of the Senior Ball she did not have a date. "Bob Halverson on the day of the ball found out and called and asked me to go with him." She attended the Graduation Dance with Jack Larson, who later became a famous textile designer. "Then, he was just a shy boy who was tall and danced well." Others said Jack often took several girls to the same dance. Sometimes they would all end up pushing his car, which apparently broke down frequently.

Rowena Harkins kept a busy schedule, too, but judging from her account she was more interested in dating than school activities. She once managed to have three dates in one night, directing traffic like a cop. She had a crush through high school on Karl Stingl, a top-flight ski jumper, and finally dated him a couple of times. "In fact," she writes, "I made an unscheduled ski jump out of the top story of the Paradise Inn on Mount Rainier one night during 'Bremerton Days.' Karl wanted to show me his skis (at least that's what he told me) and of course I accompanied him to his upstairs room to see them. When all of a sudden a bunch of Bremerton Ski Cruisers came unsteadily down the hall shouting, 'Karl, who's the girl in there?' I made Karl lock the door and I asked where the nearest exit was, which turned out to be the window. I was going steady with either Doug Lundemo or Eddie Quinn (my later true sweetheart), I can't remember, and I didn't want to get caught with Karl, who couldn't understand why I needed to make my escape. The boys said if Karl wouldn't open the door they'd break it down. Karl opened the window and out I went. Moments later Karl came sailing down in the waist-deep snow right beside me. I believe to this day that I am the only female to jump with Karl without benefit of skis."

Rowena says she probably had more fun in school with Jim McGill than anyone. "Jim took me to his Senior Prom; I was one of two freshman girls to attend. What a thrill, what an evening." She says they used to drive around Scout Tower, a favorite necking spot overlooking Charleston, and turn a spotlight on the cars. "Yes!" she says, "that was Jimmie and me!" (Later the cause of fright may have been George Meyer, said to have a siren on his car.) It's obvious from Rowena's account that she relishes her memories. "After all," she says, "those were my happiest and most romantic times." She adds: "I'm still 18. I just look older."

Gordon Lecair skied at Mount Rainier, too, although perhaps not with the same élan as Rowena Harkins. He often rode with Larry Salmela in the back of a delivery truck driven by Larry's father, owner of Apex Bakery. They would start at 5 a.m., drive to Gig Harbor, take the ferry to Point Defiance, drive through Ruston and on to Nisqually Falls. Then it was a hike up to Paradise. "To begin with," Gordy remembers, "there were no rope tows (chairs were not even thought of), so it was hike up all morning, ski down for lunch, and then do it all over again, except at the end of the day you skied down Devil's Dip to Nisqually. Most often I would be wet through and through, since I was never much of a skier. It was a cold ride home, but it was fun (I guess)."

Later, in high school, a school bus took loads of kids to Mount Rainier. "There was always a lot of singing when we left," Gordy remembers, "but on the way back it usually got very quiet as a bunch of tired guys and gals found a shoulder to lean on." More than incidentally, adds Gordon, his skiing companion, Larry Salmela, was awarded the Purple Heart and the Silver Star for gallantry in action during the Battle of the Bulge. "I believe it was the highest decoration for anyone in the Class of '42," he says.

I skied at Mount Rainier, too, usually with Jorgen Nelson, Al Blomlie, and Jorgy's father. By then, in 1938 or 1939, a rope tow was operating just above the Inn, but we often put clamps or sealskins on our skis and climbed far higher. Equipment was primitive. My skis didn't have metal edges and we thought cable bindings were a great improvement when they were introduced later. Jorgy, as blond and fair-skinned as an albino, sometimes got painful sunburns at Rainier but it didn't seem to bother him much and I was envious of the attention it brought him.

Harold Engebretson had only two weeks between high school graduation in 1943 and the start of a Navy V-12 program at the University of Kansas. "It may seem strange now but some of us organized a long hiking trip in the Olympics. The group included Don Haskell, Walter Jack, Jack Bender, Jack Keck, Jerome Herrigstad, Bob Erickson and myself. We went up the Dosewallips, over Anderson Pass to the Quinault River, down to Pyrites Creek on the west side of the valley, up Pyrites Creek into open country with lots of snow and no trails, generally westerly to a valley of Delabarre Creek, which we followed down to the Elwha River and then down the Elwha River to Port Angeles. It was a great trip into beautiful country."

Fun is where you can find it, and young adults are adept at finding it. None of those who contributed to this book complained about having too much fun; several regretted they had not pursued it more assiduously. Rose Jewett, for instance. She was married in 1942 and quit school before she got her diploma. Later she attended a high school event of her sister's and saw the excitement and fun of high school. She went home and cried all night. Her husband encouraged her to go back to school, and she did. It took a year and a half but she graduated in '45. She thinks she was the first married woman to attend BHS. She says she would sign her own absence slips; teachers knew she was married but didn't make a big deal of it.

Dorothy Fick attended both morning and afternoon shifts at high school because earlier she had missed a year after she and her brother were hit by a drunk driver. Each child broke a leg. "I look back and wonder why I went both shifts. I worked hard and didn't have time for a lot of things I should have done. I should have enjoyed more sports and fun things." Yet, Dorothy could not have been an unrelenting grind; one day she joined Bobbie Efnor in cutting Mr. Scott's biology class. They crept around the building under his window and dashed across Fourth Street to Pop's Inn. They bounded in the door and almost into the arms of Mr. Sorenson, the principal. "We about passed out. Cool and calm, he said, 'I'll sign a slip to get you girls back into class'." Dorothy adds ruefully, "I can truly say that was one of my most embarrassing moments."

Kids develop at different rates. Betty Bromley says she was shy and did not participate in any school activities. "Looking back on my school years," she says, "I do regret that I did not make friends easily." But while still in high school she started working in the Navy Yard and made close friends there. "I seemed to come out of my shyness and found that I could make friends. That was when I went to dances and learned to jitterbug and had a lot of fun."

Others dedicated themselves wholeheartedly to fun at the start. "What a place to be, and be 16, 17 and 18," wrote Florence Fraser. "All the men you wanted and then some." Shirley Sinclair says she consciously decided when she entered high school that she wouldn't try to become valedictorian because there were so many things to do that were fun. As for myself, becoming valedictorian, or salutatorian, for that matter, never entered my mind. A gentleman's C grade was entirely satisfactory. The accurate epigram chosen for me in the '44 Cat Log was "With him it's always a holiday." It should not have been a surprise when I ran into scholastic problems after leaving BHS in my senior year for the University of Idaho. In a letter home, I alibied, "Just a little bit too much fun, activities and athletics at high school, I guess, yet I can't bring myself to regret anything that I did at school."

Yes, it was sophomoric to paint '44 on the roof of the school annex as Joe Stottlebower, Don Haskell, and I did one night, and it was sophomoric that same night to paint out the headlights of a car parked near the school. It was sophomoric when I dangled a fake spider on a thread before the startled eyes of Dorothy Wilmot, who sat in front of me in Spanish class; her scream did little for class decorum. (Miss Strand ordered me to throw the spider out the window, where later I retrieved it for further exploits.) It probably didn't help my education to skip second-period study hall routinely my senior year to drink coffee and smoke cigarettes with Donna Rae Scott and LaVerne Gatlin at the Sugar Bowl over on Sixth Street. But what the hell: If you aren't sophomoric in high school, then when? (Well, OK, maybe it's a sign of retarded development to be sophomoric at your 45th reunion.)

A group of 40 or so women who attended BHS during the early '40s still meets merrily for lunch each month. They call themselves the Retreads. They also have an annual slumber party at Fort Worden, which I attended in 1994, although they kicked me out at bedtime. There I learned that Caroline Clement and Darlene Engels undertook their class's paint job on the high school, smearing '45 on the incinerator smoke stack with a vegetable brush. A group of boys, including Gene Teel, Bob Torseth, and, perhaps Darwin Gilchrist, came along while the painting was under way and insisted on helping. The boys painted '45's all over the stack, then added their initials. Word soon went out that police were investigating, and damage was estimated at $600. Carolyn told her mother, a highly respected counselor at the high school, who ordered Carolyn to confess. She and Darlene did, but refused to implicate others, who were apprehended, nevertheless. The boys were required to remove their artwork. The girls' work remained — and in fact endured after the school burned, because despite the fire the stack was left standing.

Written on the back of this photo: Patti (Scarlet O'Serry), The Raging Sensation of Stage and Screen, Frances Clement, Eleanor (The Look) Zesinger, Caroline (Hot Hips) Clement.
(Photo courtesy Patty Serry.)

I had supposed that boys were always the rowdies and girls invariably were Little Goody Two-Shoes. To my great pleasure, I have learned that wasn't true. Virginia Oass wrote of attending Frances Clement's dinner party in 1993. There, "shy, retiring Betty Schricker admitted for the first time ever that she had committed a long unsolved crime. On the urging of her rambunctious sister Frances, Betty had let out all the air in the tires of the Kiwanis Club members during their annual picnic at Cheerio Lodge 50 years ago." At the same dinner, Jo Ann Oass said Frances once had driven a Schricker Florist rattly old truck 90 miles per hour between Head of the Bay and Belfair, the longest straight-away in the area (and therefore a popular raceway for boys, too.) Speaking of highways, the favorite roller-coaster road was Chico highway near the golf course for its dips and thrills, guaranteed to put your stomach in your mouth.

Teachers sometimes had fun making a point. Girls would often come to school with pin curls under bandannas, then gather before class in the lavatory to brush out their hair. Elisabeth Benefield said Romaine Nicholson, who taught home economics and English, wore a dish towel round her head for one period. As class ended she said, "You probably have noticed that I'm wearing something on my head. I wanted you to see what it looks like." It's doubtful if her lesson, which collided with social custom, was heeded.

Someone remembered at the slumber party when Georgia Eckroat needed one additional credit to graduate. Richard Berg, the music teacher, put her at the back of the orchestra where she faked playing the bass — and got her credit.

Other stories related at the slumber party: Jo Garland said that when she and Mildred Grassness were being followed by "creepy guys," Mildred would snort loudly as though she were having a fit to scare them off. Jo said it worked . . . Jo also remembered that girls' angora sweaters shed and how difficult it was for sailors to get the hair off their uniforms . . . Once while running for the ferry, the button on Jo's panties broke — elastic wasn't available during the war — and she tried to decide whether to step out of them or hold them up. She didn't say how she decided . . . Girls remembered the curfew and how they ignored it, ducking behind cars to avoid police . . . Three of five members of the close-knit Westpark Gang admitted siphoning gasoline from cars not their own during rationing . . . Joan Evanson said her father was so busy in the Navy Yard that he didn't have time to use all his gas stamps, so gave them to Joan's boyfriends (but, alas, never to me).

Most parents were so busy with the war effort that oversight of their adolescent children was relaxed. But LaVerne Jacobson says her father imposed many stringent restrictions after the war started. "With three girls to raise in the town of Bremerton," she says, "my father became almost paranoid for our welfare and safety." For example, she was not permitted to attend public dances. "First of all, we weren't allowed in cars with other kids driving. Secondly, with gas rationing a fact of life, cars were not that available. We walked everywhere. The only dances I attended were the Senior Prom, attended with Linc Perry, and a few formal dances at the YMCA." She attended many church-related activities at the Lutheran Brotherhood Building on Washington Street and she and her sister spent many Sunday afternoons playing clarinet and saxophone at Vesper services for servicemen at the Y.

I asked LaVerne whether she felt constrained by her father's tough rules. "Yes, we resented it somewhat, and we felt we were the *only* ones who had such restrictions. Despite this, knowing my Dad's background and his age (he was 44 when I was born, and to top it off, from the 'old country' — Norway) we pretty much understood his different ideas. Actually, we felt fortunate that we escaped wearing long underwear to school all winter (to keep from getting chilblains, one of his odd or weird ideas.) Without a doubt there was a real generation gap; yet, he was a very loving and supportive parent and we loved and respected him nevertheless."

Don Rolstad's pursuit of fun sounds innocent enough. "Cruising, going to the movies, getting something to eat at a drive-in, and roller skating were my main activities in high school," he said. "I went to a few dances but did not enjoy them. I only remember one party at Maggie Ingman's. The house was full of students and we had a great time."

Jo Peterson wrote about a different variety of fun: "In September of '43 our friends from North Dakota came to help in the war effort. Palmer and Ida Tveten and five of their nine children moved in with us in our little house and stayed with us six weeks until they could get housing. Melba Tveten and I were friends from before and they became family. My Mom and Dad worked graveyard shift so Melba and I had their bed. We were really 'hot bunking' at our little house on Monsen Avenue. Brother Howard and Art Tveten would go down to my aunt and uncle's and sleep every night but otherwise we were four adults and eleven kids there for all the meals, sack lunches, baths and clothes washing — *and we had the most fun any two families have ever had.*"

A favorite relative of this period was described by Marian Booth. "My Aunt Inez, who had never worked and was in her late 50s, took a job in the sail loft of the Navy Yard, and loved it." She taught Marian how to drive by once stopping unexpectedly downtown and turning her new Ford sedan over to Marian, only 15 at the time. Aunt Inez dyed her hair red, bought herself jewelry and a fur coat and wore makeup for the first time. "She looked 10 years younger," Marian recalls. It wasn't only the free world that was liberated by the war.

Bremerton was not completely bereft of cultural events during the war. Robin Perrigo sent as proof the program of the Ballet Russe de Monte Carlo's performance at the Civic Center on Nov. 13, 1944. Performers included Maria Tallchief. Robin also speaks of Artur Rubenstein playing the piano at the high school, stopping in mid-chord when someone set off a flashbulb and warning that he would leave if it happened again. It didn't. Later, Robin thinks, Phil Thornton donned a wig and imitated Rubenstein at a school assembly.

For the past 80 years or so, during the age of the automobile, American boys have been in love with their cars. In addition to transportation, cars infuse social status, confidence, desirability — or so boys believe. I didn't have my own car until college but Cissi Loftus let me use her husband's 1932 V-12 Lincoln while he was at sea. Words cannot express my ecstasy when one day Don Haskell chauffeured me in it to high school, holding open the rear door for me as I dismounted and sauntered to class, all but regally waving to the gaping assemblage.

It's true that getting rationed gasoline was a problem — but sometimes rationing could be circumvented legally. For instance, brother Barrett was awarded 16 gallons when he came home on a furlough from the Air Corps, a practice presumably extended to other servicemen. And Harry McIntyre describes how, in working at gasoline stations, "the trick was to not drain the hoses on the last fill of the night and after I shut the station down I would drain the hoses into my gas tank. This wasn't much but it helped." Furthermore, adds Harry, sometimes a customer would ask, "What do I do with the gas stamps that I don't use?" Harry, always helpful, says, "Naturally, I would volunteer to solve the problem for him."

But black-market gasoline was sometimes available, too. Harry McIntyre again: "I had four cars between age 15 and 18 all of which, of course, required gas. Four gallons per week didn't do it so I bought black market gas at 50 cents per gallon from a little station in Charleston . . . Consequently, when the local police pulled a raid on youngsters that seemed to have all the gas they wanted for their cars my name was on the list."

Harry fingered a couple of boys who were caught up in the raid — prudence dictates their names not be repeated here — and says they spent several days in jail. "The question was asked of them, 'Where's Harry McIntyre?' They truthfully answered, 'He left for the Army Air Force last week.' How lucky can you get?"

Harry listed his four cars. The first was a 1930 Ford Model A roadster, which his father and step-mother eventually impounded because he was under age and they properly worried about their liability. The second was a 1932 Chevrolet coupe that cost $35. "If I parked it on a hill I was almost always assured of getting it started. I took a girl to a dance one night and my friends, Arlie Clark, Keith Hanson, and Clyde Wilson, pulled two of the wires off the spark plugs. Amazingly, I got the car started and drove my date to the Triple X and home before I finally figured out why the car ran so poorly." No. 3 was the 1937 Plymouth convertible costing $550 that, as we have seen, he wrecked en route to Lake Wilderness. No. 4 was a 1931 DeSoto convertible that he co-owned with Clyde Wilson. It cost $120, and came equipped with a snazzy touch of class: dual chrome-covered, side-mounted spare tires. "Fancy, except that the wooden floor boards caught fire occasionally because of a faulty exhaust system."

Because of rationing, tires were a serious problem. Patriotic motorists donated their used tires to salvage drives. "Some of those tires ended up on my cars as the stack was not closely guarded," Harry confesses.

One weekend when Alice Jane Levin's father returned to his car from a hunting expedition he found his tires had been stolen (Harry McIntyre didn't mention this, so I assume he wasn't guilty.) "He applied to the ration board and got another set of tires and the following weekend in a different place, those were stolen, too. So for the rest of that season, although I don't know what good I could have done, I took my homework and sat in the car while he gathered and hunted."

Myron Richards remembers not only his own cars but those of his father. These included a Brush, bought early in the century; a Metz; a used 1919 Franklin, which his father said was the best car he ever owned, and in 1926, a four-door Dodge sedan. "It was used to shop, go to church, drive to Mount Vernon on visits to relatives, haul firewood, and to carry goats, which we had for many years. In December of 1936, we acquired a new 1937 Plymouth four-door sedan, which was the car that I later learned to drive." Myron still has the dash-board Waltham clock from his Dad's Franklin.

Myron's own cars were a 1928 Model A Ford that he and brother Lowell bought for $15; a 1934 Dodge coupe with side mounts; a 1938 Chevrolet sedan, and, while in the Army, a 1936 Packard, plus any number after the war years.

In the winter of 1943-44, Teddy Green's father bought a big-rust colored Oldsmobile with Oregon license plates. It got him in deep trouble. Teddy wrote: "The car was very distinctive both for its size and color. About midnight one Sunday night shortly after we purchased the car my parents and I were returning from Seattle. As we turned the corner at Wycoff and Coontz — we lived at the corner of Hartford and Coontz — approximately eight men, some in Army uniforms and others in civilian clothes, suddenly circled the car, pointing machine guns and bright spotlights at us. I remember vividly the civilians were in overcoats and fedoras, just like the Untouchables. My mother immediately threw the door open and screamed 'Don't shoot,' several times and in typical teen-age disgust I told her that she was making a fool of herself. I also vividly remember that after the spotlights were pointed away from us I saw the humorous expressions on the men's faces. After calming my mother down and my father had shown the group our identification, they explained that several Gestapo had been seen in Portland in a car similar to ours."

Gestapo? In Portland? We were in even greater peril than I had realized.

Gordon Lecair received his first car on his 16th birthday, a 1930 Model A Ford convertible. Later, "I went through Fords, a '32 V-8 coupe, a '36 coupe and then a '38 coupe." Earlier, although Gordy was underage, his father would sometimes lend him the family car. "This was on the excuse that biology class was having a field trip and needed transportation. Of course, Cleo and I would take a side trip after school, probably stopping at the Triple X for a root beer." Cleo later became Gordon's wife.

It wasn't only boys who loved their autos. Geraldine Petersen diligently saved war stamps and bonds until she had enough money to buy her first car, a yellow convertible — "a prize I wish I still possessed." And when Virginia Eddy's brother Al was drafted in 1944, he sold his 1937 Studebaker to Virginia. "It cost $465, and I made steady payments to the bank, till it was all mine! I had ration tickets but I rode the bus a lot and I would come out pretty good when I had time to go somewhere in the car."

It was important to learn to drive at an early age, too — but some learned so early it was frightening. Ruby Jewett remembers growing up in Montana: "I used to sit on my Dad's lap, steer and shift when he worked the brake and clutch. It drove my Mom crazy, but I learned to drive this way. I was able to drive in

Missoula before I was of age because no one really cared in those days. When I came out to the coast I borrowed a car and took my first driver's license test. I can't believe I passed it." Same for Vi Magneson: "My dad taught me to drive in Four Town (Minnesota) at about age 7 but I didn't get licensed until after I married at age 22."

Aileen Bellinger didn't learn to drive until she was 30, but not for lack of trying. "At 16, my boy friend tried to teach me — one time only." At 18, she tried alone and got stalled on 15th. She asked a passing Fuller Brush salesman for assistance, and he helped get the car to her home on Snyder.

Jean Naish accompanied her husband from Army camp to Army camp during the war. He gave her driving lessons on their used 1941 Plymouth coupe. She made her first solo drive with an Army buddy of her husband's, near the end of which she noticed his clenched fists and a snow-white face. She reported this dialogue:

"What's the matter?" I asked.

"Have you ever driven before?" he responded.

"No, why do you ask?"

"Well, you turned onto a road and into the wrong lane, you have just gone through two stop signs and now you are going five miles over the speed limit."

What a picky person, she thought.

Virginia Oass's attempt to get a driver's license could not be called an unqualified success. She had gone with her sister Jo Ann to apply for a practice license at Head of the Bay, driving her Dad's car. "In front of the State Patrol, outside a big plate-glass window in plain view of three patrolmen, I crunched my Dad's prized Chrysler into a big truck parked behind me. How I hated to level with my Dad."

Her cover-up effort failed, too. "The first sunny day he noticed it. We should have taken it to the Chrysler agency. Their paint matched."

Virginia doesn't specify, but the same car may have been involved in this incident, which happened on September 1, 1939, the date the German army invaded Poland. The Oass family was racing to catch the Seabeck-Brinnon ferry. "Mother had just baked two cherry pies that she had taken straight from the oven to the car. In his haste to make the ferry, Dad stepped on the accelerator, careened around the last curve just as the ferry tooted its departure from the pier. The sharp turn sent the two still-warm, partially set cherry pies flying all over Mother, Dad, and his pride and joy, a brand-new, powder blue Chrysler Imperial.

During our long wait for the next ferry, tensions equaled, if not exceeded, those in Poland."

Virginia also tells about one of Jeanie Schairer's first driving expeditions, a sortie Jeanie made after promising her mother she wouldn't cross Sixth Street from the Schairer home on Gregory Way nor give anyone a ride. "To check her trustworthiness, her mother, unknown to Jeanie, fresh out of bed in her nightgown, curlers and cold cream, crouched on the floor of the back seat. Betty Shricker's at Tenth and Naval was Jeanie's first stop. Then she and Betty drove together to my house, where we chatted inside for a good half hour before my Dad, heading down the front steps on his way to work, discovered Jeanie's humiliated mother still huddled on the floor of the back seat."

Incidentally, in those days Washington state license plates identified the county of issuance. Seattle and King County license plates started with "A." Pierce County was "B," Spokane County was "C," Snohomish County was "D," etc. The sequence was determined by population of the county. Kitsap County was "I."

Harry Harkness, to whom I awarded the first *Joie de Vivre* Award for his ebullient account of his Bremerton days, tells about taking a job in the Navy Yard and picking up his final credits for graduation at night school. "With the money I earned I was able to buy my first big item, on time, of course. My Dad had to sign and was not too happy at first. Did I buy a car? Nope. Did I buy a motorcycle? Nope. Did I buy a boat? Nope. I bought a brand new baby grand piano."

Harry took lessons from Earl Brown's Music Store "and then another year of better lessons from Lila Hubbell, Hal's mother. Joann Larson, class of '42, helped me a lot on the pipe organ at the First Presbyterian Church. I was given the privilege of playing it any time I wanted and sometimes would take a date and go in the church at midnight to play for her."

My own moral disintegration got well launched in the summer of 1943. A frightening scourge of polio was sweeping the nation. Fourteen cases including three fatalities were reported in Kitsap County alone during the first 17 days of August. Local churches and theaters were closed. Swimming and dancing were banned. Funerals and weddings were limited to small gatherings. When, at last, liquor stores and taverns were closed, everyone knew the outbreak was serious.

Polio entered into the erosion of my moral fiber only indirectly. Because parents were, with good reason, frightened of polio — this was long before polio was tamed by the Salk vaccine — it was easy to persuade them to let us leave the afflicted area for a holiday. Jorgen Nelson was the key to the caper because he provided his bright red Chevrolet convertible. Joyfully joining him were Cal Christensen, Phil Thornton, Clark Dunn, and I, five members of the gang that, in high hauteur and ebullient elitism, we called the Big Seven (missing members were John Gordon and Don Haskell.) By a variety of subterfuges we collected enough gasoline to drive to Vancouver, B.C. We took a ferry to Nanaimo, then drove down Vancouver Island in glorious sunshine to a suburb of Victoria. Clark's parents, Comdr. Harry and Lillian Dunn, were staying at the Oak Bay Inn. They somehow wangled lodgings for the five of us at an adjacent annex. Then the Dunns discreetly stole back to Bremerton.

We discovered to our delight that Canadians didn't much care whether teen-agers drank, provided they didn't do it publicly or make too much noise when they did it privately. Provincial liquor store clerks issued us licenses without quibbling, although the legal age was 21 and the eldest among us had barely turned 17; two were hardly 16. Soon the bathtub was full of beer and we also had an ample stock of hard stuff. With Jorgy's convertible, it was easy to attract girls and soon we were wheeling about town, the convertible loaded to the gunwales with the five young American boys and a corresponding number of Canadian girls, several quite respectable (tradition has it that Terry was the daughter of a provincial Supreme Court justice.)

There we partied for three or four days, smoking Sweet Caparols, drinking beer in the daytime and Johnny Walker at night, entirely certain that we were suave and sophisticated and fully qualified to be playboys of the Western world.

Sure, in retrospect, it's embarrassing. Still, all but the most timid boys go through a similar Holden Caulfield phase while edging warily from adolescence to adulthood. We had left Bremerton as callow youths; we returned as callow adults. Given the times — three of us were less than a year away from wartime military duty and the other two weren't far behind — it isn't surprising that our growing up was accelerated. Nothing outrageous happened in Canada (it seldom does); there were no auto accidents and so far as I know, no one lost his virginity. I regret that I learned to smoke, a habit that continued for 17 years, and because of my precocious start, my appetite for alcohol has sometimes approached the upper limits of social acceptability.

Those regrets aside, my God! What a good time we had!

Dolores Gutoski dated local boys,
including one who sent her a dozen roses monthly.
(Photo courtesy Doris Gendron.)

• **Chapter 19**

(Headlines from Bremerton Sun in Fall of 1944)

State Estimates 71,000 Live Here ...
Ballet Russe Here Tonight ...
Army To Sell Buildings Here ...
RR Tracks Reach County Line
Nazi Scoring New Gains;
Worst US Setback Since Bataan Fell ...
Food Situation Tight; List of Rationed Items Enlarged ...

≈

I Never Dated a Sailor; Now, I Just Married One

At varying ages, boys and girls in their early teens undergo mysterious biological stirrings. Each gender becomes aware that the other isn't so bad, after all. Because of improved diet and more exercise, this biological change is coming increasingly early for girls; in the early 19th century, menarche often did not arrive for women until they were 18. By the 1990s, the average age was 12½. Still, it's usually boys who first become aware of the appeal of the other sex, although girls are more likely to talk about it.

I remember with anguish when I first became aware of the sexual attractiveness of females. I was on Pacific Avenue and Fifth Street and found myself staring at the derriere of a woman walking ahead. I was sure I was going insane, probably criminally insane. I slowly became reconciled to this attraction, however, and over the course of my lifetime I have become an appreciative girl-watcher.

Audrey Thompson remembers the first boy-girl party that was fun. It was given by Patti Serry at Halloween. "The decorations were great and we played fun games including a Treasure Hunt for odd things. Up to then I had been uncomfortable at a few parties where they played Spin the Bottle because I sure didn't want to kiss any of those yucky boys. But now — things were different."

Aileen Bellinger reacted negatively, however, when she attended a Halloween party given by Betty Lundemo. "They turned the lights off and I didn't cooperate. I thought they were awful."

She says her favorite year was when she was 14. "Had my first date. My Mother took us down to Callow Avenue to the Grand Theater with Pat Corcoran, Brian's older brother. He was later killed in the war. Went two weeks with him, what we called 'steady' and yes, we kissed but no 'touchy.' When he was killed I felt very bad and so guilty because later he had asked me for a date in high school and I turned him down."

When she was in the eighth grade, Patti Serry had a crush on the same Pat Corcoran. Their relationship was typical of the shy awkwardness of the very young who, ever so slowly, are becoming adults. "He was older than the rest of us, and bigger," Patti remembers. "Tough and muscular, but really nice. Irish. And he liked me. We never spoke. He played baseball — was very good — and he told someone he wouldn't mind if I came to the games. So Alice Jane Levin and I faithfully attended lots of baseball games. Which made all of the baseball players happy — because of Alice Jane. But everyone knew I was there because of Pat. We never spoke. But we smiled sometimes (Well, 'hi' or 'good game!')"

Pat lied about his age and joined the Army. He was sent to the Philippines and when the war broke out he was caught up in the Bataan Death March. He died later. Patti thinks she received the last letter he ever wrote. She went from eighth-grade crush to bereavement — and barely in high school.

But hearts mend. Later, when Patti zipped down the hill past Hillcrest Elementary School on her way to high school, the soldiers at the barrage balloon encampment would wave and call out her name. Trudging home, laden with books and notebooks, "I would usually have a contingent meet me at the bottom of the hill, and carry my books and flirt outrageously. I was a buxom 14 years old, but truly unaware of worldly ways. I soon found out that most of them were married and I found them very uninteresting. One sporty youth, named Peter, was probably about 19 and had an air of Bronx self-assurance. Before not too long, he alone would greet me at the bottom of the hill. He would gallantly carry my books, my coat if it was warm, and eventually he dared to put his arm around my waist to 'help me up the hill.' Soon, he was walking me all the way home, and beginning to talk romantically (which I thought was hilarious in his heavy 'New York-ese'.) Then, one day and very seriously, he asked me to marry him. Not only did he love me, he averred, but if he was married he might not have to go overseas, and while he was stationed in Bremerton he could probably live at my home with me. Now, while I was most flattered by his attention and delighted with my first marriage proposal, I really didn't like him a lot and I'm afraid I was rather brusque, alternating with giggles. He was sure of his charm, however (he *was* good-looking in a foreign way) and promised to persist in his courtship.

"When I got home I told my mother about Peter's surprising proposal, and she announced that I would either walk one block further down Callow and on the path between Cambrian and Lafayette or she would come and meet me at the bottom of the hill every day. How embarrassing! So, I started to take the longer, steeper, sometimes muddy way home. And my first wartime romance was nipped in the bud. I was very relieved!"

Don Rolstad describes more typical boy-girl relationships in high school. "I first dated in high school in my sophomore year. Since I could not drive, my dates and I used the bus and did a lot of walking. During high school I went steady for only short periods of time. Either the girl or I would want a change of scenery and that would end it. I dated one of my teacher's daughters but it did not help my class grades.

"Of all the girls I knew in high school, there is only one whom I still fondly remember. We were good friends but never dated. The only time we came close to being on a date was when we were on a school outing to Victoria. I asked her to ride a Ferris wheel with me and we exchanged kisses on the ride. She was a 1944 graduate and at our class reunions I always look forward to seeing her. She is still very attractive."

Dolores Gutoski doesn't remember her first date. "Sorry, whoever you were. I do remember that I wasn't to date until I was 15. But, my parents gave up and let me start at 14. I had to double-date and was allowed to go mostly to high school events: basketball games, school dances, football games, etc. Like everyone else, I eventually went steady. My junior year it was Al Stewart; my senior year it was Stan Johnson." Al took the relationship seriously; he sent Dolores a dozen red roses on the 28th of each month to mark their decision to go steady.

Marion Booth said her social life in high school was mostly a family affair. "We went roller skating, attended the many dances and shows at Civic Center, but always with my sister and cousins. I did, however, have one important date in my senior year. A young man named Jack Fatland invited me to go on a double date with his sister and her boy friend. We took the ferry (yes, the *Kalakala*) to Seattle and saw the Ice Capades of 1944. This was easily the most thrilling night of my life at that point and I will never forget it. Jack was almost as shy as I was at the time so I don't recall much conversation. He gave me a peck on the cheek when we got home. I wish him well wherever he is."

Geraldine Petersen readily admits that in high school boys were more interesting than studies, and that she became boy-struck. "I fell in love with a letterman. Occasionally photographing games for the year book, he became my favorite subject. Our relationship never materialized. He pursued a religion that I could not abide, being ingrained with Mormonism. It ended — but not the memory."

Audrey Thompson and Bob Landon
(Photo couresy Audrey Thompson)

In 1942, Audrey Thompson was introduced in the hallway at BHS to a senior, Bob Landon. "A special look passed between us and it was noted by my locker partner, Esther Miller. She said, 'Did you see the way that Bob Landon looked at you?' Yes, he was my special date but I liked other boys too and he never demanded that we go steady. Bob was my date for the May, 1942, Junior Prom. I was 16 and he gave me a music box for my birthday. We dated a lot and our favorite place was Perl Maurer's dance hall on Friday nights. You met all your friends, exchanged dances and had lots of fun — no liquor, just a soda, maybe. Afterwards to the Triple X for hamburgers or ice cream sodas." (It may have depended on when you went to Perl's. One girl at the Retreads' slumber party said there were boys throwing up in every corner.)

I dated Audrey in high school, too. I knew she was seeing Bob but didn't realize the seriousness of their romance until I received her Christmas package in Germany in 1945. The card was signed, "To Bob, with all my love." I realized she had mixed the cards and that our relationship was going nowhere (I'm very swift). Bob and Audrey were married on August 9, 1946, and as this is written still are. It's starting to look permanent.

If Rowena Harkins didn't date every boy in high school, it was an oversight. It started early: "As a tiny girl in Manette, I had a crush on Dick Feek, but he was older and thought I was a bother-some brat. Jack Bender invited me to a prom and I had other plans. I've been heartily sorry all my life that I turned him down. He was and is still a wonderful guy....I dated Bill Onstad (Bill wrote to me from a German prison camp) and his little brother

Rudy. (Rudy told my sister years later when he was a sedate school principal that I, Rowena, worked both sides of the bridge.)

"I dated Pat Casad, Evan Maxwell, and Phil Stewart from Port Orchard. He later became head of the Department of Fisheries in Washington State. I met him on a Boy and Girl Scout cruise on the Seattle ferry one moonlit night. Doug Lundemo's real love and later his wife was Winona Duckwiler but when they'd break up he'd ask me out and we'd go steady, then he'd break up with me and begin with Winona again. One Junior Prom he took me and after he took me home he went to Winona's house, and so it went. When they were married I was a candlelighter at their wedding. We, all of us, remained good friends all these years, and Winona and I are good friends today.

"Eddie Quinn, Doug's best friend, used to drive us around and at times I'd catch Eddie looking a me in the rear-view mirror even though he had a date up front with him. One night after a break up with Doug, Eddie asked me out — and thus began the real love affair of my teenage and beyond life . . .Needless to say I should have married Eddie. He was crushed (and in Guam) when I wrote the infamous 'Dear John' letter. I've lived with this from that sad day to this."

Rowena may not have been any more fickle than other girls. Joan Evanson wrote me in 1944, "I had to go steady with Jim Daulph to get rid of George Bottom." She acknowledged she had notified Don Haskell, who was in the Air Corps. "I hope he doesn't get mad cause I still like him," she wrote. I went steady with Joan, too; she gave back my Hi-Y pin at a New Year's Eve party at Jorgen Nelson's. So, let's see: Jim, George, Hack and me; four on the string, not counting her true love, Manford McNeill. That was doing pretty well, even for a girl as popular as Joan.

At the Retreads' slumber party in 1994, Jean Soehrs reminisced about her first love. He was a sailor who was lost aboard the *USS Sacramento*. When she came across a plaque that honors the men of the *Sacramento* in Bremerton's Ivy Green Cemetery, "I got chills." The first love, she said, is always special.

But girls had to be careful about dating sailors. At 15, Aileen Bellinger loved to roller skate, but the fun was spoiled a little "because a lot of sailors in 'civvies' went there and you had to be careful not to skate with them because if you did, you were called 'sailor bait'." Geraldine Petersen agrees, but points out the stigma waned as the war progressed. At first, "it was taboo to date the service men as you were known as 'sailor bait'," she wrote. "Then boys from back home were in the service and it was OK if you let your peers know they were old friends. I always thought this quite unpatriotic." Jo Garland remembered once running for the ferry in Seattle. She was breathless and tired but a sailor got behind her and pushed. She caught the ferry but once aboard told the sailor, "Now I can't talk to you." Rachel Morrill, walking to the Bremerton Civic Center to decorate it for a dance, was followed by three sailors, one of whom was only 17 or 18. He told her, "If I were at home a girl like you would talk to me." That gave her pause because it was the truth. So she did talk to him and they eventually helped decorate the center for the dance. "I learned a lesson," Rachel said.

Girls a little older, 18 or 19, were less likely to shun servicemen, particularly after the girls had left high school and held jobs. Virginia Eddy, for example, tells about meeting a young Marine who was stationed aboard the *USS West Virginia* while she was a shipfitter in the Navy Yard. "We dated a few times, fewer than we wished, as we worked many weekends then. We'd ferry to Seattle for a movie and dinner. I'd usually take the swing-shift bus home. Sadly, George was to be sent back to war again, this time to Okinawa. On our last ferry ride back to Bremerton, he proposed, and even though we didn't know each other that well, we had a lot of chemistry. I impulsively accepted. We corresponded all through that time, and I realized I had jumped the gun too soon, but didn't wish to send him a 'Dear John' letter. So I waited

Gordon Lecair and his then girlfriend, Cleo, now wife.
(Photo courtesy Gordon Lecair.)

till he returned, and it was one of the hardest things I ever did. Everything moved so fast then, we really never had time to know anyone that well."

Romance had not passed her forever by, however. "In the summer of 1945, I was working aboard the *USS Enterprise*, a magnificent carrier that had earned the most battle stars in the Pacific and was nicknamed 'the Galloping Ghost.' On my way up to the shipfitters' shop with two co-employees and friends, a marine and a sailor, coming off liberty, approached us, asking where we worked, etc. It seemed we worked aboard their ship. The slim, good-looking marine asked me where I ate lunch in the evenings (I was working the swing shift) and I told him 'out on the pier.' He showed up there nightly. Little did I know then he would, the following year, become my husband."

Streets were considered safe, and women felt free to entertain themselves without males. Margorie Booth noted, "Groups of us young women used to go to Seattle to attend operas and plays, usually walking from the ferry to the Opera House (probably the Moore Theater). No one seemed to be overly concerned about our safety and beyond a few hoots and wolf whistles from servicemen there was no apparent reason for concern." By the same token, doors at Jim Braman's home were never locked, he remembered, and servicemen often let themselves in, even late at night.

Many road shows came to Seattle during the war, and Bremerton residents nonchalantly flitted to Seattle to see them. Alice Jane Levin remembers Helen Hayes in "Harriett," Jose Ferrer and Paul Robeson in "Othello," Irene Hervey and Conrad Nagel in "State of the Union," the San Francisco Opera's annual trek to the Northwest, "Porgy and Bess" with Tod Duncan and Edda Moten — "great stuff," commented Alice Jane.

National studies show that marriage, birth and divorce rates skyrocketed during the war. In many areas, men became a scarce commodity. The growing popularity of going steady among middle-class teenagers was part of the cultural expression of that phenomenon, wrote Karen Anderson.[1] There was no shortage of men in Bremerton, however, and one consequence was an influx of young girls looking for relationships with servicemen. Anderson wrote that in Bremerton, such girls, who often arrived penniless, were taken to the city police station for overnight detention. That was an aspect of the city that few of us in high school knew anything about.

William O'Neill[2] wrote that marriage was the usual solution found by young men and women to the sexual problems of wartime. After Pearl Harbor, the marriage rate jumped by 20 percent. Most of the marriages lasted, too. "The war generation partied when it could, sometimes with abandon. But in the end, what men and women alike wanted was home, marriage, family," O'Neill said. (Not everyone felt that way, however. Jo Peterson remembers a teacher, Miss Anna B. Reeves, who said of being single, "It's a great sensation once you quit struggling.")

In 1942, Marjorie Lamb met a tall, curly-haired blond who gave her his seat on the bus. He was Clyde Clark, a BHS grad in 1937 and apprentice in the Navy Yard. He had volunteered for the Seabees and a few weeks before Christmas was called to ac-

---

[1] Anderson, Karen. *Wartime Women: Sex Roles, Family Relations and the Status of Women During World War II.* Westport, Connecticut: Greenwood Press, 1981:
[2] O'Neill, William L. *America's Fight at Home and Abroad in World War II.* New York: The Free Press.

tive duty. They wrote almost daily and in March of 1943 he proposed. "I thought it might be fun to be engaged, but never really thought about marriage until I got a telegram a few weeks later. He was coming home for one week before going overseas and wanted to get married. My sister took me to Port Orchard and Judge Frank Ryan gave us a waiver on the three-day waiting period. We were married in the Navy Yard Chapel on March 28, 1943 . . . When I first arrived in Bremerton someone told me nice girls didn't date sailors as they had a girl friend in every port. But that all changed after Pearl Harbor when our brothers, cousins, and neighbors joined the service. I never dated a sailor, and here I had just married one."

Other Bremerton girls married servicemen, too, and some were subjected to the terrible sorrow of losing their husbands, temporarily or permanently, while still barely out of their teens. Margorie Booth, for example: "I left Bremerton temporarily in 1944 to be married to my childhood sweetheart. In 1944, he was an Air Force fighter pilot and was shipped to the European theater that fall. I returned to Bremerton and went to work again in the Navy Yard as a stenographer. He was later shot down over Germany, rescued by the French underground and slipped back to a burns hospital in England." Happily, they were reunited in 1945.

As noted in Chapter 2, Ruth O'Grady's father was killed in an accident a month before she was born. Her mother suffered from mental illness. Affection was not expressed in her home. Then. . . well, let Ruth tell her own story:

At Bremerton High I always felt I was on the outside, looking in. I never studied enough to be "top of the class" but I remember doing homework for a lot of boys.

I met Murl Dain in Grace Ogrosky's German class. He was a little on the wild side for me, I thought. He liked to skip school and got bad grades. He had a hard time convincing me that the beautiful blonde I saw him with a lot was his cousin (Ethel Mae Munsterman, class of '42).

In one of his first notes to me he announced that he had decided we would be married one day. What a wolf, I thought. But he said he had made up his mind. Even Mother seemed to like him, and she didn't like anybody.

I believe a first boy friend can really influence a girl's outlook on boys and sex. We never did have sex until we were married. I was too scared to — and Murl said I could set the rules. He never pressed the point — well, maybe a little, even though it was very difficult at times. I kept telling him not to be so mushy because I couldn't see any point to all that hugging and kissing. My family didn't do that.

Although we met in 1940 and started going together, it was an off-again, on-again affair because his parents moved around a lot and when he was gone, I wouldn't hear from him. And when he was here, we would get furious with each other and break up regularly. But some strange magic always brought us back together. Something was going on here that I surely didn't understand.

When we were going steady, it didn't mean very much as he couldn't get his Dad's car very often so he just walked me home and we went to movies or games. I dragged my girlfriend, Hilma, along sometimes, which he didn't like but he put up with it. He taught me how to drive.

In 1941-42 I was a senior at Bremerton High school. Double shifts had started at school and I, unluckily, had the afternoon shift, which left a totally wasted day. I got in the habit of getting up late, doing a little homework, then off to school all afternoon. Many of my classmates were strangers.

December 7th and the meaning of the war only gradually sunk in. I thought of Murl (he had moved away at the time) and I was not at all surprised to receive a phone call from him about a week after Pearl Harbor, saying he had joined the Navy and was leaving immediately for boot camp. He asked if I would write and, of course, I said I would. He signed up for submarine duty, so naturally he was assigned to Navy Air Torpedo Squadron Three as an aviation ordnance man (tail gunner on a torpedo bomber), flying off the *USS Saratoga*.

I finished school but it seemed most of the school spirit was gone. Many students left early for the war and many others moved in and out with their families.

After graduating I immediately got a job as a file clerk-messenger-typist at the Credit Bureau. I didn't apply to them, they called me, jobs were that plentiful. I learned a lot there, including everyone's credit record.

About a year after he left, Murl returned from overseas, not to the parades and brass bands some of his buddies received, but back to Bremerton, just another swabbie. He had seen a lot of action but always said he would "tell me about it later." However, his mother had talked to his pilot who told her that they had been in many battles in the South Pacific. He had really appreciated letters from his friends, especially Viola Butler.

It didn't take long to know the magic was still there but he had only a short time before being sent back overseas and we thought it would be best to wait to be married until he came back the second time. When we learned he would have to leave Whidbey Island where he was stationed to go to Pasco, we decided to get married then and there so I could go with him. And besides, I was beginning to see the point in all that mushy stuff.

We lived in Walla Walla two short months before the squadron was sent back overseas. It had all been so new to me — to love somebody and to have them love you; to call somebody "Honey." I had never felt any warmth from my mother.

Murl put me on the bus for home — a sad, sad journey. We vowed to write a letter to each other every day. We did, and I still have all his letters.

This time I went to work at the welfare office, again to work with the down side of life. But I learned more about psychology and sociology than I would ever have learned in school — and I learned to type fast and use big words.

One night about a year after we were married, I woke with a start. I had seen a lifeboat with Murl in it. I wrote to a friend about it (it was all so very real) and told her I would be so glad when I got his next letter and would know it was all just a dream.

Ruth and Murl Dain.
(Photo courtesy Ruth O'Grady.)

But his letters stopped and then the telegram came — Missing in Action — followed by a letter from his C.O. and letters from a couple of his buddies. The three, pilot Frank F. Frazier, navigator Eugene Weeks, and tail gunner Murl, were seen to get into a lifeboat. Everyone had high hopes they would be picked up, if not by friendly forces, at least as prisoners. They had been flying off the

USS Yorktown, bombing Formosa. Their plane was hit but they managed to make a water landing, but there was a storm that night and the next day. No traces could be found. From then on, the days dragged. I could go to work, laugh at the jokes, and, I'm sure, appeared very normal. But inside I was destroyed. It was as though I was two people; one could laugh and talk, the other stood aside, watching. It was hard to accept — hadn't he always come back to me? I started drifting, couldn't make any moves. Everything was on hold. Every morning on the way to work I bought a newspaper to read about any prisoners being found. To this day, I have to read a newspaper the first thing in the morning.

After a year, a curt communication. Murl was arbitrarily declared dead after a year. But the uncertainty remained. V-E and V-J days were just other days. I wanted to do something, but I just couldn't move. No longer "Navy" to friends (they don't like to be reminded of what can happen), no longer a wife, and not sure I was a widow, at age 20, frozen in time. But in a letter written to me and to be delivered by a buddy should anything happen to him, Murl said he couldn't have had a better life, that he loved the Navy, loved the squadron, and had married the girl he loved.

Just a few months ago, when I read that possibly prisoners had been taken to Russia during World War II, I wondered . . . I still wonder.

Life goes on. But you never quite forget.

*Among BHS most influential
instructors and administrators
were Fred Graham, Harry Sorensen
and "Wild Bill" Carter.*
(Photo courtesy Shirley Sinclair.)

Chapter 20

(Headlines from Bremerton Sun in Winter of 1945)

Shortage of Homes Grows More Acute . . .
Meat Famine Faces Patrons of Cafes, Yard Cafeterias . . .
12 P.M. Closing on All 'Spots' Now Effective . . .
19,938 Iwo Marines Felled . . .
Kalakala **on Beach Three Hours; Freed by Tide . . .**

≈

Best Teachers Give Lessons for Life

Despite the intrusion of World War II into their education, alumni of that period give Bremerton High surprisingly high marks. Wally Ellis, class of '42, put it accurately: "Today's society would be appalled at the conditions we had, but we still received a good education." Because of the split shifts, classes were brief (45 minutes) and remained crowded. Text books were in short supply. "I still managed an 'A' from Al Hugenin in spite of having to study with a text borrowed from most anywhere I could," Wally wrote.

I asked the alums to rate their education, one to ten, with ten the best. Several gave their education the highest possible rating, among them Dolores Gutoski and Harry Harkness, although they listed different reasons. Dolores wrote, "I would rate my high-school education as a 10. I say this because of how well prepared I was to go to college (at University of Puget Sound). I saw other freshmen struggling in English classes and history classes and not being able to settle down and study. I didn't have these problems and I really attribute this to Bremerton High. I enjoyed all four years there and regret nothing."

Said Harkness: "The teaching staff was excellent." Then, perhaps thinking about urban schools of a half-century later, he added, "Nobody carried a gun or shot each other. The worst was

probably smoking behind Pop's or possibly an occasional preg-
nancy. Everyone I knew respected the entire staff and Mr.
Sorensen and Mr. Martin were to be feared."

Others gave their education during WWII a high rating, too.
Mack Smith: "I would rate my high school education as a 9 simply
because I was well-prepared for college." Vi Magneson: "I rate my
high school education as an 8 or 9 on a scale of 10 because of strict
environment." Marion Booth: "I would rank the high school very
high, at least a 9. I had some favorite teachers: Fred Graham for
literature, Miss Zlenko and Miss Woodward for art, Miss Hoffman
for shorthand and even Mr. Mykut, who predicted that most of
the girls would never learn to type because we hated to cut our
fingernails. I did, in fact, learn to type and supported myself for a
lot of years as a typist for the U.S. Department of Agriculture."

Marion's older sister, Margorie, also cited Galina Zlenko, calling her "a lovely, gracious, talented woman. She always found a
way to give kind, constructive criticism while encouraging students in their work. I have always enjoyed art and she played a
part in my attitude toward the subject. I also recall what a good
cartoonist classmate Mack Smith was." Margorie couldn't remember the name of her shorthand teacher but said she was
tough but fair and pushed her to do her best. "Nothing beat
shorthand for taking class notes! And I have used it nearly every
day for over 50 years. I've never worked for anyone with whom I
couldn't keep up and that includes some fast-talking executives,
writers, and other assorted 'dictators' whose utterances I have
transcribed."

Berenice Eicher said the only class she didn't like was typing,
then adds: "Most beneficial course? I hate to say it, but it probably
was typing. It's certainly the one I have used most." She rated
her education a 7, noting the University of California at Berkeley
gave her credit for all her classes except first-year French.

Others giving ratings included Gordon Lecair: "Perhaps an 8
with no regrets." Kathleen Shelly rated her education at 7 but
said, "Didn't like going to split shift in high school, missed out on
lots of things." Don Rolstad: "Rating of my school education
would be about a 6. Two points off for class presentation and two
points off for not studying harder. My grade average was B —
but on occasion I would pull down A's without too much effort."
Don's favorite class was Speech IV, taught by Fred Graham.
"Why was it my favorite class? I ended up being the only boy in a
class with 26 girls. Not bad odds! My most embarrassing moment was at the Gaveleers' banquet when I was introduced as the
boy who likes a good head on his shoulders — especially a girl's."

Bill Gates rated his education at 6 or 7, settling on 6½. He said he would rate it higher except he felt high school kids now are much better educated than he was. "But some teachers were sensational," he said, naming Larry Ramm and Mentha Crofoot. "I feel that way about her because she was tough. She gave me hell. She really didn't like me, I guess because I was so conceited." He remembered reading *The Scarlet Letter* and *Lady of the Lake* in her literature class.

Alice Jane Levin didn't award a numerical rating but said, "We may have suffered a bit under the shift system but all in all I believe I received a good education and most of the people I know agree." She added, with her typical whimsy, "I always hoped that our air raid drills would come during U.S. History so I could dive under the nearest table with Jack Bender."

Cal Christensen remembers that some teachers were demanding. If James Dogan, who taught chemistry and physics, thought a student had high potential, he would nag the student to work harder, as he did with Cal. Mr. Dogan named him to the Science Club, and didn't like it that Cal was involved with Vodvil and other activities. Later, when Cal was at the University of Washington in a tough Navy program, Mr. Dogan would demand, "Have you flunked out yet?"

Some years ago I wrote a newspaper column, expressing regret for all the subjects apparently taught on days I skipped school. I wrote, "I cannot read nor speak French. I do not remember the chemical formula for salt. I am unable to distinguish between ibid. and op cit. My woodworking skills are primitive, at best, and I cannot cook a soufflé. The Dewey Decimal System terrifies me." Worse, I confessed, "I cannot figure out the pronunciation symbols in the dictionary." I haven't learned any of those things since, sorry to say; I guess I would rate the education offered as a 10 — but the education absorbed at 5.

Adrienne Johnson, who does speak French, wrote that some of the teachers were real heroes, teaching the morning shift at school and then working the swing shift in the Navy Yard. "Even with shifts the classes were hopelessly crowded. I remember chemistry classes where I shared a seat with Shirley Flaherty. We had to double up because there weren't enough desks or supplies, and Mr. Dogan always tried so valiantly to forge ahead and teach us something. I think all of our teachers did as good a job as they could under the circumstances, but some went beyond the necessary effort. I recall Miss Dunlap and the Latin Club party she set up for us one evening in a downtown restaurant. We all had to wear white sheets so we would look Roman. I felt extremely foolish walking to town in a sheet, but what fun it was and Miss Dunlap (later Mrs. Justin) was so enthusiastic. Miss Strand was the same way and she too put together a Spanish party for us. Though smiling and enthusiastic, she showed her fatigue by the lines on her gentle face.

"Nevertheless, there were no mentors or anyone who took a personal interest in the individual student, no guidance in selection of subjects and future goals as far as my own experience goes. Only one teacher, Mr. Carter, the business ed teacher, walked over to my desk one day with a somewhat concerned look on his face, and whispered that he was going to impart a fact that he wasn't supposed to tell but that he thought I should be aware of. He said the result of my IQ test was one of the highest the school district had ever seen. He said I had the ability to become anything I set out to be."

But Adrienne's parents were adamantly old-fashioned. "I wanted desperately to go to college but my parents refused to help, saying that I would just get married and it would all be wasted. Such was the prevailing mentality of the time. They said I should save the money I earned, and after paying them board and room of $5 per week, use the rest for business college, which I did. The methodical, deep-rooted practice of stifling talent and intellect of girls was part of the picture in those days. Yet some overcame. My sister Fran persevered until she got a teaching certificate but it was years after she left home and had a family. The down-grading of women was another tragic loss to the country."

Gender bias cropped up among teachers, too. One of Rosalind Gillie's favorite classes was commercial law, taught by the impetuous William Carter. Rosalind wrote, "Mr. Carter paid me the supreme compliment of saying that I had a man's mind and I should practice my stenography and he would help me get a job in the county court. I am reporting this derisively with the thought that had I been of the other sex he would have recommended law school." To his credit, "Wild Bill," as almost all the students called him, was at least talking personally with his students.

In the same vein, a sad observation from Virginia Oass: "Most of us girls, regrettably, considered it rather unfeminine to be smart."

Harold Engebretson, whose IQ must surely have been in the stratosphere with Adrienne Johnson's, was under no such constraint. "My overall impression now is that Bremerton High School was very good to me. I had a lot of fun, knew a lot of nice people, and got a very good high school education. When I started college (in a Navy program at the University of Kansas) I was better prepared than almost all of my classmates from other schools all over the country, large cities and small towns. I had four years of mathematics, chemistry, physics, four years of English and literature, three years of foreign language, and four years of history and civics."

Not everyone liked high school. Myron Richards, for instance: "I always disliked school intensely right from Day One in the first grade. I consider my school experience as a mild form of child abuse, but I must admit that I was extremely lazy, and teachers kept expecting me to do things. . .The wonderful band and orchestra program in Bremerton saved my life. No school system now has a program of that quality, and if I were a student starting out today, I would not be successful at all. I learned all that I needed to know in order to be a professional symphony orchestra player, which I became, in that high school orchestra under Mr. Jackson's leadership."

Band member
Myron Richards
influenced in life by music.
(Photo courtesy Myron Richards.)

During the war, teacher turnover doubled at the national level and salaries lagged. High school enrollment dropped by one million between 1940 and 1943; by 1944, an estimated three million youngsters 14 to 17 were working. Some have called this the hidden scandal of the war.

The starting salary for teachers in Bremerton in 1939 was only $1,200. By 1945, starting salaries had increased to $2,136 — a handsome increase in terms of percentage, but still less than munificent.

After the war started, federal funds began to pour into Bremerton and it became a period of expansion and modernization. George Dewey Junior High was built in East Bremerton and the new high school was finally finished in 1945. (By the time this book was being written, the "new" high school had already been replaced.)

In 1931, during the Depression, the Bremerton School Board adopted a resolution that said, "a married woman having private means of support, income producing property or property capable of providing an income, or a husband who is physically able to support her, shall not be hired as a teacher by the District."

That was rescinded during the early days of WWII, and married women helped alleviate the shortage of qualified teachers. But turnover was high. When a husband was transferred, the wife usually followed, often on short notice.

Teachers are crucial to education, to state the obvious, and many who taught at BHS during the war are remembered fondly 50 years later. Harold Engebretson said Larry Ramm was the teacher who probably influenced him the most. He also named James Dogan, the chemistry teacher, and Paul Preus, who taught physics. "I generally did well in high school," Harold said. "With my sister Thelma a teacher there and living at home I was probably afraid to not behave and do well."

Gerry Petersen, who transferred as a junior to BHS from a small town in Utah, said, "I'm quite certain the quality of education was superior to my country school. More subjects, better teachers, and finer physical education facilities." She cited her Latin teacher, Florence Dunlap, as an effective instructor.

Virginia Oass named Louise Clement, who, as a single parent of five children, still managed to pursue her doctorate at the University of Washington while teaching at BHS — "and did all with great distinction." Mrs. Clement's daughter, Frances, wrote of her mother, "Louise first taught kindergarten, for half a day only, in the basement apartment across from the since demolished Naval Avenue School — her salary was $50 a month. This was well beneath what her M.A. degree should have afforded, but she was told that as a divorcee she should be thankful for any job at all."

Myron Richards, who, as we have seen, heartily disliked school, nevertheless praised the orchestra teacher, Vernon Jackson, and they remained friends a half-century later. Myron also praised Fred Graham, Al Hugenin, and Larry Ramm.

The good works of teachers sometimes extended beyond the classroom. Kathryn Nothwang's favorite teacher was Helen Chamberlain. "She and Romaine Nicholson did many things for students out of their own pockets. Helen also sent many children to camp from her church, First Presbyterian. I also received a two-year scholarship from her (not known at the time) to Whitworth College. I was thrilled and was one of the first ones in my family to graduate from college." (Tall oaks from little acorns grow; Kathryn became the first in her family to graduate from college. Later her son received his doctorate from MIT.) Teachers helped in smaller ways, too; Robin Perrigo remembers Grace

Ogrosky, who taught German, sewing a sock for a sailor at the separation center in the Navy Yard.

Perhaps the most visible yet unobtrusive adult at BHS during the war was the principal, Harry Sorensen. He is remembered with particular fondness by boys to whom he gave unearned credits to help them get into special programs with the armed services. Later, he helped many veterans go directly to college even though they may not have formally completed their high school educations.

He was born in Alta Vista, Kansas, on April 3, 1895, where he received his grade-school education. His family moved to Nooksack in Whatcom County and he completed high school there. He attended Bellingham Normal (now Western Washington University) and College of Puget Sound, completing his undergraduate work at the University of Washington in 1923. He was married in 1925 to Clara Kallander of Nooksack. They had two children, Bob and Barbara. He started his career in Kitsap County in 1923 as superintendent of the old Charleston district before consolidation with the Bremerton district, and became high school principal in 1929, when there were only 400 students (there were 2,100 in 1944). He often joined the vice principal, George Martin, and others in expeditions into the Olympic Mountains and regularly competed in city tennis tournaments. He was proposed for school superintendent in 1943 but the job went instead to Stanley Wynstra. He told the *Sun* in an interview in 1945, "The greatest enjoyment of my life is watching these youngsters grow up." Mr. Sorensen died unexpectedly in 1950.

Popular as other teachers and administrators were, none had the lasting effect of Ken Wills, the physical education teacher better known for coaching basketball and track.

Despite the great humbuggery so prevalent in sports, particularly at the college level, magic things can happen in athletics, as in the best relationships between a high school coach and his players. Kids are open and vulnerable in their early teens as they never are again. They have questions about themselves and sex and how the world operates, questions they would never dare or deign ask their parents. Good coaches know this. They know that some youngsters can be dealt with directly, others only obtusely. They know that the metaphor of sports as life will work indefinitely with some, only briefly with others. They know, too, that they will make a lasting imprint on many. The good coaches treasure that opportunity, for they know that in other pursuits the chance to make a significant difference in someone's life is rare.

Ken Wills.
On the back of this snapshot, Wills wrote
instructions to his players on how to
prepare for next season.
(From the author's collection.)

So it was with Ken Wills. He had played basketball for Jack Friel at Washington State College in the '30s and barely missed making the U.S. Olympic team in 1932 as a miler. He was an excellent coach, emphasizing fundamentals and defense. As we have seen, his teams won the state basketball championship in 1941, missed by a single shot in 1942, and placed a respectable sixth in 1944.

Over lunch in 1995, I asked three of his former players, Duane Thompson, Art McCarty, and Bob Romberg, to think of descriptive words for Wills. Some that they mentioned: Intense. Focused. Driving. Positive. Fair. Tough. On another occasion, Joe Stottlebower, another of his players, described Wills as dedicated and high-strung. Unsaid but understood among former players was that Wills was demanding. Sometimes during practice he would slam his megaphone to the floor and reach for his paddle. He wasn't reluctant to swat players who weren't hustling; giving hacks to players was accepted and normal practice in those days. "He was constantly saying, 'You can do better'," one remembered. He held his opinions intensely; when Art McCarty noted that Wills hated zone defenses, Duane Thompson quickly added, "He despised and scorned zone defenses." As Thompson illustrated, Wills seldom equivocated.

In 1941, he would sometimes lend his precious blue Buick to seniors for an occasional evening of dating; Art McCarty used it for the Senior Ball. When Bob Romberg wanted to borrow it, too, Wills gave him a tacit driving test. "He asked me to drive him to the high school. When I started out I laid down rubber for about three blocks." Loan of the Buick was denied. But Wills didn't encourage his players to have girl friends anyway. He once said, "Thompson would make all-state if he spent as much time in the gym as he did on the sofa." But he liked and accepted Marilyne White, whom Thompson married in 1946.

Wills was an atheist and made no secret of it. He kept anti-religion tracts on his piano bench, Art remembers, easily available to the students who frequently visited. Although everybody around Wills knew he was an atheist, he didn't proselytize. Still, he wasn't reluctant to discuss it, or to be forceful in stating his beliefs. Thompson said Wills's religious views were a breath of fresh air, "but only served to reinforce my already skeptical attitude toward organized religions."

While Bill Gates was in the Army, he corresponded with Wills. "He was in our heads," Bill said. "He was our confidant. We shared ideas and things with him. We got used to talking with him a lot, intimate things." Those things included religion. A group of us attended discussions on religion with the Rev. Wilbur Scafe at First Presbyterian Church on Sunday nights. Afterward, Bill, Xie Olanie and Jim Taylor went to Wills's for another viewpoint. Bill said Wills was circumspect. "I think he'd be even more hesitant today than he was then. But he was kind of a gutsy guy. I'm guessing he made the decision that the three of us were safe. For a high school teacher to have that kind of relationship now would be risky."

In retrospect, I'm surprised at how little stir was caused by his atheism and radical ("the munitions makers caused World War I") economic views. I'm not certain that in the lock-step, conformist eras that have followed, his viewpoints would have been countenanced.

I met Wills at the tennis courts in the Bowl while I was still in junior high. I was predisposed to like him because my brother Barrett ran the 440 on Wills' championship mile relay team and thought highly of him. I told Wills I intended to play only tennis when I got to high school but he said he thought I might want to try basketball, too. That was all the encouragement I needed.

I played on the freshman team my first year, on the B team as a sophomore and was a reserve on the varsity as a junior, the normal progression unless you were an outstanding player, which I was not. As a senior my conceit knew no bounds and I had discovered girls and other vices. In addition, I had passed a test to enter a special Army program and expected to leave before the season ended. So I didn't turn out my senior year, secretly hoping that Wills would issue a special invitation. Quite properly, he didn't. Instead (as a jock, I say this with embarrassment), I became a cheerleader, joining Clark Dunn, Phil Thornton, and Linc Perry in leading cheers from the sidelines.

Many of Wills's high school players had successful basketball careers in college, including big Roger Wiley at the University of Oregon and barrel-chested Louis Soriano at the University of Washington. "There's not been a better coach ever than Ken Wills," Soriano told sports writer Chuck Stark of the *Sun* in 1986. "Every college wanted you because you were fundamentally sound." Wiley said, "I was a tall, lanky kid and he spent an inordinate amount of time with me. Tall boys in basketball were somewhat of an oddity at that time. I happened to be the tallest one that came along at that time. He'd say, 'Just because you're big, that doesn't mean you can't do this.' And he'd have me dribble around chairs and work on all sorts of skills."

Added Soriano: "He taught us a way of life, not just basketball." Said Duane Thompson: "His work ethic reinforced the examples we saw earlier in our families and neighborhoods. His positive, encouraging style of coaching had a life-long impact on me."

Joe Stottlebower, who was named to the all-state second team in 1944, considered Wills a mentor and, I think, was one of the most important people in Joe's life. At my request, Joe wrote some of his impressions of Wills:

> He was a tireless person with energy, patience, enthusiasm, and grit who, one would think, would live forever.
>
> He was straightforward, and he possessed unquestioned integrity.
>
> He was a selfless teacher and a personal friend to many.
>
> He was a positive influence on an unusually large number of boys.
>
> At a time when each sport had a clearly delineated season, Ken pointed out that to achieve excellence in anything — playing the violin or playing basketball — practice was the key. He played the game with us in all seasons of the year. As a player he was an excellent role model. We patterned our skills after his. Though more subtly demonstrated, he taught the nuances of good sportsmanship, determined competitiveness, and sound conditioning.
>
> Ken overcame obstacles with astonishing energy and enthusiasm. He taught large PE classes of 75 or more during the school day's two shifts in the early '40s. At 4:30 p.m. when the second shift ended, the soldiers sta-

tioned with the barrage balloon in the Bowl used the boys'
PE shower facilities, which meant Ken had to coach from
6:30 to 10 at night.   One would often see him running
between his Burwell home and the school in a gray
sweatshirt, white pants, and black Converse basketball
shoes. He made time to open the gym on Sunday afternoons for all comers. He was so successful in attracting
boys to the game that he was able to split the varsity
squad in half and win two away games on the same night
during the 1940-41 state championship season.

In a game at Shelton during the 1941-42 season the
referees didn't show up. Rather than make the trip for
nothing, Ken ended up refereeing himself, in borrowed
shoes. There was no question in our minds that our coach
refereeing the games was not an advantage. We knew he
had too much integrity to give either side an unfair break.

Ken was selfless. Many friends have mentioned to me
that though they never played varsity basketball at
Bremerton High, Ken had encouraged them in different
ways. He wrote countless letters and cards to servicemen
from Bremerton during WWII. A teammate of ours from
a large family with limited funds had his wallet stolen.
Ken had his wife Thelma slip $5 in his pocket.

I have never known a competitor like him. We played
some tennis doubles together after the war. His wife
reported that after a loss in a tennis tournament, Ken
waited 24 hours before calmly leaning his racket up
against his car and breaking it in two with his foot out of
frustration.

In a game at Lincoln of Tacoma during the 1943-44
season I was sandwiched between two opposing players
with three or four minutes to go in a close game. When I
got up off the floor I saw one of my front teeth embedded
in the blond crewcut of one of the Lincoln players. I also
had a gash over my left eye. When I walked over to our
bench for commiseration, if not immediate hospitalization,
Ken suggested, "We aren't out of the woods yet. We'll
take care of the injuries after the game." He did.

It is said some people strengthen the society just by
being the kind of people they are. Ken Wills was that
kind. The secret of Ken's success in coaching was his own
example — an exceptional example.

Now we skip beyond the prescribed time boundaries of this
book to November of 1962, when Ken Wills went downtown to the

Sports Shop on Pacific Avenue, bought a pistol, went home to his garage, and shot himself dead.

In a letter to a friend several days later, Joe Stottlebower noted the funeral was held in the gym of one of BHS's successors, West High.

> Four to five hundred people were there. Fronted by wreathes of flowers and the casket, a platform was placed on the locker-room end with folding chairs placed on the floor. West's choir flanked the platform from the left bleachers — clusters of people filled the remaining bleacher space. The Rev. Wilbur Scafe made some introductory remarks. Bob Bryan solemnly praised the man: "Integrity," "teacher," "perfectionist...prepared more young men better for college basketball and life than anyone else." Scafe then briefly mentioned how Ken knew poverty when growing up in Walla Walla, giving all his earnings from farm labor to his mother. Louie Soriano and Les Eathorne were among the pallbearers....Scafe made vague inferences regarding the circumstances of the death — "mental and physical disease." I didn't look at the casket, preferring to think of Ken's jaunty walk with keys in his hand, impatience with phoniness, nervous laugh, flabbergasting determination, intense honesty and loyalty: A gentleman.

Some of his former players felt betrayed. Duane Thompson said, "He let us down." Thompson also wrote, "His suicide...was inexplicable and still hurts." Bob Romberg was angry at the public spectacle of the funeral. "It was bizarre," he said. In the 1986 interview with the *Sun*, Roger Wiley was quoted as saying, "It completely destroyed me when I found out about it. He wasn't a Christian — he was an atheist if anything —but he was a great moralist. He would get articles out of the paper and post them on the board and say this is wrong. I remember he clipped one article out about a man who had committed suicide and he said, 'This is the coward's way out.' That's a paradox I found very difficult to cope with, but I still have to say he was a great man."

I was living on the East Coast in 1962 and did not hear of the death until much later. I was shocked, and pondered it often. I wrote a column about him for the *Journal-American* in 1986. It said in part:

> So those of us who idolized Wills puzzle over the paradox of his suicide. Was there a mundane answer? He

was leaving Bremerton High to become coach at Olympic College and some say he couldn't face up to the change.

That doesn't sound right to me. I want and perhaps need to find greater meaning in his decision.

Could he have known that hundreds of his admirers would speculate and reflect over his suicide a quarter of a century later? Was he trying to tell us, with Camus, that suicide is the only moral question of consequence?

Or was he telling us only that he was human, with the same exaltation, the same depression, as others? That he was merely mortal?

I of course do not know the answers to those questions. But intentionally or not, Ken Wills is still teaching and coaching, forcing us to ask tough questions, long after his death.

Fred Sunday and Shirley Sinclair.
(Photo courtesy Shirley Sinclair.)

- **Chapter 21**

(Headlines from the Bremerton Sun of 1945)

**Local Cafes Must Roll Back Pay of Cooks, Waitresses . .
Jap Naval Anchorage Captured . . . New President Holds
White House Confabs; . . . Byrnes Offers Help . . . Yank
Entry into Berlin Near . . . All Meats But Mutton Placed on
Red Points . . . Sun Purchases News-Searchlight . . .
Hitler Killed in Berlin . . .
Peedle Weezer Tavern Razed; Loss $22,000 . . .**

We Weep for Those Who Never Came Home

In most periods of our lives, a year or two difference in age means little. Not so during the teen years. High school freshmen, for example, are much different from seniors; seniors are on-the-verge adults and freshmen are only-yesterday children.

They may tread the same halls and attend the same games but they live in different worlds. For young males during World War II, the difference of a year or two or three in age was particularly profound. The difference could mean prolonged and hazardous war duty or continuation of comfortable civilian life.

Starting in early 1943, draft age was 18. The services would accept volunteers at 17 and many of that age did enlist, usually for special programs that provided education or assured assignment to specific branches, such as the Air Corps or Marines. (At first, all marines were volunteers. Later, draftees were assigned to the Marine Corps, too). As a rule, then, males who turned 18 in 1945 did not see combat; those who became 18 in 1944 might; and those who turned 18 in 1943 or earlier were at substantial risk.

Younger soldiers and sailors are usually best. They do not fully realize they are mortal. They are more willing to take risks, to get caught up in the esprit of a unit, to believe in the righteousness of their cause, to possess greater physical strength and stamina. Older soldiers are more thoughtful, a bad trait in combat. They have sniffed at the possibility they may not survive. They are more likely to have wives and children and a white-picket-fence home to which they yearn to return. This truism holds for marines, too, who were engaged in some of the bloodiest battles of the war.

When the Germans swept through Western Europe and the rest of the world finally realized in 1940 how serious was the threat of tyranny, the U.S. Army was 227,000 men, ludicrously small for a major nation. In the fall of 1940, the United States Congress passed its first peacetime draft. All males from 21 to 35 were required to register. Some 6,500 draft boards of unpaid volunteers sent out notices that started: "Greetings: Your friends and neighbors . . ." A lottery established the order in which men were called up, but many were deferred because of defense jobs or because they were married. Much later, married men were drafted and still later the Army took married men who had children.

Training of men drafted in 1940 was awful. They had no rifles, tanks, artillery pieces, no recreational facilities, and were paid only $21 per month. Morale was terrible, too. The acronym OHIO stood for Over the Hill in October, which is where the draftees promised they would go if their one-year terms were extended. But in August of 1941, the draft was indeed extended for 18 months, slipping through the House by a single vote, 203-202. By then, some of the training problems had been resolved and General George Marshall's contention that it was normal for soldiers to gripe turned out to be correct; hardly any deserted. In truth, for many draftees, the peacetime Army was better than civilian life. They were fed 5,000 calories per day and gained an average nine pounds during their first nine weeks of service. Teeth were fixed, eye glasses provided, literacy improved. Although $21 wasn't much, cigarettes cost only 5 cents per pack. For some, it was more disposable income than they had ever had.

The ironic old joke that in time of war the Army is no place for a professional soldier turned out to be true for draftees, too. Soon after the attack on Pearl Harbor, many men drafted in 1940 and 1941 ended up fighting desperate battles in the South Pacific. Many did not survive. The early draftees were soon joined by millions of other men, both those who volunteered (they did so by the thousands after Pearl Harbor) and those who were drafted. The Army accepted volunteers aged 18 to 36; older men could enlist if they had previous service.

A quick detour for some esoterica: Those who volunteered for the Army could be identified by their serial numbers, which are an essential part of a soldiers' identity, as much a part of them as their names. Goldbrickers, who held you should never volunteer for anything, liked to scoff at those who had enlisted. But many volunteers felt patriotic and secretly proud that their serial number started with the digit "1" (for draftees it was "3.") The second digit in serial numbers represented the Army district from which the soldier enrolled. Thus the serial number of a volunteer from Bremerton would start "19;" of a draftee, "39." My serial number was 19193634. It is chiseled so firmly upon my brain that it may be the last thing I'm able to remember. Ask any Army vet of WWII his serial number and he will rattle it off. But for reasons I don't understand, don't ask me my serial number in the Korean War. I do not remember it. Social Security numbers are becoming the civilian equivalent of military serial numbers.

The Marine Corps took volunteers from 17 to 30; married men were not accepted. The Navy accepted older men, some even 50, but those over 36 had to have special skills to sign up. By the end of the war, said the book *Let the Good Times Roll*[1], 17,955,000 men had been examined for the draft. About 40 percent were rejected, totaling 6,420,000, a sad commentary on the physical and mental health of the nation. The draft was not always uniform in who was selected. In towns such as Seattle and Bremerton, many men were deferred because of war-connected jobs. That shrank the pool of eligible men and meant married men in those cities were drafted starting in February of 1943 and by the end of the year fathers were being drafted in those communities, too. In most other communities, the call for those categories came later.

In some ways, going into the service was like betting on roulette: The individual had little control. Take Bert Brown, for example. He entered the Army on April 2, 1945, and almost immediately was sent to Fort Riley, Kansas, to train with the last troop of horse cavalry in the history of the United States Army. "I had never been aboard a horse and was terrified," Brown wrote. Fortunately, he caught pneumonia and almost immediately was released from the Army. Tongue in cheek, he likes to tell of his military career this way: "I was drafted on April 2. Ten days later FDR heard about it, had a stroke and died. I was discharged on May 4. Somehow, the Germans heard about *that* and, realizing the game was up, surrendered."

Sometimes the transition from civilian to soldier occurred overnight. When Allied troops invaded Europe on D-Day, June 6, 1944, I was already in Moscow. Not *the* Moscow, but the Moscow

---

[1] Casdorph, Paul D. *Let the Good Times Roll.* New York: Paragon Press. 1989.

where the University of Idaho is situated. I was a member of the ASTRP, the Army Specialized Training Reserve Program, set up for 17-year-old student-soldiers who moved from high school to college without benefit of graduation from high school or basic training from the Army. One day we wore civilian clothes, the next day Army khaki. There was no sergeant to tell us how the uniform was supposed to be worn; we just pulled it on without regard for insignia or regulations. We looked it. The regular ASTP GIs were not reservists, as we 17 year olds were; they had taken basic training and were chosen for college education from the ranks.

One of our number in the ASTRP at the University of Idaho had been in the Civilian Air Patrol. On the dubious assumption he knew something about military protocol, he was named cadet sergeant. He marched us to class and, to the embarrassment of our civilian professors, called us to attention when they entered the classroom. I had been away from home alone only once before in my life and was dreadfully homesick. So, I think, were others.

Jim Taylor was in the ASTP at Indiana University studying engineering. "ASTP had the best system to pour a lot of knowledge in our empty heads. A section was just class size — about 20 men. We marched from class to class. No free time. After evening mess we reported to study hall and hit the books till lights out at 10 p.m. No letter writing or personal business. The rule was study only. I thoroughly enjoyed the duty at the university. The coeds were lined up Saturday nights rarin' to dance with their favorite Cadet." There was no doubt in Jim's mind who that would be.

But in 1944 the Army needed ground troops and Jim and many others were reassigned, he to the 20th Armored Division at Camp Campbell, Kentucky, and then to combat in Europe. "The things we did, the things I did, are unbelievable. What an experience. The division was a late starter but once on line (in combat) we did a great job. We gained ground every day despite heavy resistance. We'd take our losses and go at 'em again the next day. My battalion was awarded a distinguished unit badge for good work. When the war ended the 20th Tank Battalion was in Mondsee, Austria. We were waiting on the Russians. I was all over that Europe to get there. France, Belgium, Holland, Germany, Austria and Czechoslovakia."

Jim Braman studied civil engineering at West Virginia University as part of the ASTP. "This program (ASTP) over-all had negative national effects. It was founded as a means of keeping scientific and engineering talent in the educational pipeline to assure rapid post-war development of the U.S. However, the need for military manpower early in 1944 became so acute that the program was abruptly disbanded and almost all enrollees were shipped overseas as replacements in infantry and combat engineer units. This type of service inevitably resulted in high casualties, with exactly the opposite end result as anticipated, namely the loss forever of top engineering and science students."

Jim, however, went to officer candidate school and was commissioned a second lieutenant. He went overseas to Hollandia, New Guinea, in the Transportation Corps, eventually ending up in Manila. He was discharged as a captain in 1946.

To illustrate how profoundly the war affected many families: In 1944, only my mother of the six-member Wetzel family was left at home. Dad was in Illinois and then New York, recruiting workers for the Navy Yard. Older brother Scott was in the Coast Guard, overseeing the loading of ammunition in Houston. Sister Edith was in North Carolina with her husband, a Marine major. Brother Barrett was learning instrument maintenance for the Army Air Force at Chanute Field in Illinois. I was at Moscow. Still, our house on Gregory Way was brimming, not with our own family but with wives and their husbands from ships being repaired in the Navy Yard.

As soon as we in the ASTRP turned 18 we were called to active duty. A dozen of us were called up in July of 1944 and reported together to Fort Lewis. By then we knew something about the Army, including how to march, and we dazzled the other recruits with our skill at close-order drill. Is there a joy equal to possession of a skill that permits you to show off?

We were assigned to the Army Air Corps and took basic training at Buckley Field near Denver. The commanding officer at Buckley was absolutely wacko about singing. Everywhere the training companies went they sang: *Off we go, into the wild blue yonder...* and *Around* (pause) *her neck* (pause) *she wears a yellow ribbon* ...(pause) *she wears it for her sweetheart who is far, far away...* and *Wait* (pause) *till* (pause) *the sun shines, Nelly...* The poor training cadre, forced to hear the singing month after month, must surely have been driven daft.

When Xie Olanie, training at Camp Swift, Texas, with the 10th Mountain Division, heard I had been assigned to the Air Corps, he wrote, "From the flying bedpan to a fly boy — when are you going to join up?" His reference to a flying bedpan was to the patch, or shoulder insignia, worn by student-soldiers, the lamp of knowledge with wings attached. Infantrymen such as Xie looked down on less risky, less rigorous branches of the service.

Author Wetzel in Passau, Germany, on the Danube.

After six weeks of training we scattered, I to nearby Lowry Field for gunnery training. Mom entered in her diary a typical mother's reaction: "Frank's news that he is to be an aerial gunner scares me silly." She needn't have worried, for after bluffing my way successfully through one test, my color blindness was detected. I was shipped off to the Troop Carrier Command at Sedalia, Missouri, a soft billet. I was settling in nicely when the Battle of the Bulge in December of 1944 created another hurried demand for infantrymen. Mother's diary said, "Got a very disturbing letter from Frank, who is now at Camp Gordon, Georgia. Fifty thousand boys were taken from the Air Corps and put in the infantry and he was one of them. It makes me feel pretty sick." The six weeks of training at Camp Gordon were well organized but too short. Although I had never fired a gun or even held a real one until I went into the Army, I shot 192 of a possible 210 with the M-1 Garand rifle, third in my company. I'm still proud of that. Then I was off to Europe as a replacement, which meant that I would be assigned to whatever infantry division needed men.

When I caught up with my unit, the 304th Infantry of the 76th Division, on the Rhine River in March of 1945, the war was almost over. Joining a a combat unit as a replacement was like joining a football team in the fourth quarter; you knew neither the plays nor the players. Some replacements were killed before anyone but the company clerk knew their names. To this 18-year-old replacement whose boots were still new and his uniform clean, the men of Company F were grizzled veterans who commanded respect. Many had grown handlebar mustaches. They hadn't bathed or shaved in days, nor had they slept recently in a bed or with their shoes off. But they accepted me for bringing the unit back to prescribed strength and as someone with whom to share tasks and risks. In a day or two I became part of the unit. It was a treat to find a way to heat a can of spaghetti and meatballs from our C rations instead of eating it cold. Almost everyone smoked, and tiny packs of cigarettes came in our rations. So did toilet paper, which we kept inside our helmet liners. The old-timers loved to supplement their Army diet with eggs, which some learned to scrounge from the countryside with such success that they became beloved by their comrades. They were, in short, tired and dirty, and often frightened. They looked like Willie and Joe, cartoonist Bill Maudlin's doleful dogfaces, the affectionate slang for infantrymen. Before long I guess I looked like them, too, although I was never successful in growing whiskers.

Forty years later, on May 8, 1985, the anniversary of V-E day, I wrote this column for the *Journal-American* in Bellevue:

> It was no longer a war but a rout. Across Germany we raced, moving as fast as the supply of gasoline permitted, through towns and villages whose buildings flew the new national symbol: The white flag of surrender.
>
> Resistance did not crumble simultaneously. Sometimes the Third Army's Company F, 304th Infantry, for which I speak, plodding in battle formation across recently plowed farmland, was sent scrambling into the nearest ditch by the sharp crack of bullets passing overhead.
>
> One morning a single Luftwaffe fighter plane came skimming over the highway. I watched with surprise and admiration as my squad sergeant emptied his M-1 rifle at the airplane while we huddled in the ditch. Some in our squad imagined they saw smoke from the plane as it disappeared over the next hill, but we heard no crash, saw no billowing flames.
>
> When there was resistance from a town, we went from house to house, rifles at the ready, searching for German soldiers who usually had disappeared by the time we got there. Sometimes when the town had been secured, a few German soldiers would return to town, hands folded behind their heads in surrender, the heels of their boots smacking against the cobblestones.
>
> Usually they were old men (younger than I am now, but old men for soldiers; they looked to be 55 or 60) or young boys (younger than I was then, which was 18).
>
> They were frightened, of course, and sometimes with good reason. Our platoon leader, a lieutenant, slapped a young boy in uniform hard across the face because the youth would not tell us where was the remainder of his

unit. Most likely he could not understand the lieutenant's bad German.

I heard stories of others who met worse treatment but I never saw it.

If resistance continued, tanks would roll into position and pound a few rounds into a house or barn suspected of hiding snipers. Sometimes the building burned, destroying everything inside. Later we would see the owners poking disconsolately in the rubble.

But those whose houses and belongings escaped unscathed seemed relieved as the tide of advancing American troops overtook them. They knew, after six years of increasingly desperate war, that they had survived. They were afraid of us, of course, but grateful that they had survived.

As April progressed, even the sporadic resistance dwindled. Now, more often than by straggling soldiers we were met by grinning, cheering, waving throngs. They were displaced persons, DPs — Slavs or Italians or Poles who had been brought to Germany as forced laborers. From them we learned on April 15, the day I turned 19, that FDR had died three days earlier.

When April turned to May, the 304th Infantry was halted near Dresden. Other units were making contact with the troops of the Soviet Union; the convergence of two of the most powerful armies ever assembled was not achieved without concern that we would mistakenly undertake to destroy each other. So we hunkered down and waited. Forty years ago, on either May 6 or May 7 (it was hard to keep track of the exact date), we learned that the war was ending.

That night we had hot showers and a big party, celebrating with liberated wine. I don't remember much about the occasion — whether because of the wine or the passage of time I do not know. I do remember someone from another platoon yanking a towel off my neck and making fighting gestures but I side-slipped the confrontation by assuring him that I was a lover, not a fighter.

One day my best friend, Hugo Gooderum, and I, standing guard near a river, ducked into a nearby gasthaus for a cold beer. It was our luck that while inside, a Russian came wheeling past in an American-made jeep, heading for our lines.

So far as I know, it was the only contact made by our unit with the Soviets. Of course there was an investigation; how had the Russian managed to get past the American outpost?

Hugo and I were caught flat-footed. In addition to a royal chewing, during which we were told we were lucky not to be court-martialed, we spent the night scrubbing the floor of our billet.

It was that night, doing penance by scrubbing a *German* floor, for God's sake, that I realized the war had really ended.

Ten years later after writing that column, I sent a copy to Hugo Gooderum, newly found in Cathedral City, California. It was a lesson in the selectivity of memory: He said he remembered neither the Russian nor scrubbing the floor. "I remember sitting in the pub next to the bridge we were guarding," Hugo wrote. "I remember going to a nearby house and we took turns firing at dinner plates thrown up in the air. We were practicing firing at moving targets from the middle of the bridge. From this same bridge we also shot at people (size of ants) in the distance going over another bridge not guarded."

Well, I too remember firing in the air over the heads of the people on the other bridge, but I don't remember the plates.

Hugo, a lead scout who earlier had won the Silver Star for bravery, also said, "I remember the fighter plane incident differently but very clearly because I saw all the machine-gun bullets pepper the ground a couple of feet from where I lay in the very shallow and unprotective ditch. On the first pass I got no shot because I faced him. On the second pass I had my face in the direction of his flight so I was one of many who shot at him lying down. As he made a turn to make a third pass at us I saw a trail of smoke which later turned into a sudden puff. He then bailed out and we saw the parachute and the ME 109 dive into the ground. We discussed going after the pilot but decided not to as he was no longer dangerous and our mission was ahead of us on the road."

So there you are. Let the differences in memory be a lesson to all who read histories. Except this one, of course.

The war experiences of my childhood friend, Joe Stottlebower, were remarkably similar to mine. He also was a member of the ASTRP and when he went on active duty was assigned to the infantry. For this memoir he wrote:

Following basic training at Camp (now Fort) Hood, Texas, I joined the 42nd Infantry Rainbow Division as a replacement rifleman in northern Alsace in the middle of

January, 1945. The division was in reserve, reeling from 50 percent casualties suffered in bitter battles around Strasbourg.

The unit returned to the front lines February 14 in the Hardt Mountains and launched an offensive March 15 that took the division from Strasbourg through Wurzburg, Schweinfurt, Nuremberg, Dachau, to Munich and V-E Day.

Some memories:
- The loudest noise I have ever heard before or since was in France in January, 1945. A bomber filled with bombs headed for Germany collided directly overhead with another bomber returning from its bombing run.
- I discovered life is not a matter of good or bad choices, but began regarding every alternative as a trade-off in which some pluses must be given up, and some minuses tolerated. Replacements in my company were assigned the task of hiking back in mountainous terrain to pick up heavy boxes of rations and tote them back up to the front line. When the unit attacked, the veterans who had remained in the foxholes had difficulty keeping up. We replacements didn't.
- I was the most scared 24 hours after an incident. I discovered a hole in a container of canned heat I had in my backpack. Slowly I realized that a bullet from a machine gun that had suddenly opened up on my platoon the day before had entered the pack as I had dived for the ground. Shaken, I sat down on a rock, wondering at my close call.
- One of the most devastating condemnations of war I found was in the beautiful resort town of Bad Gastein in the Alps of Austria in the summer of 1945. It was used as the amputee

Joe Stottlebower of the Rainbow Division.
(Photo courtesy Joe Stottlebower.)

center for the German army, and hundreds and hundreds of men missing from one to four limbs crowded the town.

Joe also mentioned being so fatigued that even while marching he had to fight to stay awake . . . Being envious of tank-destroyer crews because instead of eating cold food they could heat their rations on the exhaust pipes of their vehicles. How heavy the bazooka rounds and the Browning automatic rifle were, and how friends in his squad traded off lugging them. . . A single bullet from a sniper that wounded three men in his platoon. . . Reading in the '50s that Maj. Gen. "Hollywood Harry" Collins, commanding general of the 42nd Division, was severely reprimanded for maintaining a paintbrush platoon to paint rainbows on architectural treasures of the Middle Ages that were in the path of the division. . .

Another dear friend, Don Haskell, had joined the Army Air Corps and took his basic training at Buckley Field. He was soon transferred and went to Europe with the 56th Armored Engineers Battalion of the 11th Armored Division. The division went into action near the Ardennes at Christmas in the Battle of the Bulge. Hack (the nickname came from his last name, obviously, but probably stuck because long ago it was slang for smooching) was hit in the left hip by fragments from a mortar shell on January 13 or 14, 1945. He was evacuated to a hospital near Nancy in France. My mother's diary for February 4 says, "The Haskells had a wire saying Hack was seriously wounded. We are so sorry for them." But better news the next day: "Alice Haskell phoned that she had a letter from Don and he is not as badly hurt as they at first suspected. He was able to write and said the shrapnel had not broken any bones or hit any vital organs. We are so happy." Hack recovered with the speed of youth and soon returned to his unit. After the war we often met in Bavaria; he was a T/5, or technician fifth grade, the equivalent of corporal, and had access to a Jeep, which made it simple for him to visit me at a former stalag in Moosburg, where I was assigned to an intelligence unit processing small-fry Nazis.

Jack Bender, who was drafted within 10 days of his high school graduation in 1943, was a radio operator with the 67th Armored Infantry Battalion of the 13th Armored Division in Europe. One day his company commander told Jack he should report to the battalion commander immediately, an order guaranteed to put fear in the heart of any private first class. Instead of chewing out Bender, the battalion commander said, "I don't know what you've been up to, but you've been ordered to West Point."

Jack, slightly dazed, asked, "Do I have any choice?"

The battalion commander answered, "Number one, you can either accept, or number two, stay and be the dumbest son of a bitch in the United States Army."

Jack accepted — and a couple of wars later became a battalion commander and full colonel himself.

In early August of 1943, Duane Thompson, Frank Pease, Jack Honodel, Max Carter, and Denton DeLong joined the Seabees, the Navy's Construction Battalion. They all served in the Pacific, although not in the same unit. Of his experience Duane wrote:

> We shipped out to the Pacific in 1944 and worked at Oahu, Tinian in the Marinas Islands, and on to Okinawa near the Japanese homeland. We touched history a bit in that the 9th Seabees helped build North Field on Tinian, from which the B-29 Enola Gay flew to atomic bomb the Japs into final surrender in August, 1945. As one of many who would have participated in the November 1, 1945, invasion, I gave thanks to Harry Truman for that decision — and a firmly extended middle finger to the apologists who knew not of whereof they speak.
>
> Being overseas and working hard in a non-military environment was not bad duty, in that Seabees were only occasionally in combat. I learned, again, that construction work is hard and dangerous, and that I ought to get a college education if possible. (I sustained a fractured pelvis in a construction accident in Tinian).
>
> I was flown back to Honolulu and spent three months on my back. Later I attended baseball games featuring pro stars, and was reunited with Kenny Larson and Wayne McNeil (both from Bremerton), both serving in the Army.
>
> I then finessed myself 6,000 miles back across the Pacific to rejoin my outfit in Okinawa, an odyssey of which I'm very proud . . . After six sweltering weeks aboard a Navy transport I reached Okinawa and went ashore I knew not where, to be greeted by an air raid. I roamed around for a few days, eating and sleeping where I could, and finally found the 9th above Buckner Bay. It was great to be back!
>
> Little did I know we were scheduled to be in the November 1, 1945, invasion of Kyushu — the southernmost of the Japanese home islands, nor that we would be bat-

tered by 130 mph winds in a great typhoon that killed many.

Years later, we received a unit presidential commendation for fast work on waterfront projects at Buckner Bay (intended to aid the invasion of Kyushu, but actually used in getting GI's home).

After Wes Wager graduated from high school in 1941, he worked for a year at Sexton Auto Freight, saving money for college. He attended Washington State College for one semester, then volunteered for the Army Air Corps. Although he wanted to fly the hot B-25s, instead he was assigned to B-24s as co-pilot. He flew to Italy in 1944 via the Azores and Marrakesh in Morocco.

Wes didn't go on his crew's first mission, a checkout flight. Their second mission was to bomb oil refineries in Germany. Over the target their plane was hit by flak and lost fuel from its wing tanks. They didn't have enough fuel to get back to Italy so looked for alternatives. The nearest possible haven was Yugoslavia. Perfect navigation under difficult circumstances put them over Croatia, where they all bailed out. Within two days, all from the plane were reunited. They spent two months with Tito's partisans and eventually connected with the Soviets, who at first were suspicious but eventually helped them get from Budapest to Bucharest, where they were picked up and flown to Italy by U.S. planes. Everyone aboard Wes's plane survived, although he contracted yellow jaundice from the terrible sanitary conditions.

On February 15, 1945 the *Sun* reported:

> Missing in action over Yugoslavia since Nov. 20, Lt. Wes Wager is safe and has returned to his bomber base in Italy. This was the first definite confirmation they (his parents) had of his safety although they had received unofficial word in a letter a Bremerton soldier, Mack Adams, had written to his parents. Young Adams wrote that he had seen Lt. Wager at an Italian hospital and that they had also talked with Bill Mahan, another Bremerton boy. Mrs. Adams, unaware that Lt. Wager was missing in action, called Mrs. Wager to inform her of the two boyhood chums' meeting and was quite surprised to discover he was reported missing. Mrs. Wager was almost overcome with joy when she heard the news that her son was safe.

The reason for the delay in notifying the parents isn't clear but may have been connected with debriefing of the crew by Air Force authorities.

Military personnel learn to live with fear or they don't survive. Fear isn't limited to the explosive moments of combat — Winston Churchill said there is nothing quite so exhilarating as being shot at, and missed — but includes quiet times when death may be present but unseen. Harry Harkness describes such a moment:

> Heard about FDR's death while sitting in the cockpit of our B-17 Flying Fortress. I had the plane guard duty that night before. This was in Italy and we were very fearful of sabotage. To me, flying a mission over enemy territory and getting shot at was less scary than plane guard. Maybe it was because you were all alone. This was a huge field out of Foggia, and the planes were parked about 200 yards apart. We were delivered out by truck and picked up the next morning. As it grew dark I saw this shepherd with his flock right near the hardstand and he looked just like Adolph Hitler. I swear. It grew darker and darker and I would sneak looks at this dude out the tail gunner's window. He didn't move and neither did the 50 or so sheep. Kept staring right at the plane. I finally managed to get some sleep but I was sure I was to be blown to bits sometime soon . . .

To digress for an instant, almost as important to servicemen as rations and sleep was the mail. Mail call, when letters were distributed, was the highlight of the day in training camps. When letters made their way to front-line units, morale soared. Soldiers overseas sent some of their letters home on V-Mail, one-page forms on which messages were written, then photographed en masse. The film reduced the bulk and eased transport. Mail from overseas was censored; sometimes lazy GIs would cut big holes in their stationery, pretending the censor had excised portions of their letter. Servicemen also had franking privileges; that is, by writing "free" on the upper right corner of envelopes they avoided postage. Many servicemen spent much of their free time writing letters and so did their girl friends and families.

Slang found in a few letters from my friends (I have kept stacks) includes "potent quotient," for big share; "strictly solid" for all right, OK, yes, indeed. "Smooth" was the equivalent of today's "cool" and was said by my gang almost as often. "Woo-woo" was what a movie comedian whose name I forget but probably was Hugh Herbert said in a popular flick of the time, and is distinguished from "pitching woo," which was necking. Letters were often coded "SWAK," which meant "sealed with a kiss." No doubt there were other coded acronyms too steamy to list here.

Sadly too many from Kitsap County were casualties to mention in detail. But for those unable to speak for themselves, here are a selected few other stories from the last months of the war:

Francis Ahearn was graduated from BHS in 1942. He was a member of the Honor Society, president of the History Council, president of the Photography Club, active in the Radio and Hiking clubs. He was an apprentice machinist in the Navy Yard until he was called into the Army in September of 1943. He went overseas with the 80th Division and took part in the invasion of France on D-Day.

On December 14, 1944, the *Sun* quoted a letter written the previous month to his parents:

> We've been making some big gains under Patton towards Germany, and weather conditions couldn't have been worse. I honestly thought it would be impossible to endure the hardships we had to take and people back home think things are going nice and easy . . . What I've been doing the last few months has been with machine guns. Yes, I know it was dangerous. Twice I was the only member to come out of small campaigns. I'm called instrument corporal and I do everything from searching newly occupied towns for quarters and Heinie equipment to stringing communications. Recently I was fortunate enough to be able to help a bunch of badly wounded fellows with a sergeant from my platoon. Conditions were a little rough and we almost got the Silver Star for it but it fell through. I'm glad it did for I wouldn't feel right to get decorated for doing a simple job that you would expect someone to do for you if you were wounded. We moved into a town amid sniper fire and finally settled in a nice house. In the ensuing two days I scoured the town for equipment of which I really found a lot, and by then the town was reported pretty clear of Germans. Anyway they said it was a complete cleanup. I came upon a very dark corridor that led into a wine cellar. I was bulging all over with booty, and I sure got mad when the straw started rustling and I couldn't see because the light was at my back. I then started cursing out loud and I guess I scared the daylights out of the two armed Heinies that were there. Anyway, they started yelling 'Kamerad' and we headed them off down the streets. I think the platoon

appreciates my talents for finding stuff now for I found them about 50 gallons of wine in all sorts of jugs and bottles and about 20 gallons of good cognac. I found even a bunch of canned goods from all over the world including some salmon and shrimp."

The occasion for the article in the *Sun* was to say that Cpl. Francis Ahearn had been missing in action since November 24. A few weeks later, he was declared killed in action.

On December 8, 1944, this article appeared in the *Sun*:

Pvt. Francis Berg, 21, has only one leg now and the Army hasn't any further use for him. He'll soon be fitted with an artificial leg and sent back to civilian life. A native Bremertonian...he lost his leg at Anzio. "That was a helluva place. We couldn't keep out of the range of the German guns, and they were pounding us to pieces. One day a few of us at the front ran square into a German Tiger tank. With three other fellows, I was trying to draw the tank's fire while some of our buddies were outflanking it. They wanted to open up with their bazookas from the side. We drew the tank's fire, all right. The first blast from the big 88mm cannon clipped off my leg, just like that (as he snapped his fingers). Then it ricocheted off the wall of a building, killed a close friend of mine and put some slugs in the other fellows." They got the tank.

On February 10, 1945, this article appeared in the *Sun:*

Fred L. Sunday is missing in action as a member of the crew of the U.S. submarine *Tang*, which is overdue and presumed lost. His parents were notified of the young sailor's fate last Nov. 26 but as instructed by the Navy Department kept silent until announcement of the Tang's loss was made this week. A native of Bremerton, he was born Dec. 19, 1924, and was educated in local schools. He enlisted in the Navy when he was 17 in August of 1942 and received training at San Diego, Purdue University and the submarine base at New London, Connecticut. He hadn't been home since he left home. His father, a 27-year Navy Yard shipfitter, is now employed at the Winslow yard on Bainbridge. Young Sunday has two brothers.

On February 13, 1945, this article appeared in the *Sun:*

Lt. Richard L. (Red) Alderman is dead, his wife has been told. The pilot of a P-47 Thunderbolt fighter plane, Lt. Alderman had been reported missing early in December after he failed to return from a mission Nov. 17. Word of his death was received from the German government through the International Red Cross. He was flying "Baby Lynn," his new Thunderbolt named after his first daughter, Lynn Sharon, 16 months old when he went down. A few days later his second daughter, Cedilia Ann, whose name he chose by mail to his wife, was born. The popular Bremerton athlete didn't know on that November day when he went out over Nazi-land that he had been promoted to first lieutenant in recognition for his valor, leadership and efficiency.

He was a graduate of Bremerton High School in 1940 and played football and baseball. He coached the "B" grid team and was a mainstay in the backfield of the semi-pro Red Raiders of the Northwest League.

A letter received by his widow from Lt. Aanenson said, "I was on the same mission from which he did not return. For security reasons I can tell you only that it was one of our roughest missions flown during very bad weather through intense flak. The last any of us heard from Dick was when he called in saying he was just going into his dive-bombing run. No one saw him go down and no one heard any message from him after that. He was leading an element at the time, but his wingman is also listed as "missing." I was the last one to leave the target area and just as I set my course for home, I tried to contact Dick on my radio. I received no answer."

On March 10, 1945, this article appeared in the *Sun:*

Jack Campbell was killed in Italy on Feb. 21. He was the son of Mr. and Mrs. Rudy B. Campbell, and had been serving as a ski trooper with the famous 10th Mountain Division, which has been leading the attack of the 5th Army in the Apennines mountains in Italy. He was born and raised in Bremerton and graduated from BHS in 1943. He was a member of the Christian Church, DeMolay, and an Eagle Scout in Troop 504. An ardent skier, he enlisted in the infantry in August of 1943 and was attached to the 10th Mountain Division. He is also survived by a younger brother, Prestley, 16, a student at BHS. The elder Campbells have been Bremerton residents for 45 years. Mr. Campbell is a supervisor in the planning and estimating section at PSNY and Mrs. Campbell is an engineering draftsman in the design section.

On April 16, 1945, this article appeared in the *Sun*:

Pvt. Wesley Canfield was killed in action on Luzon on March 19. With a field artillery battalion, he met death in his first front-line engagement. His last letter was dated March 14. The 19-year-old youth was born in Bremerton Jan. 19, 1926, and graduated from BHS in 1943 (actually, he graduated in 1944). He was employed by Lent's until he donned the Army khaki nine months ago. He was sent to New Guinea for further training early in December and went to the Philippines last month. He is survived by his parents, Mr. and Mrs. Marcus Canfield, 1802 11th St., and a sister, Mrs. Alice Dent, Bremerton, and brother, Ora, a fireman first class now somewhere in the South Pacific with the Navy.

On April 23, 1945, this article appeared in the *Sun:*

Kent Chollar, a Navy signalman third class, has died in action. He was the son of Mr. and Mrs. Sam Chollar, executive secretary of the Army-Navy YMCA. He lived here for most of his life and graduated from BHS in 1942. He also attended the University of Washington and worked part-time at J.C. Penney Co. here. One of four sons in the service, Kent is survived by three brothers, Lt. Ben Chollar, at sea with the Navy Supply Corps; Capt. Robert Chollar, in the Pacific area with the Army Dental Corps; and seaman second class Sam Chollar, Jr., now training at San Diego. Kent died while serving aboard a destroyer escort in the Central Pacific.

Kent's brother, Sam, said a kamikaze airplane hit the superstructure of Kent's destroyer escort, killing 45 men. After burial on Okinawa, Kent's body was later reinterred in the National Cemetery at San Bruno, California.

On April 26, 1945, this article appeared in the *Sun:*

Parents of Pfc. Donald Hart have been told their son is missing in action. He is the only child of Mr. and Mrs. William Hart. He has been missing in action in Germany since April 8. A combat infantryman, he served in France and Germany with the 7th Army since he was sent overseas the latter part of January. He was born in Portland but came to Bremerton as a small child. He attended local schools, graduating from BHS last January. He was active in Hi-Y. During his last two years in high school, Pfc. Hart worked as a clerk in the main post office. After graduation he was employed there until entering the service Sept. 2, 1944. He trained at Camp Roberts and Fort Meade, Maryland, before going overseas.

A few weeks later, Don was declared killed in action.

On May 31, 1945, this article appeared in the *Sun:*

Mr. and Mrs. C. A. Carlson of Kitsap Lake received a war department telegram last night notifying them that their eldest son, fireman second class John (he was always called Jack) Albert Carlson, 19, USNR, had died at sea. Details of his death would arrive later, the telegram said.

John was stationed on a battleship in the North Pacific. He began Navy service last June and had been at sea since October.

Prominent in club and sports activities at BHS, John was graduated last year. He was a member of the football team for three years and served as captain of the championship intramural basketball team last year. John had been employed at Black Ball Freight Company and a local meat market.

The Carlsons have two other sons — Robert, 17, and Jimmy, 10. John's grandmother, Mrs. Emma E. Carlson, resides at 1502 10th St.

On July 9, 1945, this Page 1 article appeared in the *Sun:*

TRAGEDY STRIKES AGAIN:
LT. "PETE" BURMASTER, FORMER
STUDENT LEADER, KILLED

Wartime tragedy struck another Bremerton family yesterday when Mr. and Mrs. Arnold H. Burmaster were notified of the death of their youngest son, 2nd Lt. Edward (Pete) Burmaster, 21, on Okinawa on May 31.

The telegram from the war department stated that the young infantry officer "died of wounds on Okinawa May 31" and that a letter would follow. He had been overseas only three months and commanded a platoon of rifle troops in the 96th Infantry Division.

One of the most well-known and popular young men of Bremerton, "Pete" had lived here most of his life. He was graduated from Bremerton High School in 1942 and during his four years there was outstanding in scholastic and club activities. He was study body president in his senior year and won top honors in numerous public speaking contests.

After high school graduation, "Pete" attended the University of Washington, were he majored in law. He pledged Phi Delta Theta fraternity . . .

He began his Army service two years ago, serving one year in Panama, where he was promoted to the rank of sergeant. While there he received an appointment to officer candidates school at Fort Benning and an alternate appointment to West Point. He was commissioned a second lieutenant. The Burmasters' other son, 2nd Lt. Arnold (Buzz), 23, is now on a special mission with the Army Quartermaster Corps in the China-Burma-India theater.

This article was in Gene Gurske's scrapbook, probably from the *Seattle Post-Intelligencer:*

PELELIU, Palau Islands, Aug. 5 (AP)-The 10,000-ton cruiser *Indianapolis* was sunk in less than 15 minutes, presumably by a Japanese submarine, 12 minutes past midnight July 30 — and the 883 crew members lost their lives in one of the Navy's worst disasters.

She went down in the Philippines Sea, within 450 miles of Leyte, while on an unescorted high-speed run from San Francisco.

One of the members of the *Indianapolis*'s crew was Eddie Scheib, who must have been only 17, a member of the Class of '45. After the war ended, according to the book *West Is the Rising Sun,* it was learned the *Indianapolis* had been dispatched from Mare Island with parts of the atomic bomb. Hence the ship's mysterious, swift voyage from San Francisco.

Occasionally, dispatches contained happier news, as this one from the *Sun* on May 21:

> Bremerton Families Rejoice over freeing of flier sons. Among those were William (Bill) Onstad, liberated from Stalag Luft No. 4. He had been a radio gunner on a B-17 and had been a prisoner for 15 months. Also Staff Sgt. Frank R. Watson and Staff Sgt. John E. (Jack) Jones were interned at the same camp as Staff Sgt. Ross Calvert, who has also been liberated. Both were imprisoned at Stalag 17-B and were released by the Russians but evidently were soon reunited with the U.S. Army.
> Sgt. Jones was a gunner on a B-17 shot down on April 29, 1944, on his fourth mission. He was hospitalized in Germany as a result of a leg injury before being sent to prison. He is a graduate of BHS at mid-term in 1944 and a member of DeMolay.

The liberated prisoners were the lucky ones. Posted in the Imperial War Museum in London are the words of Lord Macauley: "The essence of war is violence and moderation in war is imbecility." What Lord Macauley failed to say is that war itself is imbecility.

Kitsap County's Roll
of Honored Dead

At the Memorial Day Dedication Services of the Kitsap County Administration Building in Port Orchard on May 30, 1949, Robert A. Yothers, Commander of the Washington Veterans of Foreign Wars dedicated a memorial plaque honoring those killed during WWII with ties to Kitsap County

Alfred Adamson	John A. Carlson	Gordon Fox
Hubert Richard Agin	Alfred M. Carlson	Marcel J. France
Francis L. Ahearn	Jerry Carroll	Martin Franciscovitch
Richard Alderman	William Charles	William Freeman
Paul Edward Almon	Chris Y. Chen	Henry Froyen
Robert S. Anderson	Leslie R. Chilton	James A. Fuller
Trig Anderson	Kent S. Chollar	Nelson N. Gates, Jr.
Carl Arvidson	Floyd E. Christensen	Raymond H. Geist
LeRoy Ashby	Alexander A. Christie	Cecil S. Gerdcon
Earl G. Atkinson	Robert A. Christopher	Hugh E. Gillette
Samuel P. Bakshas	C. H. Cleaver	Clarence Gjersvold
Walter C. Baldwin	Lewis E. Clough	Halbert E. Gorman
Henry E. Ballard	Roger F. Coffin	William J. Gould
Charles D. Bartling	Maurice H. Cohen	Edward T. Grace
Lewis G. Beck	Willett S. Colegrove	Everett A. Greene
A. Bennett	Frank E. Coleman	Elmer W. Gustafson
Harold Bennett	Sidney P. Comley	John P. Hale
David D. Berg	Donald W. Connelly	Wesley C. Hall
Kenneth Bergstrom	Erwin E. Cooper	Robert E. Hamer
George E. Biggs, Jr.	Patrick Corcoran	Clarence J. Hamilton
Burtle Bjorklund	David W. Crosswhite	Grover S. Hamm
Hugo D. Black	Maurice Crowther	Paul V. Hanson
Richmond Blieffert	Marlene Cummings	Marlet E. Harlow
John T. Blodgett	A. Cunningham	Franklin R. Harris
Joseph Boltan	Paul F. Curdy	James A. Harris
Creed C. Boothe	Neul S. Curtis	Donald W. Hart
Karl Border	Walter J. Czarzasty	James L. Hartsoc
James B. Brandon	Murl Dain, Jr.	William Haslam
James D. Brietenstein	Frank Daman, Jr.	Charles Heath, Jr.
Ernest M. Brenden	Ace H. Dibble	Norman R. Hedrick
Robert Brooks	Elton Dicken	Irvin A. Hegland
Otto L. Brose	William C. Dodge	Jerome Herrigstad
Roy W. Browder	Delmore T. Dudacek	Walter J. Hess
Ralph E. Bryner	Henry O. Ehlers	Roger Hill
Howard M. Bullard	Kenneth N. Eide	William F. Hills
James E. Buskirk	Robert Einer	Keith Hitchcock
Sherwin E. Bumgarner	Howard L. Ellis	Theodore R. Hokenstad
Edward A. Burmaster	Bruce H. Ellison	George Holmquist
Norman Byers	Arthur W. Erickson	Robert Wesley Howard
Elmo D. Calkins	Richard T. Erickson	Joe T. Howell
Arthur C. Campbell	Frank Fenton	Jack C. Hubbard
Clinta Campbell	Robert M. Fiske	Frank Hubbs
Jack R. Campbell	Wesley Finch	Freeman B. Huffsmith
James Campbell	Henry C. Florea, Jr.	Billie Lou Huneke
Wesley M. Canfield	Louis C. Fogg	William I. Imamoto
Carl Richard Caper	Robert E. Forsman	James R. Jacobs

Elmer Jones
Leland L. Johns
Leo O. Johnson
Claude W. Jonoh, Jr.
H. Katzenberger
Ivan C. Kelly
William F. Kiehn
Frederick W. Kinney
Edward E. Kjelness
E. E. Knechtel
Elwin Knudson
William J. Koch
George A. Komedal
James O. Komedal
Chester W. Kreiling
Guy R. Laber
William J. LaCaff
Wilfred T. Lambert
Donald Larson
Vernon L. Larson
Doyle R. Lawrence
Howard LeBeck
Eugene Leggett
Gordon W. Lester
Algea Libby
Albert J. Limpp, Jr.
Albert L. Lloyd
Clyde D. Lowery
Murray Lund
Robert E. Lund
R. E. Lundgren
Estus L. Lynn
Norman M. Mackie
John P. Madsen
Hollis Martin
Terry J. Martin
Glen E. Mason
Merrell Mastick
Stanley A. Mathiason
Ronald J. Mathison
Elvin J. Matt
Clair E. Mattoon
Gordon McBride
Lee McClure, Jr.
Douglas McDonald
Lee McDonald
Michel McGuire
James McPherson
Robert McPherson
R. M. McPherson, Jr.

Robert L. Meusch
Edwin Miles
Harold E. Mitts
Dale C. Moore
Edward L. Moore
Donald G. Musselman
Edwin J. Myers, Jr.
Clyde Nelson
John Nelson
Alfred Ness
Rudolph N. Ness
Walter Niemi
Lincoln G. Nordby
Raymond Norton
Raymond J. O'Connell
Chester D. O'Dell
Elmer Odden
Adrian V. Olness
Arthur H. Olson
Warren R. Olson
Keith V. Otis
Donald C. O'Tyson
Roger B. Paddock
Thomas A. Parsons
William Perkins
Carl V. Person
Chester D. Peterman
George H. Peterson
James C. Peterson
Gerald H. Peoppel
Marley O. Polk
John C. Ravin
Otto V. Rich
Andrew W. Riker
George Riker
Richard Ronnie
Joseph J. Ruskey
Perry O. Russell
Ralph E. Salt
William Sands
Albert E. Scheib
Berl O,. Schmidt
Rueben O. Schnase
Pall B. Schroeder
Edward C. Schultz
Dorman L. Scott
Drexel T. Scott
Walton T. Seed
Clarence J. Setko
James E. Sherwood

William H. Shurts
Phillip G. Silva
Clarence F. Sitko
Elmer A. Slaton
Herman R. Slobey
Hamilton A. Smith
Thomas Smith
Oliver Spencer
J. W. Spriesterbach
Stuart Stanley
Jack E. Starkel
Robert Starevich
Oral L. Stewart
Russell G. Stewart
William G. Stillwell
John Stoddard
Louis Stornnelli, Jr.
Jack Sutherland
Fred L. Sunday
Catho H. Swalling
Charles F. Swanson
Glenn Thompson
Lester O. Thompson
Loren Thorsen
Harold W. Tiedeman
Donald Tivey
James Torpey
Lloyd R. Turk
Laverne E. Twohy
Samuel J. Tyree
Donald Umall
John D. Van Arsdale
Robert Van Klinken
Gordon V. Vestal
Oliver P. Wadley
Herman E. Wagner
Edwin J. Wallen
Warren M. Watson
Arthur M. Weiss
William R. Welch
Eugene B. Wescom
William Whitham
Earl E. Whiting
Harry E. Wilcox
Jack O. Williams
William B. Williams
Henry E. Wilson
Clarence Wolfe

Xie Olanie, Salzburg, Austria, 1945.
(From Frank Wetzel collection.)

Chapter 22

(Headlines from the Bremerton Sun of 1945)

**Surrender Accepted ... Tomorrow is V-E Day ...
Tribute Paid Old Classmates in Solemn HS Rites ...
Jap Balloon Bombs Hit US ... 6,000 More Housing Units
Ready ... BHS Will Graduate Its Largest Class ...
Butter Quota Halved; Meat More Scarce ...
Truman Plays Mozart and Visits Mt. Rainier ... Allies
Weigh Jap Surrender ... NY Sirens Signal End of War
US Begins Occupation Sunday ...**

≈

When Johnny Came Marching Home Again

V-E Day, May 8, 1945, the day observed as the end of the war in Europe, was commemorated with almost professional coolness in Bremerton. Probably the reason was that on the West Coast the primary identified enemy was Japan and a deep sense of foreboding still pervaded the region. The battle for Okinawa then under way was foretelling how bloody the invasion of Japan would be. Kamikaze pilots were taking a terrible toll of U.S. ships and men. The Japanese had employed for the first time a deadly piloted buzz bomb.

The only emotional reaction reported by the *Sun* on V-E Day was a Yard worker toting a lunch bucket. The paper said he had tears in his eyes as he explained that now he felt certain his son was safe somewhere in Europe. The *Sun* also said a sailor let out a yell in a downtown restaurant and cried, "Now we'll get those damned Japs." (But in those upright, uptight times, the *Sun* didn't say "damned"; instead, it said "d— — —")

With the war in the Pacific not yet at its climactic stage, victory seemed only half achieved. Raucous celebrations would have been unseemly. Looking back from the perspective of 50 years, we know that the war with Japan was almost over, too. But there was no way then to realize the war would end not with a whimper but with a bang — the thundering, ominous bang of two atomic bombs, one on Hiroshima and the other on Nagasaki, forever changing warfare and the world. Not having that retrospective knowledge, the United States went ahead with plans for ratcheting America's war machine even higher. On May 10, only two days after V-E Day, headlines in the *Sun* said "1,200 Housing Units Will Rise on West Side; Dorms also planned; Funds Oke-hed." Four days later, the nation's most ambitious war bond drive began; the local quota was $5.4 million and the Elks Lodge was the sponsor. And still the casualty list grew: Kent Chollar, Jack Carlson, Pete Burmaster, and Eddie Scheib, as already noted. On May 18, the Army confirmed that Pat Corcoran had died of dysentery in a Japanese prison camp. On May 31, the *Sun* added the name of Stan Mathiason, that smooth trombone player with the high school jazz band, the Swingsters, on Okinawa. The same edition said that Kenny Larson, who a year before had been playing football for BHS, was wounded while participating in the second infantry wave attacking Okinawa.

So the V-E Day observances in Bremerton were restrained. At the high school, tribute was paid to old classmates. The *Sun* reported:

> For BHS students who have seen their friends and classmates hurried off to war by the hundreds, V-E Day was observed quietly and solemnly with assemblies on both shifts today. A well planned program of music and a timely lecture by Dr. Frank E. Eden paid tribute to the 32 BHS students who have lost their lives in this war and pointed to the big job of beating Japan in the Pacific.
>
> Principal Harry Sorenson said that it was the most attentive audience he has seen at BHS. "These students have been shocked in recent months by the death and injury of many of their classmates, some of whom graduated as late as last year." He said Bremerton's list of 32 war dead started with Lt. Ted Hokenstad, who was killed in a Flying Fortress over North Africa in 1942, and leads up to the recent death in the Philippines of Wesley Canfield, who graduated in 1944.
>
> Specially arranged for the day by the art classes, the stage held a black altar on which was mounted a large white cross. On each side of the cross were table-size flags of the United Nations. On the wall above the cross

were the large block letters, V-E Day. American flags were flown on each side of the altar.

Student body president George Meyer greeted the assemblies with a brief announcement of the significance of the ceremonies and urged the students to recognize and aid the great job that is still to be done.

Dr. Eden, lecturer for the occasion, reviewed the terrific cost which had made V-E Day possible, the loss of 40 million lives, four million in concentration camps. He spoke of the reasons for the sacrifices, citing the values of the Four Freedoms — for religion and speech and from want and fear. Don Thulean sang *Thanks Be To God,* composed by Stanley Dickinson, as the musical portion of the program began. The choir presented *This Is My Country.* A murmur of pleasure and joy went through the crowd as the choir switched to *When Johnny Comes Marching Home.*

In June, the President once again visited Puget Sound — but now, for the first time since 1932, the President wasn't Franklin Delano Roosevelt, the only President many of us could remember. Now it was Harry S Truman.

Harold Engebretson remembers the first reaction at his NROTC unit at the University of Texas when FDR died at Warm Springs, Georgia, on April 12, 1945: "The room fell silent and the first words were spoken by a fellow from Missouri in the unit. He said, 'That son of a bitch Truman is president.' Most of the rest of us didn't know anything about Truman, barely that he was the vice president." Few other Americans knew much about Truman, either. He had been unexpectedly chosen by Roosevelt as his vice president at the Democratic convention in Chicago in 1944. But Truman had built a reputation during the war for ferreting out cost over-runs and war profiteers who turned out shoddy goods. He had visited PSNY on August 27, 1941, with his old friend from the Senate, Mon Wallgren. The two proposed the possibility of a government-owned ferry system, which was operated then by the privately owned Black Ball line, to serve Yard workers living in Seattle. While at the Yard he conferred with Capt. L.F. Kimball, a simply dreadful golfer who before the war nevertheless joined the Royal Foursome at 9 a.m. each Saturday and Sunday on the Navy Yard's golf course and whose caddie often was . . . But I digress.

*The late Bremerton pharmacist and Bremerton native Bob
Brown luckily drove to Gorst to wait for President Harry Truman's
motorcade to pass on June 10, 1948. The President's car stopped
and Brown snapped shots of the President, Bremerton's Mayor
"Hum" Kean and Washington's Governor Mon Wallgren. Brown
hurried to Bremerton where he photographed the throngs waiting to
hear Mr. Truman. It is commonly held that one of those standing
in the street yelled, "Give 'em Hell Harry," which became
Truman's hallmark.*

Truman, it turned out, was a common man with uncommon abilities. With scandalously little help from FDR in preparation, Truman moved into the White House and took some of the most decisive steps of the century. He approved the atomic bombing of Japan, went ahead with formation of the United Nations Organization, led creation of NATO, the North American Treaty Organization. He had also approved the invasion of Japan to start on November 1, 1945. Estimated losses would be one million or more; his awareness of how many lives, both American and Japanese, would be lost in an invasion no doubt made it easier for him to approve use of the atomic bombs.

So the bombs were dropped, first on Hiroshima on August 6, then the coup de grace on Nagasaki on August 9. Under a headline *"ATOMIC POWER SOLVED BY US"* the *Sun* said the super bomb's destructive force equaled 2,000 tons of TNT. "The age of atomic force was ushered in July 17 when a group of renowned scientists and military leaders gathered in New Mexico's desert wastelands to witness the results of their $2 billion experiment. . . Materials for the new atomic bomb are being assembled in a huge super secret government plant near Richland. The workers never knew what they were making. . . " The bomb on Nagasaki wiped out 30 percent of the city.

On August 15, the *Sun* carried this sidebar story:

It didn't take Bremerton folks long to start celebrating the occasion when the official V-J Day announcement was made by President Truman yesterday afternoon.

On three different occasions during the past week other unverified announcements had caused minor outbreaks of revelry. But yesterday when President Truman told of the official end of the war, the entire town erupted with blare and confusion, the like of which hadn't been known in Bremerton history.

The entire Bremerton police force was called out to move traffic jams downtown and watch for possible vandalism. In addition to the 37 police officers, 35 members of Bremerton's state guard unit were called out, and another 35 were on call.

Vandalism was light but the noise, paper-throwing and girl kissing continued at a fast pace on downtown streets throughout most of the night.

Word was all over town shortly after 4 o'clock that the war was over. With swing shift workers going onto their jobs and day shifters leaving with the announcement, Bremerton streets were packed with thousands of the working people who were the first line of the home-front against the Japs.

Almost immediately hundreds of automobile horns began honking. Confetti made from torn newspapers, business forms, scrap paper and everything else available, showered down from office windows. Sidewalks and streets were soon blanketed with paper.

There was barely standing room on Front Street, where Navy and civilian buses filled the area and were unable to move through the milling crowd.

Camera shutters clicked all over town as still and movie photographers caught celebration scenes.

Girls — hundreds of them —were kissing sailors until the men's faces were covered with lipstick.

Three marines were seen carrying a case of beer each — where they got it nobody knew, for taverns had long before locked their doors. Civilians threw bottles of beer to servicemen from a window of a Second Street hotel . . .

By 6 o'clock, streets were vacant — even quieter than normal . . .

The celebration of V-J Day was as exuberant as the observance of V-E Day had been subdued. The *Seattle Post-Intelligencer's* banner headline on August 15 was in white letters three inches high on a red background: JAP NATION SURRENDERS. A makeover later in the night said simply, in white letters five inches high on blue background, PEACE.

An ad in that edition for Best's Apparel said THANK GOD/THE WAR IS OVER/PLEASE GOD/THE TIME OF PEACE AND WISDOM/BEGINS. Another full-page ad, this for the Bon Marche, said only, HALLELUJAH!

A Page 1 story in the *P-I* by one of the paper's ace reporters, Stub Nelson, was headlined, "City Blows Lid/On 2-day Holiday. It started, "There will be no mail deliveries today and tomorrow, courts will be dark, liquor stores and taverns will be shut up tight. Even city parks and beaches are officially shut, in that they will be sans guards . . . Police reported a minimum of vandalism in the first hours of the peace news. Greatest traffic jams were on Third, Fourth and Fifth Avenues between Union and Pine Streets."

In Bremerton, Cathy Anderson was on summer vacation from school and working in the Navy Yard the day the war ended. "All the workers coming in for the swing shift turned around and went home, and those of us on the day shift put everything down and left early. I saw sailors going on leave making a mad dash for the gates. Some of them made it before the loudspeaker said, 'Now hear this. All leaves are canceled!' It was quite a day."

Vi Magneson: "On V-J Day (I had been working at PSNY for two months), we heard the news about 3 p.m. and hoped for an early dismissal to celebrate but no such luck. After work, everyone was hugging, laughing, shouting, and happier than they had been for a long time. What a joyous occasion."

The book *Nipsic to Nimitz*[1] quoted a worker, Ralph Smith, "It was the biggest traffic jam you've ever seen, with both shifts leaving at the same time. The (Manette) bridge was wall-to-wall people and cars. I walked home to Sheridan Park, along with many others." Parker Snapp recalled for the book, "At war's end, the shipyard emptied in a shouting flood . . . in time to board the *Kalakala* for return to Seattle. An apprentice was boosted by his companions to the canopy over the fantail. He crept forward, cut the airhorn line, tied a cord to the stub and brought it back to the stern where it was pulled taut and tied to a stanchion. The airhorn blasted for three minutes or more before the skipper and crew identified the problem." Jerry Grosso, a reporter for the *Sun,* was quoted in the book," . . . in Port Orchard, Bay Street was crowded with people whooping and cheering. Some emptied their pockets and small change clattered off store windows. All whistles on ships that could, were blown. In the shipyard, thousands of workers put down their tools and went off to celebrate, (some) not even coming back to pick up their pay."

One of my favorite celebrations of V-J Day was noted by Dorothy Fick: "Irv Hughes and I went out on his Dad's boat. That is when the Bremerton Yacht Club was out on the Navy Yard Highway to Gorst. We went on the other side of Bainbridge Island and we just drifted and listened to the radio and all the noise coming from Seattle and West Seattle. Irv was a good friend of my brothers and I guess everyone else was working that day so we had fun celebrating the end of the war."

On the way home from the Navy Yard on V-J Day, Catherine Anderson asked her car-pool driver to go downtown "so we could see what kind of a celebration was going on, but he firmly declared that downtown Bremerton was no place for a young lady to be that night and took me straight home. What a disappointment! But Dale Burklund, his girl friend (and later his wife) Margaret French, my date and I had a splendid bonfire on the beach to celebrate the end of the war and the end of an era."

---

[1] Reh. Ibid.

Adrienne Johnson's Navy husband wrote a note to her from the Stage Door Canteen in Washington, D.C., that captures the rapture of the moment:

> Darling:
>
> *The War Is Officially Over.* I just got up town about 1/2 hour ago — what a mob — what a noise — a million people are wild with joy. Just saw Pres. Truman come out of the White House and wave. There is so much noise you can't hear yourself. Am going out to look around. Ain't it grand. I love you so much. Love,

After V-E Day in May, troops in Europe were being sent home, a few for discharge but a greater number to prepare for the invasion of Japan. I had been transferred to the 83rd Division and we were preparing for the invasion of Japan on maneuvers at Grafenwohr, former training grounds of the German Wehrmacht. I sat on a cot in a squad tent, the sun streaming down outside, and listened as an assistant squad leader said "some sort of big bomb" had forced the Japanese to surrender. Although I had not fully absorbed the reality of transferring to the Pacific and invading Japan, I remember nevertheless a rush of relief in the knowledge that I had, for certain, survived the war.

The peace treaty was signed aboard the *USS Missouri* in Tokyo Bay on September 2. The date coincided with Labor Day weekend. It was the first full-fledged holiday of the post-war era. Gas rationing had already ended. The highways were jammed and the ferries full. There was a Victory Ball and floor show at the USO Club on Washington Street. Charlotte Koontz was head of the arrangements committee.

Yard workers had reason to celebrate, for they had achieved much. In all, reported the PSNY publication *Salute,* "PSNY workers repaired 31 battleships, some of them more than once, in the 44 months of the war. Five of the big fighters were repaired and overhauled in 1941, five more in 1942, and three in 1943. Then as the fleet moved closer to Japan, the number rose, in 1944, to an even dozen. Six had been repaired in 1945 when the war ended.

"Eighteen carriers received battle damage repairs and overhaul in Bremerton. Some of them visited the Yard more than once. The *Saratoga,* for instance, was in drydock three times and the *Lexington* and the *Enterprise* were in twice. The carrier repair record rose from two in 1941 and only one in the years 1942 and 1943 to five in 1944 and then, as the Kamikaze attacks increased, to nine in the first seven months of 1945.

"Hardest hit of all types of ships in the Pacific were the destroyers. Their visits to the PSNY for damage repairs were frequent enough to almost tell their stirring story in numbers. Sixty-eight destroyers were repaired in all. There were eight in 1941, six in 1942, 17 in 1943, 16 in 1944 and 21 in the first seven months of 1945."

Still, occasional somber notes intruded as delayed casualty reports continued, even after the peace treaty was signed. On September 8, the *Sun* told of the death of 1st Lt. James Fuller, 22, killed on Okinawa on August 12, only three days before the Japanese surrendered. He was an Air Force meteorologist attached to the 55th Long Range Weather Reconnaissance Squadron. He had attended Star of the Sea and graduated from BHS in 1941. He was on the honor roll at Washington State College for three semesters before entering the Army in February of 1943.

Early in September, the 13th Naval District said Navy officers and sailors could wear civilian clothes off duty. Startled shoppers on Pacific Avenue reported seeing two "civilians" saluting each other. At midnight on September 4, the exile from the West Coast of Japanese-Americans was lifted. The *Sun* reported 47,000 to 52,000 persons of Japanese ancestry were still in eight relocation camps and a segregation center.

A headline and story revealed that an air-raid shelter capable of holding 10,000 people had been burrowed deep into a hillside under officers' row in the Navy Yard. "The main section of the shelter is a 1,650-foot tunnel with four connecting laterals making a total tunnel length of 2,200 feet. The tunnels, 18 feet wide and 12 feet high, have an independent lighting system for emergencies and a complete drainage system." The tunnels were converted to peacetime uses. One portal was turned into a telephone center for ship's personnel. Another was turned into a ship's service store. The main tunnel was used as storage space.

The United States prepared for peace with the same energy and even more zest than it had mobilized for war. In late August, work was stopped on apartments for single persons at four Bremerton housing projects, Sinclair, Marion, Trenton, and the National dormitories. The double-shift system was dropped as students moved into Bremerton's new high school. In addition to gasoline, canned fruits, vegetables, fuel oil and oil stoves were no longer rationed. Printing of new ration books for meats, fats, diary products, canned foods and sugar, scheduled for distribution in December, was halted.

War industries slashed their work force as they converted to peacetime production. Boeing's employment dropped from 75,000 to 9,000 almost overnight. Professor Bridgman said the odd aspect about it was how placidly workers accepted their layoffs. "The interesting thing was that many men had worked so hard they would just as soon have some time off and they apparently had considerable savings," he said. "They welcomed the time off and knew there was a gigantic pent-up demand in the United States and they were going to need workers and they didn't know if it would be airplanes, it would be for something. In fact, the labor exchanges had plenty of jobs, they had virtually as many jobs as they had workers, and that included large numbers of GIs that were coming back."

The number of women in the work force had increased remarkably — by 47 percent from March, 1940, to July, 1944, Karen Anderson wrote in her book *Wartime Women*.[2] An ad for Magnin's, the tony women's apparel store, said "Work and run a home, too." Boeing asked in an ad, "Are you doing your part?" The allure of work at PSNY was the "glamour of the shipyard." Most women spent their earnings on family requirements. The difference in clerical and assembly-line work in Seattle was smaller than elsewhere. Clerks averaged $36.25 per week; manufacturing jobs paid $39.90. In the Puget Sound area, more than half the women worked a 48-hour week and 80 percent worked at least 40 hours per week. At the Navy Yard, both men and women worked 13 consecutive days and took the 14th day off. Women whose employment had been limited before the war to sales clerks, waitresses or maids became riveters, welders, taxi drivers, and shipfitters. Despite a ruling by the National War Labor Board that promised equal pay to women, that policy was often weakened. Although the postwar employment rate for women was substantially lower than during the war, it remained higher than prewar figures, increasing from 28.9 percent to 33 percent during the '40s, 37.4 percent in 1960 and by 1968 it was 41 percent. In the '90s, women made up about 43 percent of the total U.S. work force.

Dr. Bridgman quoted an editorial from the *Seattle Times* published just after the war ended that spoke for the people of Bremerton, too:

> We shall miss them. We shall miss the GIs with the Brooklyn accents, the WAVE with the sweet Southern drawl, and the sailor with the Midwest twang. We shall miss them hurrying along our crowded streets going somewhere and not knowing where. We shall miss them when the aftermath of the war is over and we as well as they may find that it's a little dull to settle down."

[2] Anderson. Ibid.

Al Stewart and Linc Perry share news of home when they rendezvoused in the South Pacific.
(Photo courtesy Linc Perry.)

And thousands who had come to Bremerton for the war happily returned home, as they had always intended. (But many also stayed). Employment at the Navy Yard was cut back sharply, too. The *Sun* said on September 19 that the payroll was expected to level off at 22,000, down from 32,000. That was far too optimistic. By the end of 1946, employment had dropped to fewer than 9,000 employees. Many of the ships repaired at PSNY during the war were involved in Operation Crossroads, the Bikini Atoll atomic bomb tests, and were never used again.

The Navy said in September it planned to reduce its size to 839,000 men by Christmas day. The Army and Air Force were re-leasing men rapidly, too — although not fast enough to suit those of us who remained in the armies of occupation in Germany and Japan. To the tune of *Lily Marlene*, we would sing plaintively:

Tell me, Mr. Truman, when do we go home?
We have taken Berlin, we have taken Rome.
We have conquered the master race
Why is there no more shipping space?
Oh, when do we go home,
Oh, when do we go home?

While on Tinian, Jay Atherton had seen the B-29 Bock's Car being loaded with the second atom bomb that was dropped on Japan. He didn't go home immediately, either. Instead he was posted to Korea. "I was there about 13 months and damned near froze to death the winter of '45-46 living in a Japanese radio transmitter station."

Although our return was not always as swift as we wanted, return we did, to a nation eager to get back to normal, to spend money saved during the war, to get reacquainted with wives and children, to resume or launch careers. Washington and many other states approved bonuses for veterans, and the returning sailors and GIs were welcomed home gratefully.

It was not apparent at the time, but the greatest gift from the nation (and, later *to* the nation) was Public Law 346, also known as the Servicemen's Readjustment Act of 1944. It was signed by FDR on June 22, 1944. It became known commonly as the GI Bill. But its effects were most uncommon. Of 14 million who were eligible, 2.2 million veterans jumped at the unexpected opportunity to attend college. An article in the *Smithsonian Magazine* of November, 1994, said, "It pulled a generation up by their combat bootstraps, transformed America's colleges and universities, cranked out a huge pool of trained professionals, changed the education goals of the nation, and fueled a giddy postwar boom." The cost was $5.5 billion — but it produced 450,000 engineers, 240,000 accountants, 238,000 teachers, 90,000 scientists, 57,000 doctors, 22,000 dentists, 17,000 writers and editors, and thousands of other professionals.

The main purpose of the bill originally was to give veterans unemployment benefits of $20 per week for up to a year. (Those who collected the benefits were said to be members of the 52-20 club). College provisions of the bill, added almost as an afterthought, guaranteed a year of education for 90 days' service, plus one month for each month of active duty, for a maximum of 48 months. It paid tuition (at the time tuition for many private colleges was only $300 per year), fees, books and supplies up to $500 per year. The *Smithsonian* article said single vets received $50 and married vets $75, but memory tells me those figures were increased to $75 and $90.

The GI Bill produced many success stories, including that of Jim Hathhorn, Marian Booth's husband. She wrote that after the war he wanted to attend the University of Idaho, but had dropped out of school "and had about a year of less than distinguished grades. Because he was a veteran, he was allowed to enroll on probation. We moved into married student housing and received the sum of $90 per month . . . Five years later, he graduated with honors and a brand new MA degree in education. Years and four children later, he returned to Oregon State University and earned a doctorate in education."

I don't know whether I could have managed a college education without the GI Bill. I do know that the bill made it much easier and faster. I know further that it enriched the nation, providing a much better educated work force. It also laid the groundwork for the postwar cultural explosion. Furthermore, it permitted four glorious years of fun at college. Down at the Vet's dorms on the campus of the University of Washington, I roomed for a time with Xie Olanie. Across a wing in the same dorm were Dave Poll and Bill Gates. David Leathley roomed with Gordy Lecair.

*Cal Christensen,
Frank Wetzel,
Jorgen Nelson,
John Gordon
"hamming it
up" at home.*
(Author's
Collection.)

Harold Engebretson was nearby, too, I think, as were many other Bremerton residents. Most of us held summer jobs in Bremerton, creating the opportunity for parties that became legendary in the Western world. Or so it seemed.

"The war generation partied when it could, sometimes with abandon," wrote William L. O'Neill[3]. "But, in the end, what men and women alike wanted was home, marriage, family. In the postwar world their dreams came true."

At the end of her reminiscences, Aileen Bellinger said, "Sometimes I cry for the lost times," and it's natural to be nostalgic for those exciting days. But Adrienne Johnson wisely warns against that. "The driving basso ostinato of the time was the unspeakable horror of war's death and destruction. All else was played out above that relentless dirge." She named some of those who lost their lives, and added, "The tragedy and loss are simply beyond comprehension."

Virginia Eddy agreed. "Even though we despise war with a vengeance, the feelings of WWII and its full-fledged efforts, its camaraderie, the faith, the love of country, the sacrifices of all of us, have made us 'old timers' stronger for having seen, done, and survived. We must never forget those who gave their lives for us who were given the gift to go on."

As to the city itself, parts of Bremerton always have been unsightly, remembers Virginia Oass — the tattoo parlors, pawn shops, beer parlors and smashed sailors. In her mind, however, that ugliness "was more than overshadowed by its pristine location tucked in among the snow-capped Olympics, evergreen forests and Puget Sound, and its decent, warm people."

But what of Bremerton in the 1990s? Alas, to this outsider's eyes, for an outsider I have become, it has lost its allure. Downtown businesses fled to the Silverdale mall, leaving empty buildings, footsteps that echo, a desultory, shabby appearance. It ap-

---

[3] O'Neill. Ibid.

pears down at the heels, defeated, despite efforts of the town's burghers to resuscitate it. Its status in the '90s was probably the inevitable fate of a company town in which the principle player, the Navy, of necessity took a hands-off position while the principal owner, the Bremer family, dithered and finally let the core slip away.

Marjorie Lamb saw the Bremerton of the '90s much the same way. "I'm sad when I drive down Pacific Avenue and see the old stores gone and empty sidewalks and parking spaces. I think back to the days you bumped into people just walking down the street. We waited in line to go to a show, eat in a restaurant, buy liquor or cigarettes or catch a bus. We didn't have the improved streets there now, the parking garage, the Warren Avenue bridge, new ferry landing or new YMCA. Neither did we have the crime and AIDS we see today. Yes, Pearl Harbor changed my life and the lives of my entire family. Of one thing I am sure — we lived in the 'good old days' — much better than our parents and better than our children."

Said Wayne Matz, "She is a ghost town of many memories . . . It is hollow and depressing to even drive through the old downtown, much less walk around in it."

Adrienne Johnson agreed. In 1994, she drove by her home at 927½ North Summit built by her father and learned it had burned. "Then I drove to our old high school but it was gone, too. I went to Park Avenue where it ends at Burwell, to see Craven Center where I met my future husband on April 4, 1944. That huge building had also vanished. I walked along Pacific Avenue and it was like a ghost town. Then I turned on the news one evening and saw the Commissioned Officers' Club in the Navy Yard going up in flames . . . Now all these places exist only in memory."

Ah, but we loved it once. Let Adrienne Johnson provide the final eulogy:

"When I come to Bremerton now I don't see it as it is, but as it was then. The changes don't seem to belong, and I think, 'Who said they could do this to my town?' I see the seemingly endless lines of Army Jeeps and trucks full of troops heading north in anticipation of the expected invasion of our shores. I see gold stars in windows of homes, and people suddenly bursting into tears as they walk down the street. I see young men in uniforms of different nations jostling for room along our crowded streets. I see the final good-byes to families and loved ones there at the ferry terminal as the boys leave for combat . . ."*Mais, ou sont les neiges d'anton?*"

But where are the snows of yesteryear?

War is miserable business; as bumper stickers said later of nuclear warfare, it can be hazardous to your health. We who collaborated on this book, like others looking back on their youth, tend to emphasize happy times and to forget the bad ones. But it would be a serious misconception for younger readers to decide from the upbeat recollections of its survivors that WWII was entirely a time of uniting, bonding, sharing. In truth, the war was a filthy, nasty mess. Remembering classmates who died in it is profoundly sad, and does not ease with the passage of time. We think of the great pleasures in our own lives over the past half-century, and, yes, the pain, too, and then realize all that our friends have missed . . .

While we were corresponding about this book, Joe Stottlebower, sent me two pages of epigrams about war that over the years he has collected from his voluminous reading. Here are several:

"For every man in whom war has inspired sacrifice, courage and love, there are many more whom it has degraded with brutality, callousness, and greed." —-*Omar Bradley*

"This year you're a hero. Next year you'll be a disabled veteran. And after that you'll just be a cripple." — *Doctor to World War II veteran at Army rehabilitation center, 1945*

"In war, there are no unwounded soldiers." —-*Jose Narosky*

"War, which used to be cruel and magnificent, is now cruel and squalid." —-*Winston Churchill*

"Youth? We are none of us more than 20 years old. But young? Youth? That is long ago. We are old folk...in some strange and melancholy way, we have become a waste land." —-*Erich Maria Remarque*

These men who died, these few mentioned here, barely more than boys: Was there meaning in their deaths?

The answer is not easy. The reasons for fighting World War II have withstood the test of time. Perhaps, despite the usual propaganda and exaggerations, it was indeed the Last Good War. But while remembering these young war dead, it is appropriate to ask: At what cost? Was it worth their lives? We call up their images and remember them with joy as they were. But we weep over who they never became, what they missed, and we yearn for a world in which we can be a pacifists. But we cannot be, not yet, not until all nations forgo war. And that time probably will never come.

Still, war is madness. Complete madness.

Appendix

In 1993 I asked about 600 men and women who had attended Bremerton High School during World War II how they had heard about the Japanese attack on Pearl Harbor.

More than 150 former students responded in writing. Many took the occasion to expound upon their experiences in Bremerton during the war. Although not always completely accurate, their reminiscences offer a complementary kaleidoscope that in aggregate recaptures the atmosphere of December, 1941, and sometimes beyond. Some of these accounts duplicate material elsewhere in the book. Here are a few, edited only for brevity:

Class of '42

Nelda Allen Goff: I heard about Pearl Harbor Sunday morning with my boyfriend. Came straight home to listen to the news. What a shock because of relatives on the ships in Pearl Harbor. I must have been 16. So many people moved in; we had the 4Fs coming from all over the USA to work in the Navy Yard, had Army, Navy, Coast Guard, Marines all in town.

I left school in my last year. Didn't want to go to school. Took a test and went to work for the Navy Yard. I worked in the shipfitters' office as a messenger, then worked as a shipfitters' helper on the ships. Then took a class for a burner on a destroyer. Worked on a ship in summer, in winter in a plans shack.

What a place to be living and be 16, 17 and 18, etc. All the men you wanted and then some. I was always popular in high school. It was fun years for me and my sister and her daughter.

I remember getting food stamps. Candy was in short supply and people would line up for different things; even shoes were rationed.

My older sister worked in a bar and they were always crowded. Even going to the shows you waited in line. Meeting all the service men and having them leave was so sad. They had songs in those days that were so pretty and made you think of your loves overseas or going overseas. I wonder how many I knew in those years who didn't come back? What sad memories.

One cold winter day with snow on the ground (which was unusual) the Army marched into town and made their headquarters across the street from our house. It used to be *our* junior high school (Washington school). They were the balloon barrage unit. When we or they thought we were in danger, the balloons would go up. Their main gate was right across from us — so every morning I would say hello to them. They would count my boy friends who came to see me and tell me later. We were good to them all in the service. My sister's daughter Ginger, whose father was killed on the *Arizona* — she got to know all of them, she must have been 7, 8 or 9. Then she used to sing, "Remember Pearl Harbor."

I remember working in the Navy Yard and we had a bond rally. Lana Turner, the famous movie star, came to see us, to buy war bonds for our country.

I remember being in the fourth and fifth grades at Hillcrest school (which no longer stands), we used to save tinfoil wrappers of candy and gum — to be sent to help Japan. Then around seven years later they bombed us.

My high school years in the war — it was crowded. A to K went to school in the morning, L to Z in the afternoon.

Places were hard to get to rent or buy. It was a boomtown and I went to our 50th reunion in 1992 and looked at the town so small. Streets look like alleys and most of downtown moved out of town with malls, etc.

PS: In 1945, I moved to California as my sisters all married sailors and moved to Long Beach. I have been up to Bremerton many times, but still live here, where there were more jobs after the war.

James D. Braman: The family was in our living room just after returning from church. Our next-door neighbor rushed in saying the Japs have bombed Pearl Harbor. Her husband was a sailor on the *USS Houston* and she didn't know if it was in Pearl (it wasn't).

Margorie Booth Poleson: Radio announcement in West-end drug store. My cousin, Vera Adams (now deceased) and I had walked from home on West Cambrian to the store. The place had a great soda fountain and we usually had a milkshake (25 cents) whenever we went there for any reason. We were stunned to hear such horrible news and wondered what it would mean to us.

Dale C. Burklund: Al Erickson and I had decided to take a ride around Hood Canal to Lilliwaup Falls and watch the salmon work their way up the falls. It was a convenient reason to get the Ericksons to allow Al to borrow the new Pontiac and take our girl friends on a full-day outing. Al was dating Louise Koch and I was dating Marjorie Kleisath.

We stopped by the Lake Cushman Dam and then went on to Lilliwaup Falls. Al had his new portable radio with him so we could have some music. It was one of those first portables with large batteries. You could hardly lift it.

We watched the salmon at the base of the falls for a short time and then Marjorie and I walked up to the top of the falls to watch the salmon jump their way to the top. It was a beautiful, sunny crisp day. The setting was peaceful and lovely. I think the last thing from our minds was war and an attack by anyone. We heard Al yelling but couldn't make out what he was saying. He and Louise had stayed in the car listening to the radio and we thought he might have had a problem. We finally made out that the Japanese had attacked Pearl Harbor. I don't know that we believed the report but the news kept coming about the attack.

By the time we got back to Hoodsport they had someone guarding the generating plant. One older man was walking up and down the causeway carrying a big double-barrel shotgun. As we got closer to Bremerton we were very anxious as we expected the Japanese would attack the Bremerton naval base next. It was obvious the base and the country were vulnerable and unprepared.

Doreen Burton Schau: I was at home listening to the radio when the news came. I remember being very frightened because of the Navy Yard. I really thought we were in danger of being bombed. (As time went on, those fears lessened.)

I didn't know I was going to graduate in '42 until about three weeks before. Way back when, you could start school in January and September. I was always a half-year student (smaller class). We were called into the office (I'm not sure how many) and asked if we wanted to graduate with the class of '42. I had enough credits; some others, I believe, attended the ceremony and then took a course at night school and received their diplomas later. I was happy to graduate — going to school in shifts wasn't much fun.

Ed Drouin: It was a bright Sunday morning. I had a day off from the shipyard. I was helping my father clean out the basement. First word by radio, then an "extra" from the *Searchlight.*

Les Eathorne: I was heading for the gym for Sunday basketball and I could hear radios along Warren Avenue. People were out in their yards talking about it. Decided to go on to the gym at high school. Coach Wills opened gym as usual and we played. War went on that day without us.

Wally Ellis: I arrived in Bremerton, a mid-term junior, in 1940, worked for butcher shop in the old Farmers Market on Fourth Street after school, played French horn in the high school and Elks bands, and otherwise led pretty much a dull life up to mid-term senior year, when I left school for the seemingly more fruitful rewards of an apprenticeship in the local shipyard. I had more than enough credits to graduate with the rest of the class.

As to the crowded conditions, yes, they were crowded along with a shortage of text books. I still managed an "A" from Al Hugenin in spite of having to study with a text borrowed from most anywhere I could. Today's society would be appalled at the conditions we had, but we still received a good education. I guess the summation here is that I didn't spend any more time at BHS than necessary.

I don't recall too much about hearing the news regarding Pearl Harbor other than I was working on my car in the garage when the radio interrupted to announce we were at war, running up to tell my folks and then spending the rest of the day listening to news reports like millions of others were doing.

Harry B. Flesher: Our family was out by Union City for a ride in my uncle's new '41 Pontiac — first car radio we had. We heard it on a special news bulletin.

Billie Hill Christensen: I was in the living room of my parents' home at 1134 Bloomington Avenue in Bremerton listening to some music when the program was interrupted by the unbelievable news that Pearl Harbor had been attacked, and we were at war.

Your inquiry started me reminiscing. I was quite a nomad during the war years. Worked at PSNY in the mail room and radio material office for awhile, then got bored and went to work at the Naval Ammunition Depot operating a fork lift loading ammo into the barges, warehouses, and railroad cars (had to do something for the war effort). Then Jo Winkenweder, Myrtle McFee and I (I was 17) went to San Francisco. Worked for the Navy in the A.I.M. office (construction) in the Ferry Building at the end of Market Street.

Six months later I got homesick so came home, but home then was Farragut, Idaho, where my Dad, Jesse Hill, US Navy, was training recruits. Stayed there a few months where I worked in the PX, then back to San Francisco where I got my old job back. Hung out with Nadine and Vi Malstrom. Then my sailor came into Bremerton on the *Enterprise* for repairs so back to Bremerton where we were married August 11, 1945, about the time the war ended with Japan. Then we moved to Hollywood, California (couldn't find a place to live), so back to Bremerton, worked at R.S. Hayward for two years, renewed friendships with Marge (Lamb) Sullivan and Carmen Ensign.

Anyway, except for the war, I had so many wonderful times and friendships, so many fond memories. Been looking through all my annuals and reunion books today. The day has passed but not wasted. Wouldn't trade my youth with anyone.

Joann Larson Gillis: I was at First Presbyterian Church, Wilbur Scafe's first Sunday as the minister there. Next evening went to an orchestra rehearsal at old Bremerton High — Vern Jackson was the teacher. Al Erickson's mom had to drive me home in a partial blackout. Slow going. Most people tried to cover their windows that night. I remember I heard Harry Sorensen (principal) say later to the class president, "Have you prepared your class in case of an air raid?" I gulped at that.

I worked at the Naval Ammunition Depot 1942-1945. Nice place to work. Towards the end — spring of 1945 — the office personnel started Bangor in our offices. Sometimes we had to hang on to our equipment!

Frank D. (Dave) Leathley: I was with Doug Jones, a Royal Marine from HMS Warspite then in the yard. We had my Lionel train set spread out over most of the living room floor when my mother came in from the kitchen, where the radio was on, to tell us we were at war with the Japanese. They had just attacked Pearl Harbor. Doug Jones spent most of his weekends or other days off with us. My Father and Mother were originally from Yorkshire in England. They had decided to invite Doug and another Marine shortly after the Warspite came into Bremerton. The other Marine was sent back to England very shortly but Doug, from Coventry, stayed assigned to the ship and left with it when it again returned to sea. He was 19 to my not quite 17 years and had a good two years of combat service by then. He used the extra bed in my room when he stayed over and told me quite a bit — being dive-bombed by Stukas in the Mediterranean Sea, and other combat experiences. Had quite an impression on me.

I also recall walking all over Bremerton locating each barrage balloon site, noting whether it was black or silver and locating it on a map I had traced from a city map using some of my good mechanical drawing vellum. I don't recall how Dad found out about my map but he was very upset by it and had me destroy it, said we couldn't keep information like that in wartime (Dad had seen four years of service in WWI with the Canadian Army Engineers). One of the balloon sites was just across the road from our house (now Marion Ave.), another was just a few houses north of us also on Marion. Maybe enough folks still remember other locations and we could recreate the map — if no one else did as I had done but kept it secret.

Maury Olson: I was a soda jerk at Graham's Malt Shop on Pacific Avenue. Have memories of night of December 7 turning off lights, working in Graham's and driving around Bremerton with Harold Bob Wintermute with no lights on '31 Model A. Had some problems with British Navy, at malt shop.

I joined Navy in November '43, spent two years in South Pacific on ships. Hit most islands.

Myron Richards: In 1941 my brother Lowell was a student at the University of Washington majoring in journalism. He was a member of the Bremerton High School band under Wally Hannah all during his high school years, and so when he went to U of Dub he played in the band under Walter Welke. The university band was scheduled to play a concert in Meany Hall the afternoon of December 7, and my parents and I had not heard the band before and so we were on our way to the concert on the *Chippewa*.

The ferry had just emerged from Rich Passage and was heading for Seattle when the captain announced the attack on Pearl Harbor over the ferry's public address system. I was more astonished by the realization that the ferry had a PA system than at the news, because I had ridden dozens of times and never heard it used. Details of the incident were not part of the announcement so we had no real information of the seriousness of the attack. Our family was not in the habit of listening to the radio for news, and so probably had no other information until the *Seattle Times* was delivered on Monday afternoon. I was still in high school and delivered the Times on a route that started at Burwell and Callow.

My brother and I read in the paper one day that some federal agency was going to spend some money in Bremerton for recreation for the huge numbers of people flooding the area. We learned the name of the person charged with administering the money and visited him in his office at city hall. Our suggestion was that a conductor be hired and a local symphony orchestra be started. Both my brother and I were amateur musicians and besides having played in the high school band and orchestra, had also played with the Port Orchard town band under the direction of Ed Benson. Our selling pitch was based on the fact that we had direct contact with enough musicians to furnish a complete instrumentation for an orchestra and would contact the necessary players. The administrative person (whose name I don't remember) agreed that such a program was within the guidelines of authorized expenditures, a man was hired to conduct and the orchestra became a reality. I believe that orchestra still exists in Bremerton.

Donald Serry: I was working for Rumsey Puget Sound Construction Company and was hanging crossarms on 70-foot lighting poles around DD #5 when it was announced that Pearl Harbor had been attacked. This event changed the whole direction of my life and I'm sure of many others.

Jo Lauth: I don't seem to remember too much about that particular time period. I think it might be because I lost one of my two brothers in the war. Clarence went down on a destroyer in the South Pacific, April 12, 1945. The war ended soon after that. I do have papers that tell all about it. That had a devastating effect on my parents and me.

Gordon D. Solie: It was a warm sunny Sunday. My parents and I were standing in the front yard. The phone rang and my mother went in to answer it. In a minute she came to the door and said, "It was Wayne McNeil. He said he heard on the radio that Pearl Harbor had been bombed." We were stunned. Although none of us had ever been to Pearl Harbor, we knew where it was.

Donna Tierney Wakefield: Several friends and I had gone to Fort Lewis to visit a boy friend of mine who was stationed there. We got on base and as we drove to the barracks we noticed all the groups lined up with full uniform, etc.

Dick managed to get to our car and said, Pearl's been bombed. We're on orders. The Military Police came by and asked us how we got on base and we told them through the main gate. They sent us off base and later Dick's first letter came from Alaska. Later Dick (Urich) became a doctor at Mayo Clinic.

I lived at 3723 D Street (middle of street). Barrage balloons were at foot of D Street in Westpark Community Center. Later after I married in January of '43 I went back to Bremerton when my husband (Navy) shipped out and I worked at the Supply Building for Lt. Biggerstaff. We used to watch the ships leave the dock and any wife working in Supply was allowed to stay on the dock until the ship pulled away.

I was in Bremerton at the dock when President Roosevelt pulled into dry-dock. Also when the English ships came in — one with 240 dead sealed in her hold.

My father worked for Navy Yard and on the barges that came in from Bikini.

When I moved to Bremerton 1939 nice girls did not talk to Navy personnel. Most of us married civilians and wound up in the Navy anyway. Dancing was our recreation. Perl Maurer's two nights a week. Saturday — regular shift — swing and graveyard. Other than movies that was it.

Bernice Welch Workman: Sitting in theater watching movie. Announce-ment came. We all left stunned. Service personnel told to report. The most dramatic — besides blackouts — was a barrage balloon that came down on house next door and engulfed the home. We all had to leave area while multi-Army personnel arrived.

I worked in commandant of yard (admiral's office), handled secret and confi-dential material. Met many celebs — Walter Pidgeon, Ginger Rogers (her slip showed) while on war bond rallies. Met Eleanor Roosevelt at Admiral Taffinder's home on base. Thought she was the homeliest woman in the world — but quickly became aware she was the most beautiful woman I had ever seen.

Bob Schutt: Skiing on Mount Rainier. I was at the top of the rope tow and the news rapidly filtered up the slope. I left BHS in fall of '41 to attend the U of W. I technically hadn't graduated (3½ years student) but Harry Sorensen ar-ranged it so as to avoid the double shifting due to start. So only returned on oc-casional weekend. I remember a barrage balloon at end of Marine Drive adjacent to my folk's place, and the mushrooming of the area with Westpark, Eastpark, etc.

Class of '43

Catherine Anderson King: We were reading the Sunday papers when Max Peabody, a quarterman at PSNY and our next-door neighbor, came down and told my father, "The Japs are bombing Pearl Harbor." I had just turned 16, and can remember it as clearly as if it just happened.

Incidentally, my father was always firmly against interning Japanese resi-dents. He said that if we were going to evacuate Japanese-Americans, we had to do the same to descendants of German and Italian citizens. His sense of fair play was outraged.

Both of my parents were immigrants — my father came to the U.S. from Norway before WWI, and served at what was then Camp Lewis before the war ended. My Mother was from Scotland, and had four brothers, mother, and a sister still living in Great Britain, so they both followed the news closely from 1939 on. We often had men from British minesweepers who were in the yard for repairs over to our house for dinner. There were anti-aircraft guns up on the hills behind our Phinney Bay home.

As you know, we couldn't take photos of barrage balloons but I remember clearly the ones on the football field at Washington Junior High School.

I was working in the Navy Yard the day the war ended — on summer vacation from school — and can describe in detail what happened there as all the workers coming in for the swing shift turned around and went home, and those of us on the day shift put everything down and left early. I saw sailors going on leave making a mad dash for the gates. Some of them made it before the loudspeaker said: "Now hear this. All leaves are canceled!" It was quite a day.

Hazel W. Butler Presley: I was walking across the Manette bridge to my home on Ironsides and someone in a car shouted to me that Pearl Harbor had been bombed. I certainly remember the pall that came over the town when the survivors from the Enterprise came to town.

Gerry Calder Allen: Most of my memories have to do with the war effort (e.g. victory gardens, blackouts, air raid drills, barrage balloons, and most of my friends either joining the services or the work force to help in whatever way they could).

Frances Clement McConnell: I was baby-sitting at the home of the head of the Marine Barracks in the Navy Yard when I answered the phone. It was the first call into the yard from Washington, D.C., and gave the news of the attack. I woke the colonel to answer it — but I didn't know what it was until I got home that afternoon when mother told me what had happened.

Ellen M. Davis Willis: In 1941 I was 17-years-old. My boy friend and I went for a ride and wound up at Paradise Inn on Mount Rainier. After walking around we passed a car with people clustered around. On top was a radio. . . The Japs had bombed Pearl Harbor. Everyone was stunned. I felt like I'd been kicked in the stomach. All we wanted to do was go home. There were tears and total incredulity. My father was a quarterman in the Bremerton Navy Yard; my oldest brother was in Reed College in Portland; my younger brother was in the Navy. I still had a year of high school to finish; and I went to school in the mornings . . .

My first husband, Les Plaeger (deceased), was working in the Navy Yard when I met him on the only blind date I ever had. That was April 5, 1942. We married on August 5 of that year. I had gone to summer school so I only had a half-year to go for a diploma. I went back and finished. Because of the war, they no longer expelled married persons. I was the second girl to get married in my class.

Virginia Eddy Trammell: I was a sophomore at South Kitsap High School (Port Orchard). It was discussed in class and needless to say this news dominated the day. Apprehension and numbness were ours. At that time we hadn't a clue if we would also be attacked as suddenly as Pearl Harbor. Somehow we hadn't heard this news till Monday, at school!

I spent my senior year at BHS on the first shift. After graduating in '43, joined many grads in applying for work in the PSNY. Was hired as a "shipfitter helper." Worked aboard damaged ships beginning with *USS California, USS West Virginia, USS Tennessee* (spent New Year's Eve there, on swing shift!) and many carriers. Ended up in supervisor's offices, some on the piers, some aboard ship, etc. Sold War Bonds.

Bremerton exploded. "Recruits" came in from many states. Housing projects were built, servicemen were all over town. Everything thrived — there was electricity in the air. Gas, food items, nylons, shoes, etc., were suddenly rationed. Early on we had "brownouts" — no lights were to be exposed at night. All shifts worked around the clock, and many worked seven-day weeks for months at a time.

I could go on — there are so many stories — our Dad's mom owned and operated a resort on Hood Canal — "Doc Eddy's Rose Point" and we housed Navy Yard-wartime families there, too.

Harold J. Engebretson: I recall riding around that morning with Bob Pettengill of BHS when we heard news on the radio. It is possible that he had heard the radio and came by to tell me about it. At my house we got a call from the Navy Yard wanting my father to report to work. He was out on the North Shore of Hood Canal working on a house that he had built the previous year for my sister Thelma. Bob and I drove out there to tell him to go to the Navy Yard. There was no phone at Thelma's house then. He returned to the Navy Yard and did not get home for about three days. Apparently they were trying to get information from Pearl Harbor and make initial plans for whatever repairs could be made.

Later that day, I was called to work at a small grocery store in Charleston where I had been working part-time. It was a very busy day at the store with a continual crowd buying 100-pound sacks of sugar, flour, potatoes, cases of tuna fish, and everything else. By late afternoon the Army units started to roll into town past the store with anti-aircraft. . .

Ida Greyell Boss: I was at a Christmas program practice at our church. Our pastor's son, who was always playing pranks, etc., came rushing in to tell of the attack and we didn't know whether to believe him. He finally convinced us that it was true.

Rowena Harkins Henshaw: My mother was postmaster in Manette through WWI and WWII. I had been out on a date Saturday night (can't remember who) and was trying to sleep in Sunday morning. My Dad came in and said that I should come quickly and listen to the radio, that something terrible had just happened at Pearl Harbor. What a tremendous shock! That whole day was total confusion for everyone! I was told recently that US Marines were aboard the Black Ball ferries shooting into the water, wondering if there were enemy subs already in place. My Dad, U.S. Army captain WWI, disabled, medically retired, tried to enlist.

We in the Bremerton area certainly saw as much action as any place in the US. Those were bittersweet, frightening, passionate, exciting, romantic, heartbreaking times for us all. And tension ran almost unabated. It was the one time in our lives that everyone pulled together — and cared . . . Even my German Shepard dog, King, was father to two "sons" serving overseas — K9 Corps.

Harry L. Harkness: It was about 11 a.m. Sunday at our home on the Navy Yard Highway close to the Bremerton Yacht Club. Dad was reading the Sunday *P-I* and I was settled into the comic section. The radio was on but ignored by those in the room or nearby. Then the startling words, "We are interrupting this broadcast. . . The Japanese have just bombed Pearl Harbor — the USS *Arizona* has been sunk along with the *Oklahoma*." Dad jumped up from his chair and said, "Oh, my God, my God." I said, "Dad, what is, where is Pearl Harbor?" He said, "That is our navy yard in the Hawaiian Islands."

My dad was a 20-year truck driver for the Navy. Within an hour our telephone rang and it was my Dad's supervisor, Mr. Duane. Mr. Duane said, "Get into your work clothes, pack a change or two for an overnight stay — you're driving our largest flatbed to Astoria to pick up ammunition and return as fast as you can. You'll lead the group followed by your buddies Art Ward, Al Bard and as many as we can muster up. It's a dangerous trip but it looks like we may be going to war. Expect you in less than an hour." (Clunk.) Needless to say our household was quite a bustle for the next 30 minutes.

As the empty flatbed trucks, complete with tarps, ropes, cables and special danger signs headed for the Montgomery Street gate of the Navy Yard, the captain of the yard, Captain Dowell, I believe, stopped the procession of trucks to thank the drivers and then whispered to my Dad, "You know, Harky, we have just enough ammunition aboard our ships here, at NAD (Naval Ammunition Depot), Keyport (torpedo station) and in our supply department to hold off the Japs for just 20 minutes." Can you imagine the panic in Bremerton if that news had gotten out? I didn't see much of my Dad, Ryle G. "Harky" Harkness, for the next 60 days. The thought of sabotage and the drivers being blown to bits was ever in my mind.

Following the declaration of war that Monday, crazy things were happening in and around Bremerton. Our little two-lane highway leading into Bremerton from the Head of the Bay right in front of our house was crowded with Army personnel and supply trucks, headlights on during the day bringing equipment, guns and soldiers. These would be located throughout the Navy Yard, greater Bremerton, Naval Ammunition Depot, Manette and Keyport. Some short time after this our two-lane highway was straightened out and enlarged to four lanes. We no longer had a swimming beach, oyster beds or clam digging. There was a war on!

Jay Hendrick: We had been to church and had just got out a little after noon on that Sunday. We heard about it on the car radio as we went home. I remember the deep snow of 1943 when the Army had to pull the transit buses over their routes to pick up and deliver the shipyard workers to and from their jobs. . .

Francis Johnson Shaffer: I worked at the telephone company and remember trying so hard to get calls through for sailors who'd just come back or who were about to leave and needed to contact family. It was always difficult to obtain a circuit so at times while our "customer" was talking on his call, we'd check with the operators around us to see if they were waiting for that kind of circuit so they could use the one we had as soon as the current call was completed.

One day I was on the dock, the old ferry dock, and the *USS Mississippi* had just dropped anchor off the end of the dock out in the middle of the bay. It had been badly damaged and looked dark and ominous to me. Some of the sailors were coming ashore in an open boat. They were wearing dark work clothes and even had dark hats, too.

When we had the blizzard one winter, I remember that some of the soldiers gave Mama a ride home on Capitol Hill in a Jeep because the buses weren't running and she was trying to carry groceries home from Sixth and Callow.

Phyllis Johnson Fowler: My mother and I were sitting in our dining room listening to the radio Sunday morning. My mother started to cry, since she knew what war would bring. I was 15 and it didn't seem real to me.

Barbara L. Van Wert: My older sister Virginia (Kingman) Hill was on duty at the time of the attack at the telephone company downtown. When news came through she said "all the lines lit up like lights on a Christmas tree."

Ellen Leathley Winters: My parents were English, so we had one of the Marines from the English battleship *Warspite* out for the weekend (he spent most of his time with us). He and my father and brother had walked to the drugstore to buy the Sunday paper, and Mother and I were preparing dinner. Mother always had to listen to H.V. Kaltenborn with the news as she wanted to know what was happening in England — she had a sister still there. So we heard about Pearl Harbor on HV's program and then had to tell the rest of the family. Of course the radio was on the rest of the day, and they kept announcing for the different military personnel to return to base but they never mentioned the Warspite, because no one was supposed to know about it being in Bremerton. However, my parents and Doug (our Marine) decided he should go back early, too. The next day Mother went out and bought lots of black yardage to make blackout curtains (she'd been bombed in England in WWI). My brother recorded the President's declaration of war — I think he still has the old record. And in school that first week, every time I'd hear a truck grinding up the Fourth Street hill I was sure it was a Japanese plane coming to bomb us.

Boyd McCaslin: I was working at Fourth and Park Safeway store part-time as a junior in high school. That Sunday morning some of us were working at the closed-on Sunday store mopping and scrubbing the floors. We went up the street toward Pacific Avenue late in the morning and saw the news of the Pearl Harbor attack on the Teletype set up in the front window of the *Bremerton Sun* office.

Toni (Frances A.) McHale: Walking home from church I passed Donne Clayton out mowing the lawn who told me of the bombing. Once home we turned on the radio and let the news sink in. I believe my father was called into work or went with co-worker Frank Higgins, a neighbor.

BHS went into shift sessions in my junior year. Though I had some interesting classes and teachers, I felt very disconnected from my long-term friends, and school accomplishments were not inspired. For my fourth year I convinced my parents to let me accompany a younger sister, now deceased, to a boarding girls' academy in Vancouver, Washington. It was a valued school year — a graduating class of 18, virtually private instruction with a coordinated curriculum. Though located near the Vanport community, Portland and the shipyards I felt quite safe in the town and the fortress-like academy building in the shelter of Fort Vancouver, adjacent.

Our family did well in the rationing, probably because of our number (seven children, two parents), Mother's victory garden in the parking strips, and generally modest living habits in a stable environment. We had never been used to free use of the auto, but felt safe on the streets going with another to games, scouting events, etc., walking or busing. More affected probably were my younger sisters and brother — their grade school classes were suddenly more crowded, maybe hours shortened for shifts, and their lives were more disrupted at home — father working longer hours, different shifts, in the first six months of wartime sent to a relative's farm out of Chehalis for safety —because of the fear of bombing Bremerton — probably a release for her.

Virginia Oass Steffensen: Pauline Schairer and her daughter Jeanie had driven my mother and me home after attending Sunday Mass. My dad, hearing the car drive up, came out on the porch and shouted that the Japanese were bombing Pearl Harbor!

My mother, Jo Oass, was captain of the Red Cross Motor Corps. That evening she had us all lay out our clothes for a quick evacuation during the night, if necessary. We secured the blinds, prayed, said good-bye to her not knowing if we'd meet again. Dramatic!

The next day at BHS a real pall seemed to hang over the old familiar sights. The student body was subdued, sober, wary. After school Jeanie Schairer, Betty Lou Schricker, Betty Jane Crawford, Frances Clement and Toni McHale (I think that's right) accompanied me to downtown Bremerton where we dropped in for cherry cokes and French fries at a hang-out across from the Rialto Theater. A sailor wondered in, dropped money in the juke box machine and played God Bless America. We all sat in the booth staring at our French fries soaking in ketchup and cried!

Beatrice (Bee) Parsons Morton: On car radio coming home from a movie date — Nils Burckland my date, was on his way to join the Coast Guard. I was living in a tiny mountain town in Colorado, Cotopaxi. Soon our family was on its way to Bremerton — me to finish high school — all of us ended up working at PSNY.

Being from the tiny town of Cotopaxi, Colorado, and our small high school — I think there would have been 12 in my graduating class — Bremerton High was overwhelming and exciting and I loved it. I loved and love Bremerton — but at that time I imagined it to be the most exciting place on earth and at the same time we were all so dedicated and serious about winning the wars on both sides of our country. Now, since living in Los Alamos, I realize Los Alamos was an exciting place, too. BUT they didn't have those crippled ships coming in and the Navy Yard sending them off again all repaired and ready to fight again. All the military activities around us.

My husband, William H. Morton, was deferred from the military as he was considered more important to the war effort in the Navy Yard than in the military. The minute the war was over he was off to Japan in the Army with the Army of Occupation. Bill was born and raised in Tacoma, took the apprentice program in the Navy Yard and became an instrument maker. I met him working on the fifth floor of the Machine Shop there. We were married March 24, 1946. I was an engraver in the Machine Shop — went to work about two days after we graduated in 1943.

My Mother worked up to be a leadingman out of the rigger shop in the Navy Yard!

Robert W. Romberg: I remember helping put up blackout curtains on the windows, the rumors of a giant burning arrow in the Port Angeles area pointing to Bremerton, a feeling much like the one we had when Orson Welles' "War of the Worlds" broadcast scared us all — only this time it turned out to be real!

Class of '44

Lorraine Allison Faulds: My family was over at my aunt's in South Colby, just outside Port Orchard, a post office-store combination. My cousin heard it at the store and came running home. No one believed him until the radio was turned on. As I recall it was the same night we woke up to Army trucks coming up Burwell Street.

I went to the morning sessions of high school and during my junior and senior years worked in the Navy Yard as a messenger.

Joan Baer Hansen: A typical lazy Sunday in December. Dad was still in pajamas and robe. We hadn't even turned on the radio. The Marine next door pounded on our door and asked, "Mr. Baer, have you heard? The Japs have bombed Pearl Harbor!" At first, Dad thought he was joking but the Marine's obvious nervousness and paleness of face soon convinced my Dad. He quickly got into uniform and drove to the base. We didn't see him (or the car!) until Dec. 12. We were fortunate. Our Dad stayed in Bremerton through the whole war, much to his disgust and our relief. He was a WWI veteran and felt that he could fight as well as any of the younger men! We were glad he didn't have to!

Stan Baselt: Riding out on Hood Canal highway, Hoodsport. Had radio on in Model A Ford car. Came home, sold *P-I* papers end of Manette bridge till 11 that night. New papers came over every 2-3 hours. 5 cents a copy. Made a lot of money . . . 16-years-old.

Ed Bejeault: I was coming down from the woodshed (it sat on a hill above the house) with wood and coal for our kitchen range, a huge insatiable monster with two ovens, when my mother heard the news on the radio and yelled at me to come in the house. We lived on South Lafayette overlooking the west end of the Yard and the beautiful golf course. We kept our ears glued to the radio and our eyes glued to the skies over the yard. We expected to see Jap fighters and bombers at any minute!

There are other items that I can think of about those days regarding the war, but I doubt if any are unique to Bremerton.

Like swiping the rubber mat off my mother's bath scales to throw in the rubber collection at the corner gas station.

Like taking any table-sized radio I could find or pick up to give to the war effort; there was 10 or 12 pounds of aluminum in them. Later, I wised up and sold them as scrap for about 10 cents per pound.

Like making more money than I had ever seen before, selling "Xtras" about the war news. They came out every night and my area was from Burwell to Farragut/Montgomery to Lafayette —Wuxtra! Wuxtra! Everybody up and down the block would come out of their houses to buy a paper! I forget how much I sold them for —probably five cents, but I sold so many each night that I thought I was really rich! Just the names of the streets probably are unique — on the west end of town at least they all seem to be Navy heroes or admirals or something.

Like seeing a boat in the bay that came out of the water and ran along Charleston beach on wheels but nobody would believe me — the start of amphibs?

Like the admiral who had a big, beautiful (at that time) house up the block from us on the corner of Rodgers and Lafayette. He had numerous swabbies there all the time washing windows, trimming hedges, cutting grass, painting, etc. One would have thought that corner was an extension of the Navy Yard.

Aileen Bellinger Epling: Our family had moved from Navy Yard City to a beautiful home (burned down in the 1960s) at Chico and I remember I had on a pink outfit and as a 16 year old was caught up in the bombing tragedy without really understanding "the tragedy" of it.

Since my brother and I didn't want to go to Silverdale High we walked to Kitsap Lake to catch a bus to take us to Bremerton High, and with gas rationing and the different things that us kids were involved in — my Dad caved in to the pressures and we moved back into town. We thought gas rationing was harder on us than food rationing.

We moved back to Snyder Avenue which made it possible to do a lot of things by walking, my Dad into the Navy Yard and my dear Mother even took a job in the Navy Yard. She was *not* the working away from home type — but became a riveter catcher. My Dad was a riveter. Probably the strangest thing about those early times was my Mother tying up her hair in a scarf and going to work in the Navy Yard. Double shift at school meant having a job for lots of kids at first if your name began with A through K. School in the morning 8-12 left me with the chance — so I had a couple of jobs as soda fountain girl and then at the Arctic Lunch on Fourth Street. My honor roll status slid with that job (started at 35 cents an hour and my boss liked me so much she upped it to 50 cents an hour — very good at the time). We had to clean up on our own time and lots of times it was midnight or 1 a.m. when I got home. I remember going to sleep one time in Miss Wagner's class (English/Lit) and she was my favorite teacher and that made me feel really bad . . .

The first deaths of people I knew hit hard also — Kent Chollar, Pat Corcoran, Larry Andrews — and I know I wasn't alone in that. And the others — our family was spared and we lost no one. My brother Keith, Class of 1945, went into the Merchant Marine.

Marian Booth Hathhorn: My sister Marge and I were driving to Brownsville with another friend and heard the news as we turned right onto the Manette bridge. I was 15 and Marge was 17 —our lives were changed forever. . .

Shirley Braendlein Sketculey: In those days, the radio was on constantly so that's how we hard the unbelievable news. At first we thought it might be another Orson Welles' stunt. What a shocker!

Sam Chollar: On Dec. 7, 1941, I had just gotten home from church when I heard of the attack on the radio. Memories of the barrage balloons in the high school practice field, blackouts, gas rationing, and food stamps flooded my memory. The third day after I graduated I was on my way to boot camp. Wow! What lovely (lonely?) times. Four stars in the window at home, one gold.

Edna Eastwood Shroy: I was asleep, my dad woke me up and told me the news. Before moving to Bremerton in 1940 I lived in a small railroad town in Northern Idaho. My dad and I would see many flat cars heading west, loaded with scrap metal and he would say, "There goes another load of scrap that the Japs will shoot back at us one day." Of course we all know, that's exactly what happened.

After school, twice a week, I would go to Naval Avenue school and answer the phones for the barrage balloons that were stationed there. My mother took a course at the Red Cross and our family helped wherever possible in the war effort. My mother also took a job as a sheet metal worker at PSNY.

Cleo Fellows Carpenter: On December 7th the attack had been announced on the radio while I was on an errand. I did not comprehend what it really meant. I was just involved in my errand. My Mother had sent me to deliver some club papers to a committee member. It did not impress or frighten me at the time. I just did not realize the gravity of the action and what it would mean to my future life. I worked four hours a day (summers eight hours a day) in the PSNY's I.D. office during the balance of my high school years. I worked full-time one year after graduation until I left to marry Ensign Kenneth S. Magelssen.

Myrtle Forbes Kressin: My mother came to my bedroom and told me the Japanese had bombed Pearl Harbor. I had one brother on the *Lexington* and we didn't know where the ship was at the time. We learned later that the *Lexington* had just left Pearl Harbor. It was later torpedoed and we received a telegram that my brother was missing in action. We later learned that he swam to an island called Tonga. Another brother was in the Army. Two more joined the day after Pearl Harbor, so it was a very personal scary time for a 15 year old. We had barrage balloons in our block.

Diane Gillette Grant: I lived in Quarters B in the Navy Yard at Pearl Harbor. My stepfather was manager of Pearl Harbor, a Navy captain. I was to be on the *Arizona* December 7 for lunch with ten of my friends, guests of Capt. Vallenberg.

Patricia Goodwin Trent: Heard about it on the radio after lunch. Later on the way to the Roxy Theater with my friend, Reggie Saunders, we saw an English soldier who was staggering down the street saying, "It's about time you blokes got in it. Should have been in it a long time ago."

Chris Gourlie Rennick: I was living in Orient, Washington, and we were celebrating my Mother's birthday when news of Pearl Harbor attack came over the radio. We moved to Bremerton in February as my father was called back to work at PSNY after the Pearl Harbor attack.

Gene Gurske: I was part of the double shift at Bremerton High School. In my machine shop class there were sailors from the Navy Yard also taking the course. As a result, we high school students were unable to use the metal lathes because the sailors had priority, so we never had much hands-on experience.

Our high school shop teacher sent us out in the community gathering scrap metal that could be used for the class and for the war effort. On one occasion, we went by truck to the Waterman Beach in South Kitsap to gather metal.

Going to school in the mornings gave me and other students a chance to work at the Black Ball Ferry Dock. I worked there for nearly two years, until I joined the Navy in 1943 in the middle of my senior year.

There were five ferries running from Bremerton to Seattle. They were the *Enetai, Willapa, Chippewa, Kalakala,* and *Malahat.* My job was operating either the car ramp or the passenger ramp and then taking the tickets. I remember gangs of sailors would run for the ferries, or they would jump into the back of a truck. That made it nearly impossible to take tickets. Sometimes it paid to look the other way.

When I first came to Bremerton in 1941, my folks and I lived in a tiny World War I-style house with just one bedroom. I slept in the car until Sears got in a shipment of army cots. Then I slept on the cot in the kitchen for a few months waiting for contractors to finish building our Eastpark government housing unit.

I was an air raid warden in Eastpark and made the rounds enforcing the blackout. If I saw lighted windows, I knocked on doors to remind residents of the blackout requirements. The Army raised and lowered a barrage balloon at dawn and dusk every day next to our housing unit.

Doris Harkness: What a time we had — a 15-year-old girl surrounded by every young male in the U.S.! We had a barrage balloon virtually in our back-yard. We lived at 2513 East 16th and the balloon was on the Manette school grounds

When my Aunt Birdie called on that dark Sunday morning to tell us what she'd just heard on the radio our family was traumatized. My dad was on the *Enterprise*, stationed at Pearl Harbor. So for weeks the rumors were flying about the Big E being sunk.

Dick Kint: My most memorable experience was one night when we were heading out to Madrona Point on Sixth just before Naval Avenue when there suddenly appeared draped over the hood what we all recognized as the broken cable from one of the barrage balloons. Without giving it a second thought I jumped out of the back seat, grabbed the cable, pulled it clear and Dad drove free. Almost immediately — and who knows how much embellishment has developed over time, I want to say a split second after I let go —blue sparks danced between the cable and the concrete street. I crawled back in the car and as I remember it, it was a few minutes before anyone recovered enough to say the first word.

I went off to Kemper in mid-January 1943, came back that summer, when I worked for Johnson Lumber and for a few weeks drove their oldest truck — a bit before I had a license. I was back for a couple of weeks in June of '44 before joining the V-12 training program and Central College, Fayette, Mo.

Alice Jane Levin Begg: I came home from Sunday school and Mom and Dad were sitting in the living room with dazed expressions on their faces. Dad told me what had happened and of course the radio was on with the local newsmen of the day, and then he left immediately to the naval shipyard, where he was chief electronics engineer and began a long siege of seven-day weeks filled with 12-hour days.

I remember the rationing, of course, saving fats and tin cans and waiting for hours for sugar stamps because Mom made so much jam and canned so much fruit. My Dad had always kept meticulous records of this and we had no trouble getting the sugar, but I did use all of my shoe stamps for school shoes and had to buy unrationed shoes for graduation. A heel fell off just as I stepped up to accept my diploma.

We had three lady teachers who went into the service: Thelma Engebretson, Army, Patricia Skinner and Jean Strassman, Marines.

I remember the barrage balloons, swing shift dances, those ridiculous submarine nets and the A gasoline cards with the guys siphoning gas and pooling their efforts. Your date always tasted like gasoline.

Remember the air raid drills at school? And the "Commando" training in the boys' PE classes? When we were indoctrinated into the Naval Shipyard, we had to go through a gas chamber and snatch off our masks at the last second so that we would recognize the smell if we happened to encounter it.

Dorothy M. Williams Baker: I was shaking a rug on the porch in Yakima. I was one of those wartime new arrivals to Bremerton in 1942. I met and married a local man, Roy H. Baker, Class of '42. My family came to Bremerton by degrees because of the housing shortage. We lived like the homeless in basements, etc.

Betty Loftus Berreth: I was on the Seattle-Bremerton ferry. First announcement I ever heard over public-address system. Total shock and silence. Then strangers talked to strangers, fearfully. Were we far enough away? Were we next?

Later, barrage balloons were on hill across road from us. My parents welcomed the men, told them they could use our beach anytime, invited them to dinner. We were not permitted to take pictures.

I took the ferry to Seattle every Monday for a music lesson. Always had to wait for the nets — how stupid! Any sub could lie in wait and go through with the ferry.

I remember one air raid drill — late at night. We were never sure it was a drill. Knew if anyone ever hit the ammo dump a couple of bays over, Seattle as well as Bremerton would be gone. It was scariest moment.

I brought a pair of shoes in Victoria that didn't quite fit, but they *were not rationed*.

Carol McCaslin McDougall: My parents were away for the weekend. I had a girl friend staying with me. During breakfast we turned on the radio, which, in itself, dates the circumstances. The news was especially frightening, not having my parents at home. We went to my girl friend's home to be with her family until my parents arrived home . . .much earlier than planned.

Jorgen Nelson: I was practicing basketball at BHS when Les Eathorne arrived saying, "Boys, we're in the war."

Geraldine Petersen Snow: I do not remember so much on the actual day. Of course it was a shock. My father had left Utah and our farm to work in the Navy Yard as an electrician. In September of '41 my older brother had been killed in a farm accident so we no longer could run it and therefore sold and moved to Bremerton in a housing unit in 1942 at Eastpark (temporarily). My parents could have purchased a home then but we didn't know how long the war would last. The kids at BHS who were long-time residents were quite clannish. But I made my friends and thought I fit in fairly well.

It was taboo to date the service men as you were known as "sailor bait." Then boys from back home were soon in the service and it was OK if you let your peers know they were old friends. I always thought this quite unpatriotic.

Coming from a small Mormon town I saw for the first time a girl smoke, for the first time saw taverns (viewed from the outside on First Street) Never had seen drunks before.

Crossing the ferry with nets protecting us from subs was exciting. I never dreamed I would be rich enough to live on the water, which was one of the most beautiful sights I had ever seen. I'm on Henderson Bay now and it's still the most beautiful place on earth.

I worked in a bank after graduation and thought a mortgage of $15,000 would never be paid off *in this lifetime.*

To date an officer and go to the Officers' Club made me ecstatic. Movies were our main entertainment; they featured love shows or war pictures. I don't remember much about rationing, we didn't go on trips, but we seemed to have plenty of food and gas to get around. Stockings were scarce and we put some kind of make-up or coloring on our legs to simulate stockings. I guess that's what made the seamless come into their own. Shoes were plentiful but the unrationed variety had cardboard soles and fabricated tops. No leather was used.

I'm sure many of the transplants are like my family. We still visit friends and relatives in Utah but after 51 years in Washington it is our home. As for the war years, it was my youth and like youth I looked for fun and friends and found both. The only sad part is when the bombed ships came in for repair and the stories of the killed and wounded became known. Otherwise, I'm glad we came here to stay. So be it.

Jo Peterson Spencer: At the time I lived in North Dakota. We were out walking after church on Sunday and one of my girl friends mentioned that Pearl Harbor had been bombed. I didn't think it had anything to do with me — besides I didn't even know where it was. By the next day of course we all knew what it meant. We had heard of close families that had sons on the *West Virginia* and other ships in Pearl Harbor. Then by the next fall my oldest brother was in the Navy and my father left to work in the war effort in Bremerton and we followed (mom and six kids) in February of '43.

Don Rolstad: My folks were out of town and I heard about it on the radio. Gordon Personius and his folks were neighbors. When I went there for dinner, I told them about it. We were not worried about a Japanese air attack until the anti-aircraft gun placements and the barrage balloons suddenly appeared.

I went to high school in the mornings and worked in a grocery store, wholesale grocery warehouse and at the YMCA over a three-year period before going into the service August 7, 1944.

The increase in Bremerton's population from about 12,000 to about 85,000 in a short time amazed me. Food rationing led to many interesting stories. Gas rationing was a pain but we managed to survive.

Richard W. Sanders: I remember the visit of young sailors from *HMS Warspite* to our high school classrooms. In 1941 they were already war veterans, about our age. There were 13 barrage balloons surrounding the Naval Ammunition Depot station near Madrona Point, where we lived.

Some tradesmen that were our neighbors would suddenly leave for a place called Hanford, with their families. No one seemed to know what went on there. These men had, I believe, draft deferments and had to leave PSNY for the atomic energy project or go in the Army.

Part-time jobs were plentiful in the war years. I worked in the afternoons at a Safeway store in Charleston. We all remember the split shifts at high school. My weekly hours almost totaled 40 hours working. I and others should have spent more time at our studies and school activities.

My war experience was from 1944 to 1948 in the U.S. Merchant Marine. Fortunately, I was able to travel to many world ports even if it was in the wartime-built Liberty ships.

Bette Jean Spotts Lietz: We had a barrage balloon, anti-aircraft gun emplacement and a machine-gun right under my bedroom window . . .

Susan Swanson Matison: A newsboy ran down Gregory Way yelling "Extra, extra." My dad went out and bought the paper that announced the attack. Then we heard it over the radio. Later I went to visit my girl friend, Pat Bryant. Her folks were sitting at their kitchen table, very quietly, stunned. I asked why people made war on one another. Mr. Bryant said, "I don't know." That's the first time I realized that adults didn't have all the answers. I grew up a lot in that instant.

Helen Jean Stubblefield Boyer: That stirs up a flood of memories, all swirling around and getting tangled up in each other. It was the day the world invaded my comfortable space and made me look and think outside of my immediate circle of family and friends.

My mother and father and I were out at our beach cabin on Hood Canal. It was Sunday, after church, December 7, 1941. I was 15-years-old, a freshman at Bremerton High School. We had gathered evergreen boughs and were nailing them up round the eves of our porch and stringing lights in preparation for some Christmas parties. My folks were making plans for a gathering of their friends, and then there was to be a small dance party for me and my friends during the holidays. We were playing Christmas records when our neighbors, Alma and Al Bard, came running up the hill and pounded on our door. They were as white as sheets and Alma was crying.

Al said, "Turn on your radio, Pearl Harbor has been attacked by the Japs and we are at war." My father went to the radio and I remember my mother slumping onto the couch with her face flushed and Alma beside her. It was obvious to me that we had been notified of a dramatic blow that had been delivered not just to Pearl Harbor but to us individually, and I had yet to sort out what it meant.

We knew where Pearl Harbor was, for it had not been long since our friends, Del Barnes and his wife, had had a going away dinner party at our home before he had gone with the *USS Arizona* to Pearl Harbor. It was supposed to be great duty and she was hoping to be able to join him there. Even in peace, military service had hard times of separations. He was extremely handsome, with a mustache and they were as close to Nick and Nora Charles (William Powell and Myrna Loy) as anyone could want if you were casting "The Thin Man."

The rest of that day and into the night we listened to, and stared at, the radio. Everyone spoke in hushed voices and took only short spins about the room to deliver coffee or make sandwiches. The radio became the focal point. The Bards remained with us. There was a feeling of need for companionship and support as we waited for what we were to be told next.

I was seeing my parents from a different perspective. My father, whom I viewed as confident, successful, with a wonderful sense of humor, I now found re-impacted with a sense of inadequacy because he had not been accepted into the military during World War I because of his poor feet. He was now a doctor of optometry with a family and he was wondering what would be asked of him now and was he up to it.

Alma and my mother had both lost brothers in WWI. They had known pride of country, noble causes and personal losses. Now they were looking at me, and hugging me, as representative of the next generation and wondering what I would see and experience. They were expressing love, mixed with tears. I cared, but there was no way that I could comprehend.

When we went back to our home in town, everyone felt the need to phone and make contact with family and friends. Phone lines became jammed and again it was the radio that became our director, instructing in the necessity to limit phone calls to emergencies.

There were air raid drills, blackouts, blackout inspectors wearing gas masks, out patrolling the street for violators that let any light slip through their windows. Slogans like "a slip of the lip will sink a ship." My Aunt Minnie was a comical sight for her block patrol.

Mom took first-aid classes from the Red Cross and then taught first aid. She joined the Gray Ladies at the Navy Hospital and organized recreation activities and events for the hospital corpsmen and patients. We regularly entertained military men in our home. We saved fat and tinfoil. We wrote letters. But I wasn't to date a Navy man, because "only seagulls follow the ships. And no daughter of mine was going to be a seagull."

My cousin Vera Cellars came from Montana as the Bremerton school system was strained to the breaking point. She was an outstanding teacher and one of the first women principals, along with Lillian Hendrickson. Vera at one time was acting principal of four schools at one time, and got extra gas rationing so that she could drive from school to school and do her administrative chores. This also included war bond and stamp sales in the school system. Once every week, she carried a lot of money on the days of war bond sales.

This is just a jumble of stuff that came to mind today as I opened your letter. It was an amazing time that would be hard to capture the drama and emotion of the hour. But it did bond us, didn't it! What other old gals in their 60s would get together and have an annual slumber party like we gals of Bremerton High

School do at Fort Worden. Also regular lunch dates that gather 30 or more at a crack. We are all a fascination to our kids.

Wanda Thomas Mosbarger: My dad seldom went to church with us but that particular Sunday we had pressured him to go with us. When we got home Dad turned the radio on and we heard about Pearl Harbor. Dad's comment was, "I knew something drastic would happen if I went to Church."

Audrey Thompson Landon: It was Sunday morning and my Mother and I were reading the Sunday paper. Dad was working in the Navy Yard and he called to tell us about the bombing of Pearl Harbor. By nightfall, armed guards were patrolling the downtown streets of Bremerton and within days Army trucks were pouring into the town, setting up barrage balloons on every vacant lot in the whole town.

In looking back, I am most impressed by the way we carried on our normal activities in spite of the war. Life went on and we still had high school elections, junior and senior proms, Vodvil, football and basketball games and tournaments, etc. If there were problems such as shortages and curtailments, we knew that that was a small price to pay.

I remember going to the Red Cross and picking up olive drab wool yarn and knitting countless 6-foot long scarves that we were told were needed by the servicemen, especially airmen. Since there were so many jobs to be filled, it was easy to find work even for a few months. Though I was only 16, I worked the summer between my freshman and sophomore years as a clerk-typist in the personnel office in the Navy Yard. I held other jobs every summer and worked afternoons my senior year as secretary to various high school teachers such as Miss Dunlap and Miss Kern.

I have dug into an old trunk and have found a scrapbook of my high school days. There are momentos of all our BHS activities as well as newspaper clippings about the whereabouts of our boys in the service. Some tell happy news that Lt. Wes Wager is no longer missing but has been found well and alive but then, sad news that Francis Ahern has been killed in action. I have a clipping of a letter that you wrote from Germany describing Buchenwald.

We've noticed how so many of the BHS grads have kept in touch with each other and remained good friends through the past 50 years. I wonder if this is because we shared a special time and era in our history.

Class of '45

Eleanor Boyle Ogg: As usual when my family wasn't around the radio was on. I wish I could remember what song was playing when the announcer interrupted with the news of Pearl Harbor. We had always lived on Oyster Bay and Dad was on the beach cutting wood. I called to him repeating the bulletin and asking what it meant. My father never used profanity around his family but he swore at me, said I'd heard wrong. Nevertheless he ran for the house and before he could change his clothes the phone rang and my father, a master moulder in the Navy Yard, left and didn't return for three days. When he came home again it was only to shower and pack his bag for an even longer stay. Many months were to pass before my brother and I were to learn what had taken place in those awful first weeks of the war — but I will always remember my father, who probably didn't even know how to use it, wore a gun.

Carolyn Clement Ball: I was singing in the junior choir at the Chapel in the Navy Yard when an officer came into the church to speak to the admiral. The admiral then came to the front of the Chapel and interrupted church service to announce that all officers should report to their duty stations at once, and that everyone else should go home immediately — the Japanese had just attacked Pearl Harbor.

John E. Fick: Sunday midday, I was with my Dad — was having a basement excavated for a house at 1241 10th Street (since torn down). A neighbor said, "Maybe the Japs will drop a bomb and you won't have to excavate." The news had come on about Pearl Harbor and we spent rest of day listening on radio.

Florence Fraser Petry: I was in North Dakota, working for my room and board in order to go to high school, had the radio on, was dusting the fireplace mantel when I heard. I had no idea where Pearl Harbor was, but did know it was a bad thing and would affect everyone. I do remember that I started to cry, don't ask me why, guess I was smarter than I thought I was.

Do know that all the girls either worked at Olbergs' drug or in the theaters here. Oh yes, the lines, to get into anything. If you saw a line, you asked what was selling and if it was something you wanted or needed you got in line, mainly if it was stockings. Never had enough of them as they did get runs in them. The women's underpants didn't have elastic in them, either a button (which always came off) or they tied. Oh, what fun.

Jo Garland Larsen Ekroth: We were at the Braman's house mimeographing some freshmen class election material. Mrs. Braman told us as soon as she heard news on radio.

Our house was so close to the Navy Yard. Just the shifts of workers had a great impact. I recall someone asking Dad why we didn't move to a safe location. He replied that he believed that our moving would possibly trigger other moves and would be bad for morale.

Dad served as attorney for conscientious objectors with the draft board. He was proud of that service, and I know the objectors were well represented.

Doris Gendron Brandstetter: We were a unique group of young people. In the past 50 years I have never met anyone who shared the same experiences that we did. There are two areas of particular interest.

One is the group of young people who lived in Westpark. We were from many different states and were transplanted to Bremerton because of our father's employment at the shipyard. We have more or less kept in contact the past 50 years and in 1993 gathered in Bremerton for an evening reminiscing about our Westpark Gang. We feel very close to one another and I think this is because we were all young teen-agers in a strange town, school and environment. We were lonely and sought strength in each other's companionship. We were struggling to find new friends and our place at BHS.

The other area would be the young girl students who gave of their time to be junior hostesses at the YMCA and USO. I recently renewed my friendship with

Gen Meyers, who was the social activities director for the YMCA. She is now 80-years-old and confirmed my feelings that indeed Bremerton was an exciting place filled with drama during WWII.

Frank Harlow: I was 13, and a freshman at the old Bremerton High School. We lived on Chester Avenue between Sixth Street and the Hospital. My younger brother, Bruce, and I living with our Aunt Bessie. My Dad, who lived a reclusive life in a tiny shack by Kitsap Lake, took me out to cut a load of wood on that Sunday morning of December 7, 1941. When we returned home around noon, Aunt Bessie met us at the front door with such a serious expression on her face that I immediately was filled with chilling concern. She told us the news about Pearl Harbor and the convening of Congress at the earliest possible moment. After stacking the wood we hovered that afternoon around the old radio, and I remember my Dad saying that this was the beginning of awful times for the world. The next day at school we all gathered in the auditorium to listen to President Roosevelt's speech, his call for a declaration of war, and his request for immediate extraordinary wartime powers. (It was the same auditorium where Eleanor Roosevelt spoke to us in person a year or two later.)

I have numerous sad and serious memories of the following years, our older classmates going off to war, the mushrooming growth of Bremerton, the ferryboat loads of workers commuting from Seattle, attending high school in the 8 to noon shift, the barrage balloon moored across the street from our house, delivering prescriptions for Olberg Drug Store on my bicycle, and enlisting in the Army shortly after turning 17 in January, 1945. It was surely an awesome time. Bremerton changed fast during those war years: Eastpark, Westpark, thousands of sailors, the USO in the old YMCA building; it certainly was very different from the days when my grandfather was a pioneer doctor for Bremerton and Silverdale, and also became one of Bremerton's first mayors.

Patricia Henning: On Sunday, December 7, my Dad, George E. Henning, USN Retired, told us what was going on. He made us hang blankets at our windows and stay indoors. On Monday he immediately went into the Navy Yard and came out of retirement. It was very somber in our little town of Illahee. After about a week we began returning to normal.

We lived in Illahee where there was a Navy installation called a deperming station. That consisted of one small barge with a one-man crew (A.H. Emerson, Boatswain First Class) who later became my brother-in-law. Out in the channel between Bainbridge Island and Illahee there were a series of buoys at which the Navy brought ships to be depermed or degaussed. Before December 7 it was only the one-man crew. Right after Pearl Harbor the Navy added a much bigger barge and some motorboats plus many more personnel, one of whom I married in 1943. The dock that we had used for our own fun was now a Navy base.

I worked in the Navy Yard from '44 to '45 for the Supply Department. In spite of war conditions, Bremerton was so much fun. There was a lot going on; USO dances, ship's dances at Craven Center, DelMarco, picnics, beach parties, etc. In high school I attended the first shift from 8 to 12. We didn't get a lot of time between classes so we studied a bit harder — but school only a half-day — wowie!

The hardest thing for me to understand during this period was watching what happened to the Japanese on Bainbridge Island. Some were friends and I couldn't understand why they were uprooted when they were American-born.

Rose Jewett Cobb: I was on the bus coming home from a movie in Missoula, Montana. Someone commented how terrible the war was, and I agreed, thinking they were talking about Europe. I didn't understand until I got home and talked to my mother. She explained how it would affect our town. I never dreamed how it would totally change my life.

Ruth Jewett Madden: I started high school in Montana in 1941 and came to Bremerton in '43. In Missoula, Pearl Harbor was a big shock, but not as impressive as when we moved to Washington (my father needed work). The biggest change in my life was the half-day shifts at school. It made it so difficult when I started the University and they put us in the same lecture classes as the brilliant Navy V-12s.

Gordon Moen: My Dad and I were in our backyard digging a sewer trench. My Mother had the radio on. She heard the news and called us inside. At age 14 I really had to think for a moment how this would affect me. Well, four years later, on my birthday, I left for boot camp.

Moulton Phelps: I remember how lucky we were supposed to be because the *HMS Warspite* was here and they had the only anti-aircraft guns around.

Elaine Richard Jacobson: I was returning from church when a neighbor and friend, Janice Michel, came running over to tell us about the attack. The rest of the day was spent glued to the old Philco radio for more news.

Nigel Tugby: Was playing tennis with Don Conant at Warren Avenue playfield. When we got back to Don's folk's place they had the radio on and were talking about the attack on Pearl Harbor. It was midmorning on Sunday.

Duane A. Wells: Another classmate and I left after church for Seattle to check out First Avenue and the wonders of all the arcades, etc. Newsboys were hawking extras, *Times* or *Post-Intelligencer*, of Pearl Harbor bombing. We didn't let it spoil our day, but did get more excited as day went on, as everybody was talking about it and rumors started to circulate.

I worked at Navy Yard cafeteria at 14 busboy after school, 1 p.m. to 5 or 6 p.m. Worked at Kelly's Mobil, Sixth and High or Veneta, not sure of street. Lied about age one summer — worked for County Road District as helper in shop — grease trucks, etc. They needed truck driver and since they thought I was 16, I was chosen. I hated to see that summer end. Worked at Kerr Motors and at 16 got job in Yard as mechanic learner, $4.64 per day for eight hours. Worked graveyard all of senior year. Worked up to helper second class in Shop X51 (Electrician) at $7.12 per day. Slept a lot in some classes and took a lot of hacks from Coaches Wills and Johnson for not suiting up for physical education. All my effort reflected in my grades. I think I had a high D average when I graduated. I enlisted in the Navy and was gone before graduation ceremonies but did get my certificate.

INDEX